APR 1 0 2018

Homeward Bound

Homeward Bound

Modern Families, Elder Care, and Loss

AMY ZIETTLOW

AND

NAOMI CAHN

OXFORD
UNIVERSITY PRESS

OXFORD
UNIVERSITY PRESS

Oxford University Press is a department of the University of Oxford. It furthers
the University's objective of excellence in research, scholarship, and education
by publishing worldwide. Oxford is a registered trade mark of Oxford University
Press in the UK and certain other countries.

Published in the United States of America by Oxford University Press
198 Madison Avenue, New York, NY 10016, United States of America.

© Oxford University Press 2017

CIP data is on file at the Library of Congress
ISBN 978–0–19–026109–2

9 8 7 6 5 4 3 2 1

Printed by Sheridan Books, Inc., United States of America

CONTENTS

ACKNOWLEDGMENTS

This book would not have been possible without the generous support of many institutions, colleagues, and our families.

Thank you to the Lilly Endowment for funding the research and to the Institute of American Values for serving as the fiscal agent for the project.

We are grateful to Elizabeth Marquardt for her role as co-investigator and for her ongoing engagement with this project. We also thank M. Christian Green, who supported this project at its conception at a law conference in November 2008, "For Children's Sake: A Summit on Marriage and Family," and has continued to be involved, providing a close and critical reading of the penultimate draft of *Homeward Bound*. She brought her intelligence, keen eye, and real-life experience to our work.

We thank the *Homeward Bound* advisory group, Dorothy Bass, David Blankenhorn, Daniel Callahan, Guido DeJesus, David Eggebeen, Kathryn Grigsby, Mark Kantrow, Mary Ellen Konieczny, Michael Karunas, Kevin Noble Maillard, Loren Marks, Suzy Yehl Marta, Stephanie Paulsell, Thomas Long, Alicia Saverese, Tracy Stephenson Shaffer, Charles Stokes, Judith Wallerstein, Barbara Dafoe Whitehead, and W. Bradford Wilcox, who supported the project in various ways from conception, construction, implementation, and dissemination. We also thank Josephine Tramantano, Charity Navarette, David and Amber Lapp, Andy Kline, Jonathan Rauch, and Jody Wood for their support for the project over the years. We also thank Sarah Gelfand, Kerri Mullen, and Mary Spargo for their research assistance, and Mary Kate Hunter at George Washington

University for tracking down hard-to-find sources and statistics. Friends and family members have graciously discussed and read early versions of chapters; we thank Tony Gambino, M. Christian Green, Michael Karunas, Alicia Kelly, Elizabeth Marquardt, and Richard Ziettlow. We are thankful for the support of Dave McBride, our editor at Oxford University Press, and Kathleen Weaver.

Several chapters drew on the work done for previously published articles.

Chapters 2 and 3 draw on our work previously published as "The Honor Commandment: Law, Religion, and the Challenge of Elder Care" in the *Journal of Law and Religion*, 30, (2015) pp. 229–259. Our thanks to Silas Allard, M. Christian Green, Marie Failinger, and Bob Tuttle for comments, and to the organizers of the "Feminism, Law, and Religion" conference at St. Thomas Law School in March 2014, where an earlier version of the content was presented.

Chapters 4 and 5 draw on a paper presented at a University of Illinois Law Review symposium on Law, Religion, and the Family Unit after *Hobby Lobby* in September 2015 and published as "Religion and End of Life Decision-Making," at 2016 *University of llinois Law Review* 1713, and as a chapter in an edited volume forthcoming from Cambridge University Press. We thank Robin Fretwell Wilson for her support in those projects. For their comments concerning the content of that work, we thank Richard Kaplan, Chip Lupu, Liz Sepper, and Bob Tuttle.

Chapter 6 builds on Ziettlow's clinical experience as a chaplain and chief operating officer of The Hospice of Baton Rouge and pastoral-care work as a parish pastor. Ziettlow thanks her many mentors in hospice and bereavement support, Kathryn Grigsby, Dani Pecue, Denise Pollyea, Rick Pitcher, Suzanne Abercrombie, Florence Scarle, Denise Domingue, Portia Henderson, and Rae Centanni. Pecue and Pollyea introduced her to Worden's *Grief Counseling and Grief Therapy* as a basic orientation guidebook for every chaplain and social worker at The Hospice of Baton Rouge.

Chapter 8 draws from "Making Things Fair: An Empirical Study of How People Approach the Wealth Transmission System," published at 22

Elder Law Journal, 325 (2015). For their comments, we thank Dirk Hartog, David Horton, Alicia Kelly, Nina Kohn, Peggie Smith, Reid Kress Weisbord, and participants at the Law & Society 2014 Intergenerational Care panel; and for research assistance, Jodi LeBolt.

Our respectful thanks and appreciation to those who chose to be interviewed for *Homeward Bound*. It is your stories of home and the many ways to which we are bound to the people, places, and ideas we name as "home" that make this book possible. Your caregiving work, wisdom, and resilience inspire us. Thank you.

Homeward Bound

Introduction

I don't want my ex-stepmother to be alone.

—*JULIE*

In 2008, our friend, Julie,[1] called Amy with a caregiving dilemma. Julie's ex-stepmother, Tina, who lived several states away from her, needed to undergo a routine medical procedure the following week. Julie wondered what care Tina might need before and after the surgery, and what role she should play in helping to provide that care for her stepmother. As Julie talked, Amy began sketching Julie's family system on a piece of scratch paper as a way to understand her kin connections.

A loose genogram representing Julie's kin by blood, by marriage, and by choice took shape; multiple circles containing the names of stepparents, ex-stepparents, cohabiting significant others, half-siblings, and stepsiblings, with dates and lines of connection and disconnection, spread down and across the page. As she sketched, Amy realized that this family system differed greatly from her own. Amy's parents dated in high school, married soon after, and remained married to that day. She had one brother. Her family drawing required four circles, one for each parent, one for herself, and one for her brother, with clear lines of connection. And yet, even without the complicating lines and circles of family members related, and unrelated, by divorce and remarriage, thoughts of family-coordinated elder care were overwhelming to Amy, as they are for many people.

As the two friends worked through the dilemma at hand, it became apparent that Julie's concerns extended beyond dealing with the present crisis. Her worries about elder care were much bigger. How would she balance caring for her parents, stepparents, ex-stepparents, and possibly a parent's boyfriend or girlfriend as they age over the next thirty years? How would she pay for the care, funerals, and burials they would all inevitably one day require? What role would her half-brother, half-sister, stepsiblings, and ex-stepsiblings play? What role would her parent's current spouse, ex-spouses, or boyfriend play in those decisions? Despite the whirlwind of questions, what Julie really cared about was making sure her ex-stepmother was not alone. She wondered what other ex-stepdaughters like her were doing. Did they share similar concerns?

Julie represents one face of the new normal in American families. Julie's parents are Baby Boomers, born between 1946 and 1964. This generational cohort's large size and penchant for rewriting the rules regarding marriage and family combine to diversify and potentially complicate how families provide elder care. Historically, most elder care has been provided by spouses or by adult children. Changing family structures challenge the existence of these traditional sources of care:

- By 2029, the over-65-aged Baby Boomers will comprise 20% of the total US population.[2]
- Eighty-seven percent of Baby Boomers had married by the age of 46, but almost half of those marriages ended in divorce.[3]
- Baby Boomers are continuing to divorce as they grow older. Assuming that divorce and widowhood rates do not change, then the national divorce rate will hover around 52%.[4]
- The percentage of older people who have divorced has doubled since the 1980s,[5] and the divorce rate for those 65 and older tripled.[6]
- The number of divorced Americans over the age of 50 is, for the first time, higher than the number of widowed Americans.[7]
- Although Baby Boomers have higher rates of remarriage than earlier generations,[8] approximately one-third of Baby Boomers

are single.[9] And remarriages have a projected divorce rate of almost 60%[10]

Moreover, the low fertility rates[11] of Baby Boomers, with their smaller family sizes, have reduced the other main support for elder care: the adult child. A quarter of all Baby Boomers never had children.[12] The decreased birthrates of the Baby Boomers have affected the old-age-dependency ratio. Whereas in 2014 for every one hundred working-age people, there were nineteen people aged 65 to 84, this ratio will jump to over thirty by 2028.[13] And the number of 75-year-old Americans who do not live within ten miles of a spouse or a child (the two most common intrafamilial caregivers) will increase dramatically, more than doubling when it comes to a spouse, and potentially increasing six times when it comes to the adult child.[14] Among the 22 million unmarried adults over the age of 65, the majority (55%) lived alone; the overall figure masks a gender divide, with women constituting a larger percentage of those alone, and men more likely to live with a spouse or a grown child.[15] As a result, Baby Boomers may not just "bowl alone,"[16] they may die alone.

These demographic characteristics of the Baby Boomer generation and their families are profoundly affecting aging in America. Baby Boomers are now working their way through the countless legal policies and procedures that support and guide the healthcare decision-making, burial, and inheritance processes, and dealing with ethical and religious conceptions of life, death, and life after death. And, just as they have challenged so many other institutions, so too are they challenging end-of-life care, and, in turn, they are forcing their grown children to adapt to those changes as well.

How do grown children, like Julie, manage caring for and grieving for their Baby Boomer parents? In-depth, qualitative interviews with more than sixty participants whose mother, father, stepparent, or ex-stepparent died serve as the base for our three-year study, which was funded by the Lilly Endowment and based at the Institute for American Values, a New York–based think tank.[17] With the consultation of a board of scholarly advisors, drawn from law, sociology, religion, and public policy, we chose to examine a seven-month period in 2010–2011 in the racially diverse, midsize American city of Baton Rouge, Louisiana.[18] Interviews were conducted in year one, and Naomi joined the project in year two when analysis of the transcripts began. She brought her expertise in family and elder law as well as trusts and estates to Amy's background in end-of-life care and pastoral ministry.

At first glance, the idiosyncrasies of Louisiana in general and Louisiana law in particular may seem like stumbling blocks; unlike those of other states, Louisiana's laws are drawn not just from the British common-law system but also from the French civil-law tradition, so, for example, it is the only state that protects children against disinheritance (at least until they reach the age of 24). Nonetheless, the dilemmas of elder care transcend geography. Moreover, the location was chosen for several reasons. Procedurally, conducting the qualitative interviews in person was a top priority. Because one of the principal investigators, Amy, was the chief operating officer of a hospice organization in Baton Rouge, this regional proximity to decedents enabled 80% of the interviews to be conducted in person. Demographically, Louisiana presents some of the greatest challenges to end-of-life care in terms of high poverty rates, low education levels, and high out-of-wedlock birthrates.[19] Moreover, our intent was not to reform Louisiana law, medical practice, or religious life, per se, but to analyze human behavior within the caregiving, mourning, and wealth transfer process as seen from the perspective of a grown child. Given our goal and the size of our sample, we did not formally survey the race, class, religious affiliation, and other demographic characteristics of the interviewees, although we highlight where these factors may have affected their experience.[20] The specific legal, medical, and religious frameworks were less important than investigating the parameters of medical, legal, and religious knowledge, examining what people knew or did not know, and the formal procedures and tools they accessed or did not access. Our goal was to understand what role their family structure played in how they responded to the serious illness and death of a parent or stepparent.

Participants were aged 28 to 49 years old, had played an integral role in caring for their now-deceased parent or stepparent, and came to the

interview around the one-year anniversary of the death. The family structure of the respondents reflected current Baby Boomer family demographics: for one-third, their parents had remained married throughout
their lifetimes; for one-third, their parents were single; and for one-third,
their parents had divorced and were remarried at the time of death. Our
study focused almost exclusively on different *nuclear* family structures.
As a general matter, we use the term "family structure" throughout the
text to refer predominately to the parent–stepparent–child–stepchild
circle, although we mention the supporting or complicating roles played
by grandparents, aunts, and uncles, where appropriate. As interviewees talked about what actually happened while they provided care and
planned funerals and searched for (often nonexistent) life insurance policies, the work that society must undertake to address the issues presented
by the growing number of older persons with differing ties to other family
members became apparent.

Interviews began with a family picture drawn by the interviewee as a
springboard to explore their childhoods, focusing on the home as a place
where family norms, or a "shared understanding about family responsibilities,"[21] develop over time. These mutual expectations served to create a core family identity based on a common definition of insiders and
outsiders, shared and recognized patterns of communication, acceptable
expressions of emotion, and mutual understandings of a family's identity
and priorities. Norms such as eating together, expectations for worship
attendance, holiday celebrations, finding time alone, and sensing the conversations that are off limits converge to create a unique family character
that was cataloged by the grown child. Interviewees described how the
marital choices of their parents affected the development of these norms
and how these norms both guided decisions and came under pressure
during the caregiving process, as families made treatment and end-of-
life decisions. Should we pursue aggressive or palliative care treatment?
Should mom stay in the hospital or come home? If going home, whose
house—the second spouse's or the daughter's? Do we need a second medical opinion? Should we remove life support? At the deathbed, can we
sing, pray, wail? Who inherits dad's dress clothes? Where will mother

be buried? Whose preacher presides at the funeral? Increased family complexity tended to complicate answers to these common caregiving and loss questions. Family structure profoundly influenced not only how interviewees and their families answered these questions but also whether formal tools, such as an advance medical directive, were called on to resolve any disputes.

RESULTS

Three salient and overlapping lessons emerged: 1) family structure affects the level of shared norms, and norm coherence has an impact on all aspects of the caregiving and mourning process, 2) formal tools have not yet fully adapted to changing family forms, and 3) Baby Boomers are not dying alone, although the structures of caregiving are changing based on changes in family form.

First, caring for a seriously ill and dying loved one presents challenges for *all* families. Regardless of family structure, virtually all those interviewed found meaning in the elder-care experience and felt that any efforts they made were worthwhile. However, the contours of the family shaped how the grown child understood and managed the challenges of care and loss. Family structure often determined the level of what we labeled "norm coherence,"[22] defined as a high level of shared values, customs, and traditions within the family system, as well as a shared history of overcoming difficulties together. A relatively coherent sense of norms often contributed to a caregiving and grieving experience that was similarly coherent, with family members making decisions cooperatively and supporting one another. In addition to the quality of the experience, higher norm coherence was often associated with resilience: The family adapted to the loss together. Norm coherence was highest in married-parent and single-parent families. For the most part, remarried families tended to experience low levels of norm coherence. Grown children struggled to understand the wishes and decisions of the family members involved, to predict what would happen next in the care and grief trajectory, and to manage what role they could play during stressful moments of care, decision-making, and mourning. After the death, they tended to separate from any stepkin.

Resilient family systems tend to share these attributes in relationship to the caregiving and loss experience:[23]

1) *Understandable.* The grown child understood the implicit and explicit rules and expectations of his or her family system. If the parent became incapacitated or died, the interviewee understood the values and wishes of the parent figures.
2) *Manageable.* The grown child felt a sense of control within the caregiving, medical decision-making, and funeral planning process. The grown child was able to contribute money, time, effort, or emotional support during the experience.
3) *Meaningful.* The grown child felt that providing care was worthwhile. He or she incorporated the experience of support and loss into his or her sense of self and the family story.
4) *An Expectation of Ongoing Relationship.* The family members, narrowly or broadly defined, remained in contact a year after the death.

Almost half of those interviewed could be considered to have all four elements, with more than half of those coming from married-parent families.[24] Contributing factors included the following:

- close geographical proximity to the parents, with many grown children living with the parent during the care window;
- a high level of family norm coherence such as a history of family rituals: celebrating holidays or significant family events together, including special foods, preparation routines, anticipated and expected traditions, and family identity defining memories shared by all members;
- the ability of the grown child to contribute to the care of the ill parent through money, action, or presence;

- a history of financial and emotional support between the grown child and parents/stepparents (reciprocity);
- shared religious beliefs and practices;
- a shared family story of overcoming hardship, struggle, or loss together, and
- in remarried families, the ability of the grown child to empathize with the parent's spouse or significant other and see the surviving stepparent through the eyes of the parent and to value that stepparent as a human being.

In addition to the details of the story, norm coherence showed in the pronouns used by the interviewees to tell their story of family, care and mourning: *We, I, She, or He.* The pronouns used to tell their stories shifted based on the marital status of their parents at the time of illness and death, which reflected how the weight of care and loss was distributed.

Grown children from married-parent families as well as from families with intentionally shared norms used "we" to tell their story. They carried the weight collectively, even though legally "we" didn't do anything, because the legal decision-maker was the surviving spouse, most often the other parent of the grown child. The pronoun "we" was used whether the family experienced harmony or dysfunction during the caregiving and mourning journey.

Grown children from single-parent families, even when surrounded by siblings, aunts, and uncles, and even the behind-the-scenes presence of their other parent, used the pronoun "I" to tell their story. They carried the weight of elder care and loss narratively alone. The pronoun "I" often pointed to feeling isolated.

Grown children from remarried families tended to use the pronoun "he" or "she" to tell the story of their parent or stepparent's illness and death. The third-person pronoun pointed to the spouse of their parent or to their parent caring for a stepparent and denoted distance. In stories where the "he" or "she" was a stepparent making decisions, distress, exclusion, and ill will defined the story. In stories where the "he" or "she" was the parent making the decisions, distance and objectivity defined the story. In both cases, participants indicated that it was the surviving spouse who was carrying the responsibility alone and thus highlighted both the spouse's and the grown child's isolation.

Family structure thus shaped not only how participants told their stories but what normative and legal responsibilities they assumed. Family structure affected our respondents' relationship to formal tools, whether established by legal, medical, or religious professionals. For example, when it came to wealth transmission or medical decision-making, family members often relied on nonlegal mechanisms. They were guided by informal conversations with other family members, by shared memories of past crisis care decisions made by the incapacitated individual, and by ethical and religious beliefs and practices related to the best interests of the parent to make substitutive judgments regarding caregiving and wealth transmission. They used formal tools only when they reached an impasse, a conflict escalated, or when professionals were required to confirm death or an asset transfer. The formal tools that exist today are based on a presumed familial structure that did not describe most of the participants in our study—and that does not fit the lives of most Americans today, in which less than half of children under the age of 18 are living with parents in their first and only marriage.[25]

Historical and current practices in end-of-life care presume a coherent family system that assumes that private ordering will be the norm and that conflicts within the family about treatment, surrogate decision-making, funerals, or inheritance will be handled, for the most part, privately. Consequently, elders and the seriously ill won't die alone, and families will figure out how to make that happen without outside intervention. Married-parent and single-parent families continue to fall within this expectation. However, as family structures diversify, a presumption can no longer be made that family norms will do the heavy lifting of holding a family together at the end of life. Systemic resilience in remarried families requires a higher utility of formal tools and the mediating presence of the helping professions.

Finally, although most Baby Boomers are not dying alone, some are. In our study, the situations of those who died alone involved drug and

alcohol abuse, homelessness, and extreme poverty. One death was a sui-
cide. Regardless of family structure, troubled people died troubled deaths.
The grown children who came to tell the story of their deceased parent or
stepparent who died alone told of the difficult and often isolated lives led
by parents with addiction, who were incarcerated, or lived with mental
illness. Much could be done to better support families of those who are at
risk for dying alone.

Homeward Bound unfolds chronologically. Each chapter focuses
on an element of the caregiving and grieving process, beginning with
an anchor story that highlights a particular family structure as it inter-
acts with the applicable legal, medical, or religious frameworks for that
event. Additional stories show alternative knowledge and interpretations.
Chapter 1 describes the "new normal" in American families and how
those family structures intersect with the new normal in end-of-life care.
Chapters 2 through 5 follow the typical chronology of elder care, beginning with physically providing care, then financing of care, making care
decisions with and for a loved one, and preparing for death. Chapter 6
describes the transition from care to grief. Chapters 7 and 8 focus on life
after loss, beginning with honoring the life of a loved one after death and
settling the loved one's estate.

The final chapter concludes with recommendations concerning
current policy and practice inspired by the lived elder-care and grief
process. These recommendations focus on which legal or formal processes are needed to help people access the full range of private ordering
options, ranging from designating a surrogate healthcare decision-
maker to maintaining insurance to distributing property. Background
laws, such as ones that require consensus among surviving grown children, may also need to evolve to reflect changed family forms. We advocate increased public support.

More families need to tell their story using "we" as their pronoun, but
now "we" must be intentionally named and sought and include the presence of more public, legal, and religious resources. Elder care has always
been a delicate dance between public and private rights and responsibilities. We write to offer critical, interdisciplinary insight into the future of

elder care, and, ultimately, to give guidance and hope to our friend, Julie, and to other families like hers.

A Note to Readers: We have learned through the writing and review process that although the book is academic in nature, the themes and stories hold the potential to intersect with a reader's personal experience of elder care and death. In our writing, we have tried to be mindful that certain sections of the book may evoke personal memories and strong emotions in a reader. Although we did not intend to write a self-help tome, readers may find helpful tools and suggestions for their own journeys of care and loss. We hope that the stories of those interviewed reassure readers that they are not alone as they honor the care needs and memories of loved ones.

The New Normal in American Family Caregiving

We began our research with certain assumptions concerning how demographic trends have defined the "new normal" in American families and how end-of-life care has changed. What we didn't know—and set out to study—was what happens when the new American family meets the new end-of-life care. Peter, Rhonda, and Michelle came to the interview to talk about caring for a Baby Boomer parent in the context of their married-, remarried-, and single-parent families, respectively.

Peter came to the interview after work at the local community college. He was 42 years old, Caucasian, and married with two elementary school–aged daughters. Dressed in khaki pants and oxford shirt, he talked of how he grew up in Baton Rouge, attended Louisiana State University (LSU), and had held the same job since graduating college some twenty years ago. He now lived in the same house where he had been raised. His wife and children moved into the family home after his parents downsized to a condo. Peter couldn't remember a time when his parents weren't married and didn't live close by. His father's sudden heart attack, hospital stay, and death upset his family, but a year later he felt a renewed closeness to his mother and siblings. The lifelong marriage of his parents created stable norms that dictated what role he could and needed to play in caregiving and grief.

Rhonda arrived at the interview wearing blue jeans and a Halloween-themed sweatshirt. She lived within fifteen minutes of her sisters, half-siblings, and widowed stepmother in a small bayou community south of Baton Rouge. She was 48 years old, Caucasian, and currently single after two divorces. She had been looking forward to the appointment because she wanted space and time to reflect on her family once anchored by her now-deceased father. As a stay-at-home mother, her flexible schedule had helped make caring for her father at home with hospice possible. And now, her mother, whose health had begun to fail in recent months, had moved into her home. She also worried about the health and well-being of her widowed stepmother. Caregiving was her life, and the marital choices of her parents shaped what role she could and needed to play. She saw herself as a family hub trying to balance the needs of different siblings and parent figures.

Michelle arrived to the interview with plans for a lunch date with a new beau afterwards. She was 42 years old, African American, divorced and single, and mother to three children, one of whom died in infancy. She was striking in a gold lamé cowl-neck sweater, black pants, and high-heeled leopard-print shoes. Her two phones and beeper rang and dinged throughout the two-hour interview. She apologized, but as a regional manager of a small private investigation firm, she was always on call. She described herself as the responsible one in the family both before her single mother's death and after. Yet she lived with constant financial strain, trying to support her own children as a single parent and act as a parent to her two siblings. As was true with those of Rhonda's father, the marital choices of Michelle's mother shaped what role she could and needed to play.

In this chapter, we explore the assumptions about contemporary aging that frame our analysis, many of which are illustrated in the stories of Rhonda, Peter, and Michelle. We first focus on the general changes in family structure over the past half-century, from a society dominated by married-parent families to a society in which married-parent families are a minority and in which children are highly likely to spend time living in a single-parent or remarried-parent family. We next show how end-of-life care has also seen seismic changes during this same period. We then close by addressing the intersection of the two trends, showing how they have resulted in a new normal in American family caregiving defined by differing types and potentially increasing numbers of kinship connections that may nonetheless be weak or ambiguous.

THE NEW NORMAL IN AMERICAN FAMILIES

Almost all the deceased parents and stepparents in our research fall into the oldest segment of Baby Boomers, a generational cohort born in the United States between mid-1946 and mid-1964.[1] At its peak, there were almost 80 million Baby Boomers in the United States.[2] The first Baby Boomer turned 65 in 2011; the last Baby Boomer will reach 65 in 2029 when one in five US residents will be over age 65, comprising 72.8 million people.[3] Their experiences of growing old in America and facing serious illness will be defined, in part, by their marital practices and fertility rates:

- The Baby Boomer cohort was the first to experience high divorce and remarriage rates during their early adulthood, and almost 40% of all Baby Boomers have been divorced.[4]
- Baby Boomers continue to divorce in high numbers, leading to rising numbers of "gray divorce."[5]
- At least half of them have remarried, and many more have cohabited.[6]
- One-fourth of all Baby Boomers never had children.[7]

As family patterns have changed, contemporary understandings of kin have expanded beyond the traditional nuclear family.[8] Indeed, changes in the structure of the American family over the past half-century are causing a cultural rethinking of what constitutes a *family*. In 1968, the famed anthropologist David Schneider was able to proclaim that Americans define "my family" as "a unit which contains a husband and wife and their child or children."[9] Today, with more than 40% of children born into nonmarital families and more than 40% of Americans counting "at least one step relative in their family,"[10] our conceptions of "family" are based not just on biological and marital ties, but also on legal, functional, and social ties.[11]

THE NEW NORMAL IN HOW WE AGE AND DIE

Coinciding with general demographic trends in marriage patterns and a diversification of family structure, there has been a series of equally dramatic changes when it comes to end-of-life care:

- Medical changes: Society has seen a steady rise in hospice and palliative care utilization.
- Financial changes: Society has increased its reliance on Medicare and Medicaid to fund necessary medical treatment and caregiving support as well as increased its awareness of the high costs of care at the end of life and the potential limits of public funding to cover current practices.
- Cultural changes: Overall awareness of end-of-life issues has increased.

Medical Changes

Over the past century, life expectancy has changed dramatically. In 1900, the average American could expect to live to be about 47 years old.[12] Today, life expectancy is almost 80 years (rates vary by sex and race).[13] Although Millennials, the birth cohort born between 1981 and 1997, have now surpassed Baby Boomers as the largest generation, Baby Boomers will still be our largest generation of elders to date.[14] And many of those Baby Boomers are currently caring for their own parents. AARP reported in 2015 that "14.3% of all American adults are a caregiver to someone age 50 or older."[15] From within the elder-care context, Boomers and their grown children are starting to contemplate their own end-of-life issues.

Over the last thirty years, end-of-life care has become increasingly associated with hospice. The National Hospice and Palliative Care Organization estimates that in 2014, more than 1.6 million patients were served by hospice.[16] Hospice care provides comfort care in the last six months of a terminal illness. Care can be provided in a private home, a nursing home, or a hospice facility. The hospice philosophy of care acknowledges that pain can be physical, emotional, financial, and relational; thus hospice organizations utilize an interdisciplinary group of specially trained providers who respond to and treat dying patients' pain and other symptoms, but do not cure the underlying disease. Unlike all other expressions of medical care, the hospice approach considers the patient *and* family to be the unit of care.

Hospice itself has shifted its focus in the last two decades as people now live longer with diseases and conditions that were once considered acutely fatal. Hospice admission depends on a physician's certifying prognosis of six months or fewer to live. Many of the diseases that clearly fell into the six-month fatality window when the hospice benefit began in the 1970s, such as cancer and heart or lung disease, can often be treated now as chronic conditions for many years before causing death, thus complicating the predictability of an accurate six-month prognosis of mortality.[17] In answer to these changes in mortality, palliative care has separated itself from hospice to offer comfort care that can be prescribed long before a patient meets hospice admission criteria.[18] While palliative care includes various medical options, such as surgery, chemotherapy and radiation, and management of their side effects, it also includes a focus on the patient's physical status and emotional well-being, such as how much suffering the patient is willing to experience, the effect of the illness on family members, and legal, insurance, and religious issues.

Financial Changes

As professional services providing support for aging, serious illness, and end-of-life care have grown, so too have the costs. The triple-legged stool of private retirement sources, such as pensions, private savings and investments, and public programs, including Social Security, Medicare, and Medicaid, has come under increasing pressure. The large number of Boomers combined with increased economic inequality has caused wide-spread concern about the financial insecurity of aging. Almost half of those who are 65 or older are poor or are at economic risk.[19]

Apace with elder-care needs, the number of informal, family caregivers continues to grow as well. Pew Research reported in 2013 that "36% of US adults said they provided unpaid care to an adult relative or friend in the past year, up from 27% in 2010."[20] As the number of caregivers grows, the awareness of its costs grows as well. Caregiving for an aging or ill adult can be costly for the caregiver on a number of levels. First, nearly half of all caregivers spend more than $5000 annually on care-related expenses.[21] These monies can cover medications, medical bills, in-home care, and nursing home care. In addition to money costs, a physical cost can be incurred as well as caregivers often meet a wide array of tasks from yard work and home maintenance, transportation, medication management, and grocery shopping to more vulnerable and time-intensive tasks such as bathing, dressing, toileting, and walking; these activities may require the purchase or rental of medical equipment or may necessitate hiring someone else to perform custodial care services. Emotional and profes-sional costs can be incurred as well. Scholars describe family caregiving as a "chronic stress" situation affecting physical health and well-being and causing a secondary impact on the professional life of the caregiver.[22] On average, caregivers serve 20.4 hours per week, thus impacting their ability to work and producing long-term effects on their Social Security payments and lifetime wage earnings, personal savings, professional advancement, and earning potential. Over a lifetime, caregivers lose on average $659,139 in wages, Social Security, and pension benefits that they would have otherwise received.[23] Employers also pay a price when an employee takes on elder-care responsibilities. Caregiving affects the health and productivity of employees. Meeting family caregiving demands causes higher rates of absenteeism, turnover, and early retirement, and costs US employers between $11.4 and $29 billion annually.[24]

On the other hand, this informal care has benefits beyond those for the actual care recipient. First, replacing this uncompensated care with compensated care would cost approximately $522 billion, costs that might well require additional government expenditures.[25] Second, informal care effectuates cultural preferences to remain at home, with support by loved ones.[26] The costs in the final year of life continue to be the most expensive of all medical expenses for individuals and society. For more than a decade, Medicare has spent approximately one-fourth of its total expenditures on patients' last six months of life.[27] Part of this cost can be attributed to the percentage of people in the intensive care unit (ICU) in the last month of life, which has been steadily increasing since 2000.[28] Medical professionals and journalists alike research the high costs of care, criticize contemporary billing practices, rue the lack of physician generalists and gerontologists, and propose advanced-care planning and increased hospice and palliative care services as potential solutions.[29]

Cultural Changes

In addition to the growth in financial costs of elder care and in the availability of professional and medical resources for the terminally ill, society's awareness of end-of-life issues has grown as well. Some awareness has been positive, such as advocacy efforts to increase awareness of completing advance-care planning documents. Popular on-line projects like "Death Over Dinner" and "The Conversation Project"[30] provide outlines, questions, and conversation starters, even coordinating national conversation days. Many of these efforts have been guided by the concept of "the good death" as shaped by the pioneering work of Dr. Elisabeth Kübler-Ross, as well as the more recent work of popular physicians like Dr. Atul Gawande[31] and celebrated memoirs such as Mitch Albom's *Tuesdays with Morrie*.[32]

However, some public attention has been negative. The term "death panel" entered the public consciousness in 2009 in response to proposed provisions in the Patient Protection and Affordable Care Act (ACA) that would have permitted coverage of voluntary consultations with doctors concerning end-of-life decision-making.[33] These rumors distorted the counseling process itself, creating an illusion of panels of governmental authorities deciding on life or death rather than celebrating the individual doctor/patient relationships. Despite these misleading rumors, beginning January 1, 2016, Medicare began reimbursing for doctors' appointments so that patients could discuss various advanced-care issues ranging from advanced medical directives (living wills, healthcare powers of attorney) to Medicare coverage of hospice and palliative care.[34] However, the phenomenon of death panel mythology serves as a reminder that the human capacity to deny death can take many forms and that any efforts to stress the practical and legal importance of planning for end of life, efforts that may demand increased support and influence by professionals or the government could be met with emotional, often irrational, resistance.[35]

All three changes, medical, financial, and cultural, served as direct or indirect background to the experience of care reported by the adult children we interviewed. In many ways, the sample set reflected the new normal in end-of-life care, although not the new normal in longevity. Compared with other states, Louisiana ranks close to the bottom on a number of quality-of-life measures such as life expectancy at age 65,[36] the percentage of adults ages 25–59 who are married, median family income, and percentage of population with a college degree or further education.[37] It also has one of the highest teen-pregnancy rate and birthrates in the country as well as one of the highest nonmarital birthrates.[38] Hospice utilization was relatively high, with one-fourth dying either under hospice care at home or in a hospice inpatient facility. Almost half of all deaths occurred in a hospital setting because of sudden and traumatic causes. Palliative care played a consulting role in many of the deaths in an acute-care location. Contrasting with general trends in longevity, the deceased

Baby Boomers died relatively young. The parents of study participants were under 70 years old, with the average age of 62. The causes of death were predominately traumatic events: cancer, complications following surgery, or related to substance abuse. Because of the acute nature of the terminal illnesses, the caregiving window was relatively small, unlike national trends of lengthier final illnesses. Interviewee demographics reflect a fair level of gender and race diversity, with the majority of the parents and grown children falling in the poverty to middle-socioeconomic class. To this general background, each interviewee used his or her unique family history as a lens to interpret the role of caregiver.

WHEN THE NEW NORMAL IN THE AMERICAN FAMILY MEETS THE NEW NORMAL IN END-OF-LIFE CARE

Our research studied the convergence of the two demographic trends: shifts in family structure and changing practices in end-of-life care. Although relatively little research has been done qualitatively on this convergence from a legal or religious perspective, sociologists have explored this topic and reached varying conclusions. Sociologists Suzanne Bianchi and Judith Seltzer studied how the demographics of Baby Boomers families altered the family safety net for aging and sick family members.[39] They suggest that the existence of stepfamilies can expand the list of available caregivers, with both full siblings and half-siblings as potential sources of support, but they also note that ties within families created by a parent's remarriage are not as strong as those based on biological relationships. Consequently, questions of who is entitled to receive care and who feels obligated to provide that care become more complex as family structures themselves become more complex.[40] Indeed, sociologists Marilyn Coleman and Lawrence Ganong have found that family ties created through marriage may be ambiguous or weak.[41] Yet they also find enormous variation in stepfamily relationships, ranging from acceptance to ambivalence to rejection, with stepparent–stepchild closeness affected by children's perceptions of the support they and their parent receive from the stepparent as well as by the child's age when the parent remarried.[42] Thus, for example, stepparents who appeared early in the child's life were more likely to be accepted as a parent, although even older stepchildren might move from suspicion of, to bonding with, the stepparent.

Nonetheless, in their numerous studies of intergenerational obligations to provide financial and physical support, Ganong and Coleman found that stepkin fell to the bottom of the list of potential caregivers and inheritors, unless the quality of the relationship was high or the relationship replaced—rather than supplemented—a biological tie. Similarly, other research finds that when members of the general population are asked to rank their level of obligation to provide financial and practical care for a family member, they place their parents first, followed by grandparents, siblings, and in-laws; stepparents and stepsiblings fall to the bottom of the list, ranking just above a "best friend."[43] Because research on the incidence of stepkin care is still in its early stages, our study sought to include stepfamilies to examine this aspect of the new normal in elder care, as care is provided in first-time-married families, single families, and remarried families. We listened for the ethical, legal, and religious influences regarding why grown children and stepchildren did or did not provide care in order to highlight what is working and to learn from the gaps in support revealed.

Our study population reflected the demographic changes in contemporary American society. The new normal in US families came to life in the stories told by interviewees like Peter, Rhonda, and Michelle, introduced at the beginning of the chapter. The sample set included almost equal representation of married-parent families, single-parent families, and remarried-parent families. One-third of those we interviewed came from what previously have been called "traditional families," a mother and father who marry before the birth of children and remain married until death parts them. These families are similar to Peter's. Peter's mother and father, Barbara and Leonard, met in high school when a friend set them up on a blind date after a football game. Peter recalled the oft-repeated story of his parent's courtship and marriage: "[T]hey hung out and said, 'Hey, we like each other,' then they got married, then they had me and my

siblings, and then they were together from that point on" for more than
thirty years of marriage. Their shared family history and norms shaped
how they experienced Leonard's sudden heart attack and death at the age
of 60. Although most adults and children lived in such families in 1960,
today, as noted earlier, less than half of children live in first-time-married
families.

One-third of those we interviewed came from divorced- and remarried-
parent families like Rhonda's. Rhonda was the second of three daughters
born to Evelyn and Ronald. When Rhonda was 13, her mother announced,
"We're leaving." They abandoned everything in her childhood home with
her father, including their dog. Although relationships were tense at times,
Rhonda's divorced parents tried to keep the children central, even celebrating holidays together throughout her teenage years. Her father remarried
and eventually started a new family. Two half-siblings were born. When
asked to draw her family as a part of the opening, warm-up questions,
Rhonda included her father, mother, and two sisters, but not her father's
second wife of more than thirty years, Judith, nor her two half-siblings,
Jackson and Laurie. She conceded that her stepmother eventually "grew
on her," but she "never called her Mom." Without the connective role of
her father, she didn't think that she would have associated with her stepmother. Although Rhonda worked with her stepmother and half-sister in
coordinating care for her sick father, that coordination fell apart after her
father's death.

One-third of those we interviewed came from single-parent families. These families were formed by lifelong choice, divorce, or death of
a spouse. Michelle's mother, Dorothy, was both divorced and widowed at
the time of her death. Dorothy and Michelle's father had lived in New York
until Michelle's fifth birthday, when they moved to New Orleans to be
closer to her father's extended family. Michelle was the baby of the family, with an older brother and sister. Her father left the family soon after
they moved to New Orleans, and Dorothy remarried the following year.
Michelle called her stepfather her "dad" and spoke at length about his
death in 1992. Her mother never remarried nor had a significant other
after the death of her second husband. When Dorothy became sick in

2010, Michelle and her sister shared caregiving responsibilities, with their brother supporting their efforts where he could. Even though the siblings shared both a mother and a father, that bond did not prevent them from experiencing conflicts during the course of their mother's treatment over where Dorothy would reside under hospice care and over the costs of paying for Dorothy's burial.

Other single parents had a significant other, like Nancy's mother, Shannon, who died at age 61 from complications following a stroke. We interviewed Nancy, who explained that when Shannon was 18, she married Nancy's father, Steve. They had two children, Nancy and her brother. Shannon and Steve then divorced, and Shannon married J.J., with whom she had another son. Shannon and J.J. were divorced, and, at the time of her death, Shannon had been living with her boyfriend, William, for ten years. Throughout the caregiving and mourning process, Nancy mediated decisions among her brothers, her mother's boyfriend, her father, and her mother's second ex-husband. Even though her siblings bore equal responsibility legally, Nancy considered herself to be the "next of kin" because she was on site and because, personality-wise, she was the sibling who tended to take the lead during family crises. Because of William's different opinion about life support, Nancy felt forced to explicitly express to medical personnel—as well as to William—that she was the next of kin and that William had no recognized right to control her mother's treatment. Nancy attempted to include other family members in the various decisions that needed to be made for her mother because she felt it was the right thing to do. However, Nancy found that having more kin connections to include compounded the stress of the situation. Consulting each person required phone calls and face-to-face visits during which family members expressed strong emotions. Nancy felt obligated to divert her attention to comforting and calming the other adults when she would have preferred to use that energy on making decisions about her mother's treatment. Even while she tried to be strong for her family and clearheaded for her mother, Nancy felt isolated.

As can be seen in these snapshots of the families of Peter, Rhonda, Michelle, and Nancy, the kin networks contract and expand in relation to the marital choices made by the Baby Boomer parents. Caregivers' roles and feelings varied based not only on their family structure but also on the strength of their connections to, and within, stepfamilies. Depending on the family structure, the grown child could take on varied roles in providing care from serving as the primary caregiver and decision-maker, to consulting and supporting a parent or stepparent as the primary caregiver, to being excluded by or in conflict with the parent or stepparent in the lead role.

CONCLUSION

Overall, today's Baby Boomer faces a potential constellation of kin support that includes paradoxically both fewer and more people bound to home. Stepkin, half-siblings, significant others of parents, ex-kin, and grandparents are now all available to help carry the caregiving responsibilities.[44] On the other hand, these increased connections may be ambiguous, tenuous, untested, or fragile.[45] In addition to more kin relations, there are more professionals involved in end-of-life care than ever before though hospice services, nursing homes, Medicare and Medicaid home health providers, as well as social and legal resources that encourage advanced-care planning. Conversely, geographical distance, changes in civic engagement, and a general decline in religiosity have isolated many older and midlife adults. We can no longer presume a woman will be at home to take on the full-time caretaking duties. The rise in single parenthood and divorce has led to many single elders. Smaller family size means fewer siblings to share the obligations of care, with or without a parent's spouse or significant other.

However, we remain homeward bound both because that's where we want to be and because that's where we create our first family relationships. Those bonds may be expressed in different ways than in previous generations, but they remain foundational.

Caregiving Begins

I believe it's our responsibility to care for our parents.

—*DANIEL*

Brady arrived at the interview at a local library wearing flip-flops, cargo shorts, and a T-shirt touting the boiled shrimp of a local restaurant. He worked as a welder for a local offshore rigging company, while Caterina, his second wife, was getting a degree in education. He was 36 years old, Caucasian, and remarried with no children. Brady's father, James, had been married three times and was estranged from his third wife when he was diagnosed with terminal cancer at the age of 63. Brady described his dad as a hard worker, even refusing to go to the doctor until his livelihood was threatened:

> My dad worked until the day he found out he had cancer. On his way to work, he kept havin' to pull over to the side of the road to throw up, but he was still going to work. He wasn't gonna let it stop him 'cause he knew he had a job to do. He couldn't afford not to work. My dad's boss told him, "Either you go to a doctor and find out what's wrong or I'm gonna fire you. You're not coming in doing this every day. . . ." My dad wasn't about to get fired, so he said, "Okay, I'll go to the doctor."

Brady called his father's boss a "God-sent person" not only for finally getting his dad to go to the doctor, but also "because even when my dad got
down to the point that he couldn't work, he still paid my dad. He paid him
part of his paycheck every week until my dad got on the Medicaid or some
other financial help." After his diagnosis, James called a family meeting
with Brady, his brother and sister, and his two stepsiblings, and told them
"all of his appointments and what needed to be done once he was diagnosed." Brady and his siblings stepped in to coordinate the care: "[W]e
would schedule [in terms of], if this person had off, this person could go."

Throughout his chemotherapy and radiation treatments, James was
determined to remain in his home. James lived alone in the woods, with
only a wood-burning stove for heat. When James could no longer drive or
walk without assistance, Brady's stepsister, Sally, moved in with James to
help, and Brady speculated that she did so "cause she was in between jobs
at that time." With his stepsister living with his father, Brady described
how a routine of arranging visits and phone calls took shape among all of
the siblings. Brady assumed the responsibility of chopping wood for the
stove, keeping up the yard, and buying and delivering groceries. His older
sister would come by on her day off each week and stock the refrigerator
with food. And Sally, who "did more of the taking care of him," managed
his medications, helped him with personal care, and cooked his meals.

Brady's father's wish to stay home during his illness and the family's
caregiving are typical of what happens during end-of-life care. Not only
do most people want to age in place, but also they are overwhelmingly
likely to receive most of their care from family members. Approximately
one out of five adults is providing care to another adult.[1] National surveys find that the typical caregiver spends on average twenty-four hours
a week helping care recipients with at least one activity of daily living,
such as medication management, meals, bathing, dressing, or mobility
assistance.[2] Beyond providing for basic physical needs for safety and helping with daily survival, caregivers advocate for medical care services, provide transportation, and more than half even provide some basic medical
care, such as injections or tube feedings.[3] Most caregivers have no formal
training in how to provide care; instead, people assume responsibilities

because, as Daniel's quote at the beginning of the chapter explains, they believe it is the right thing to do.

Several US laws support family caregiving, such as the federal Family and Medical Leave Act and comparable state laws,[4] and others penalize failing to care or providing abusive care, such as filial responsibility laws[5] and elder abuse laws. On the other hand, the dimensions of family caretaking in the United States and the lack of enforcement of filial responsibility laws[6] suggest that consciousness of these laws is not a motivating factor in providing care. As Robert Ellickson pointed out in an analogous context more than twenty years ago, investigating the law in action shows how people act based on informal social norms and shows that issues are resolved not only without the coercive effect of the law, but also in ways that might be different from what the law imposed.[7] Indeed, in our interviews, we found little acknowledgment (or even awareness) of secular law. Nonetheless, by setting out basic obligations, the law reinforces these informal norms and serves an important supporting role, a role that could, and should, be strengthened because caring for aging and ill parents can impose burdens on the caretakers that secular laws often fail to alleviate. In the next few chapters, we address applicable laws that encourage, support, and protect caregivers and care recipients.

In this chapter, we follow the chronology of caregiving, and, where relevant, tie steps in the caregiving process to background laws affecting hands-on care. Becoming a caregiver typically begins when the parent shares the news of a serious illness or terminal condition with the family. This information serves as a catalyst for all members of the family to focus on the needs of the seriously ill parent. In the following sections, we explore how families managed the demands of time and energy that hands-on physical and medical care required.

BECOMING A CAREGIVER

"I have some bad news. . . ." A tumor has been found, that pesky cough is more than just a cold, an unthinkable accident has occurred, or the surgery did not go as planned. Immediately, a parent's serious illness demands the family's full attention. Although spouses are the most likely caregivers, children, like Brady and his stepsister and siblings whose story opened the chapter, provide a significant source of support, especially when spousal care is unavailable because of death, divorce, estrangement, or incapacity. In instances such as these, in which a spouse is not involved, adult children assume the bulk of elder care. Although national statistics indicate that a daughter is more likely than a son to become a caregiver,[8] sons like Brady are increasingly taking on more responsibility—although it was his stepsister who actually moved in.

Most of those interviewed accepted the need to provide the kind of care at the end of life that parents are expected to provide for their children at the beginning of their lives. They carved out time from their own family routines and work schedules to provide the support that their parent needed. Little of this care was outsourced to paid professionals, sometimes because of choice, sometimes because of economic necessity. Indeed, nationally, only 9% of people who live at home pay for all of the care they receive, while two-thirds receive virtually all of their care from family members. Instead, study participants shared care with other family members or took on responsibilities alone. In this section, we explore the types of hands-on care that were provided.

Assuming caretaking responsibilities can include episodic tasks such as yard work, transportation, and grocery shopping as well as the core activities of daily living, such as meal preparation, eating, bathing, dressing, toileting, and mobility assistance.[9] Many grown children accompanied parents to physician visits, researched disease-specific information and side effects to treatment options, and acted as an advisor to the parent directly or as part of a family discussion. For example, Carla was 50 years old, African American, and married with three children when her mother, Latonya, was diagnosed with low kidney function and heart disease. Although her mother had been single and living independently for many years, her ability to walk and drive started to decline after her diganosis. Carla began transporting Latonya to her physician visits. Carla prided herself on inheriting her mother's eye for detail, so she found it easy to follow her mother's organizational system for tracking her tests, visits, and questions. As a stay-at-home mom and homeschooler to two teenaged children, Carla's schedule accommodated the sporadic, ongoing needs of her mother. She provided updates to her sister and brother, both of whom lived nearby but worked full time, concerning their mother's condition, any medication changes, and treatment options they were considering. Carla started to keep a personal caregiving notebook when her mother became ill, and she brought the notebook with her to the interview. The notebook contained dozens of pages, cataloging medication schedules, research of different treatment options, and records of her calls to the insurance company. During her mother's illness, the notebook stayed at her mother's house and thus allowed her siblings to stay informed and note changes they saw when they stopped by to visit their mother, who lived independently until her death. Carla's notebook was a visible reminder of the time and energy commitment caregiving can require, but Carla also treasured them as precious relics of her care for her mother.

Other grown children became not just extra support to a seriously ill parent living independently, but also took on the role of homemaker and nurse. Angela tended to the day-to-day needs of her single father, Roberto. Angela was 45 years old, Hispanic, and married with two grown children. Angela held a part-time job as a cashier at a local hardware store and also picked up freelance jobs in plumbing or small construction. Her schedule was relatively flexible, thus enabling her to be present for her father's care needs. When she first offered to provide care, he refused; eventually, however, he relented and even moved his trailer into her backyard to make it easier for her to provide the support he needed. She explained how this close proximity allowed her to balance responding to the needs of her father while protecting her and her families' personal boundaries:

> I would always go and clean his trailer. My husband does most of the cooking, so we'd cook and bring him food. I'd wash his clothes, you know, I took care of him. Him in the trailer was good because me and him in the same house was never good. I insisted on no smoking in the house. Then, he always had to tell us how to do things. You

know, "You're not doing that right," or he would make a comment about one of my kids, which would be very insulting. Then we'd get in a big argument and he'd get mad and leave for his trailer.

In time, her father's personal-care needs exceeded what she could provide, and Angela's brother paid for home health services. Still, her father's location allowed her to continue to be involved and to manage the care providers.

FAMILY STRUCTURE AND THE PRIMARY CAREGIVER

As care needs arise, one family member typically steps forward, assuming the role of primary caregiver. This family member delegates responsibilities to others and acts as the primary advocate for the seriously ill loved one. As kinship structures become more complicated,[10] selecting the appropriate individual to fill this role becomes more difficult. If the care recipient was married, then a spouse tended to be the primary caregiver, unless the spouse's physical or mental capacities were compromised in some way. However, as the Baby Boomers age, this trend will change. In 2015, a national caregiving survey reported that less than one-fourth of elders were cared for by a spouse whereas 60% were cared for by a grown child.[11] The marital status of the seriously ill and dying parent as well as the quality of relationships among the family members each played a significant role in determining how the family provided hands-on care.

In first-marriage families, the spouse and parent tended to take the lead in coordinating care, although study participants used the pronoun "we" to describe how care was provided, reflecting the high level of norm coherence within the family. That was how Paula explained her family's caregiving experience. When her father shared the news of his diagnosis with the family, she knew that they would care for him as a family team, with her mother as captain. Paula's parents included her and her two brothers in all major decisions, seeking their advice and support and delegating to them specific tasks and responsibilities. Paula lived in a trailer behind her parent's home, and she and her mother, both nurses at the same hospital, worked with their boss to adjust their schedules so that one of them could always be home with her father. Paula drove him to appointments and treatments and even had a baby monitor in her trailer so that she could keep tabs on her father at night:

> When he couldn't call, couldn't holler loud enough, . . . we always had the airhorn thing, kept it by the bed. I said, 'Nothing else, Daddy. Blow your airhorn. That wake me up.'

Her brothers took charge of meals, which became a family joke because their idea of cooking meant dropping off McDonald's cheeseburgers. The brothers also took over caring for the yard and house, so that their mother and Paula could focus on the medical care for their father.

Grown children in families in which the parents were in the first and only marriage were also often trusted to make critical financial decisions on behalf of the family when the spouse wanted to focus on sitting vigil with the dying person. Clay's mother, Linda, was diagnosed with breast cancer more than a year before her death. For most of that time, she was able to live at home with home health nurse visits several times a week. During that time, the whole family (his father, Clay, Clay's wife, and his younger sister) learned to provide complicated medical care at home. He spoke with pride of how the

> home care nurse gave us an IV class. We learned how to give her Heparin and then flush it with saline. It had to be done 'round the clock. We had to give her a bag in the morning, a bag at night, had to flush it and keep it clean so it wouldn't get infected, and wash up her ports for the chemo.

When Linda's condition worsened, they took her to the hospital. Jerry, her husband of more than forty years, Clay, and his sister took turns sitting at her bedside. When doctors informed the family that Linda would most likely die in the next few days, a nurse pulled Clay aside and explained that the hospital did not have a morgue so the family needed to make their funeral preparations expeditiously. Clay immediately went to his father to find out what the arrangements were, only to learn that, as is true for most people,[12] none had been made, and there was no life insurance that might help pay for the burial. His father did not want to leave his mother's side, so Clay was entrusted with taking care of everything. Quickly, Clay interviewed different funeral homes, making the most economical choices while reflecting the personality and values of his family. When his mother died a few days later, all the arrangements went smoothly. "By the time all that was over I was numb to everything that had happened. I don't want to say I had to step up and be the parent, but I had to be the gatherer, the one who had to put everything together."

In both Paula's and Clay's families the siblings and parents worked together harmoniously. Care in other first and only married-parent families was not always so cooperative; yet, even when the family members experienced conflict with one another or had a history of estrangement, interviewees still used "we" to describe caring together for their parent. For example, April lived next door to her parents and described herself as a "daddy's girl." When her father became terminally ill with congestive heart failure, she was ready to help care for him. However, she had repeatedly clashed with her mother and sister, in part because her sister had struggled with pain pill addiction for many years and she felt that her mother enabled that addiction. April respected the care choices made by her mother and attempted to involve her sister in the day-to-day care as best she could, but she experienced a great deal of frustration with them during the process. However, in contrast to conflicting relationships in single-parent and remarried-parent families, the predominant pronoun she used to tell her story was "we." Biological ties connected family members despite a low quality of relationship.

In single-parent families, a grown child tended to become the parent's primary caregiver. For only children and for those interviewed who had a contentious history with their siblings and half-siblings as well as extended family, the pronoun "I" was often used to describe taking responsibility for caregiving tasks. This choice of pronoun reflected a predominately solitary caregiving experience. Although they sought various levels of informal support from their spouse, siblings, and other parent (ex-spouse), they assumed full care responsibilities. For some, this role evolved out of an already-existing, emotionally close relationship to the single parent. For example, Chloe described her single mother as her "best friend." Caring for her mother and making decisions on her behalf came naturally to Chloe. For others, who were estranged from the single parent, the role was thrust on them by default. Some relied on the support of aunts and uncles, cousins, and grandparents, but ultimately they saw these relatives as advisors and not as people who could actually share the burden of providing or paying for care. And for some, extended family members (cousins, aunts and uncles, and even grandparents) provided antagonism and criticism, rather than support. Chloe, mentioned previously, honored her mother's wishes to end curative treatments and to enter a hospice inpatient unit, even though her aunts and cousins disagreed vocally and threatened not to visit Chloe's mother after her move to a hospice inpatient unit. And then, after her mother's death, they disagreed vocally with Chloe's choice to follow her mother's wishes for cremation because they wanted her embalmed so that they could "see her one more time." Chloe followed her mother's choices despite her extended family's lack of support and direct challenge.

The second element of cooperation—the quality of relationships among the family members—often determined whether siblings cared together as a "we" in single-parent families. For example, Will was the middle son of William Sr., a divorced and retired state employee. Will and his two brothers got along well and shared responsibility for the day-to-day care of their father. Will's older brother, Rick, took the lead in adapting his house to accommodate his father's personal belongings, hospital bed, and other medical equipment. Will, who had recently moved in with his brother, Rick, was able to help bathe and dress their father each morning. Their youngest brother, Hank, lived close by and assisted with picking up prescriptions and taking their father to treatments. The three also relied on their mother, their father's ex-wife, to help by staying with him a few times a week, making meals, and providing general emotional support. Their teamwork spanned their father's illness through his burial to settling his estate. The quality of the relationships made serving as a "we" possible.

For some grown children of single parents, their use of "we" included the ex-spouse of the ill parent. Ex-spouses did not serve as primary care-givers, but they could play an ancillary role, even following a conten-tious divorce. In 20% of the forty single- or remarried-parent deaths, an ex-spouse assumed some responsibilities during the caregiving process. A few ex-spouses took an active, hands-on role with both the grown child and the dying parent by sitting with the dying ex-spouse, regularly mak-ing food, and even playing a decision-making role after death. A few were even present at the time of death. For example, Will said of his mother, "She was amazing when he got sick. She's retired now, so she had a lot of time, and she was able, during the week, to run errands and help around our house." She made meals for the brothers as well as for her ex-husband and delivered them each week. She sat vigil with her sons at the hospice inpatient unit at the hospital after their father lost consciousness and was near death. She also accompanied them to the funeral home and helped them pick out the casket and burial plot.

Most ex-spouses, though, provided support to the grown child but assumed a more tangential role with the dying ex-spouse. Their focus was on the well-being of their grown child. Despite the level of involve-ment, no ex-spouse incurred any financial or legal rights or responsibili-ties on behalf of the dying or deceased ex-spouse. For example, Brady's mother, his father's first wife of three, supported her son emotionally through phone calls, but did not offer to provide any direct support to her ex-husband.

In married-parent and single-parent families, the shared norms and history clearly defined how the family as a unit would work together to care for the sick parent or respond to a healthcare crisis. In contrast to that clarity, grown children in remarried families often experienced ambiguity and even frustration concerning their prescribed family roles versus the role played by a parent's spouse. They needed the common point of connection, the dying parent, to help them understand how to work together. The dying parent was often too debilitated to play that clarifying role. Caregiving and the surrogate decision-making process either reinforced familial coherence or reflected existing conflicts in remarried families. As research predicts, particularly when the stepparent entered the child's life after elementary school, the grown child tended to feel excluded from the family unit. Interviewees often used the pronoun "she or he" to describe the caregiving experience. They did not see themselves as part of a family team; they were *not* connected to their dying parent's spouse as a "we."

Exclusion could be painful when interpreted as intentional on the part of the stepparent. For example, Georgia's stepmother served as the primary caregiver for Georgia's biological father. Georgia was 50 years old, African American, and married with three grown daughters. Georgia felt a certain fierce connection to her father because she had not known him while she was growing up. In her mid-twenties, she sought him out. Georgia's mother had been 13 and drug addicted when she became pregnant after a one-night stand. Georgia's father knew she existed but had never tried to find her. After more than twenty years, Georgia expected her father to turn her away or deny his paternity. To her great amazement, he welcomed her connection to his family. Extended family members affirmed her ancestry:

> He introduced me to everyone. They picked up on some of my ways and the way that I handled myself. They said, "Oh, definitely. She's a H_, she's a H_." I look exactly like the family, with hair exactly like the family. So they all accepted me . . . I look more like him than any kid that he has and he has four kids and an outside one, besides me.

Georgia relished the time she was able to spend with him as an adult. However, his wife was not as receptive to her involvement in the family.

> She was so protective of him. She didn't want me around. Because it was his wife, I tried to develop a good relationship with her. I respected her and everything and if I needed something from my

daddy, I would always try to go through her first, but my dad said, "No, if you need something come to me." So I started going through my daddy, but I felt bad about doing it because I didn't wanna disrespect her.

When her father became ill with cancer and homebound because of his deteriorating health, Georgia researched his cancer and the available treatment options, and she wanted to be included in providing hands-on care. Georgia's stepmother refused to allow her to visit or talk with him, let alone consult her; Georgia recalled climbing the fence of her father's house and pounding on the front door, begging to speak to him. During his final week of life, he was transferred to a local hospital, which Georgia counted as a blessing. Her stepmother could not ban her from the hospital, a public place, without just cause. Georgia sat vigil at his bedside, offering simple acts of care, "We would wipe him down if he messed on himself. Hold his hand. He started picking at his covers. He would look up at us and smile. His lips were cracked. I would put some Vaseline on them." Although Georgia was able to care for her father on his deathbed, the quality of her relationship with her husband's wife caused her to feel excluded and to use the pronoun "she" to describe her caregiving experience, an experience that carried over into burial and funeral choices and inheritance.

Protecting the Care Recipient from Abuse

We listened carefully to participants' stories for any signs of abuse from them or from other family members, and, although we heard about difficult to manage verbal and physical behavior on the part of the seriously ill parent, we did not hear about elder abuse. No one self-reported engaging in abusive behavior toward a parent.[13] The absence of any signs of elder abuse is atypical. The US Administration on Aging defines elder abuse as "any knowing, intentional, or negligent act by a caregiver or any other person that causes harm or a serious risk of harm to a vulnerable adult."[14]

Studies report that one in ten elders over age 65 experiences some form of mistreatment.[15] Perpetrators of elder abuse are most likely to be adult children—that is, from our survey population. Elder abuse, which ranges from physical violence to financial exploitation to neglect to self-neglect,[16] was certainly a potential problem for our population. The Louisiana Department of Health and Hospitals reports that "over 7,300 cases of abuse involving older and vulnerable adults are reported in Louisiana each year."[17]

More generally, it is hard to know about the incidence of elder abuse in American society.[18] Professionals may miss incidents of elder abuse because of their own "lack of awareness and adequate training on detecting abuse," and the elderly may not report abuse because of their dependence on the abusing caregiver or because of limitations in their own mental or physical abilities.[19]

Elder abuse statutes seek to protect the vulnerable elderly, although the statutes may be too piecemeal and political to set a floor of acceptable behavior for caregiving.[20] Every state has enacted laws that are designed to prevent elder abuse, and elder abuse statutes apply to both family and to nonfamily members.[21] Abuse includes physical, sexual, and emotional abuse, exploitation, neglect, abandonment, and self-neglect. One form of elder abuse laws establishes reporting requirements: Specific individuals must report certain forms of mistreatment. These reports are typically owed to the state's adult protective services unit. A second type of law imposes civil or criminal sanctions on those—not just family members—who mistreat older people.[22] In Louisiana, people over the age of 60 are protected from various forms of abuse, including from a caregiver, under a statute titled, "Cruelty to persons with infirmities."[23] Family members commit most elder abuse, women are more likely than men to experience the abuse, and the incidence of abuse increases with age.[24] Particularly as the number of families with elder stepparents increases in the future, so too may the risk for abuse; stepchildren are at greater risk for abuse, so the converse may also be true: Stepparents will be at greater risk for elder abuse.[25]

Overall, no one mentioned explicitly an awareness of elder abuse laws.

CONCLUSION

Family caregiving is a hands-on endeavor that can demand a high level of energy as well as respect for the independence and wishes of the parent in need. The caregiving role emerges as a response to the specific needs of a seriously ill or hurt parent and is characterized by the ethos and shared norms of the family system at hand. Although secular laws attempt to enforce, encourage, and protect the giving of this care, most grown children are willing to serve without coercing, oversight, or public support. However, even though the needs of care recipients may be met, the needs of the caregiver may be overlooked, a topic addressed in the next chapter.

The Costs of Care

Give me the strength to deal with this because I'm losing it. I'm losing my strength.

—*Michelle*

Michelle served as the primary caregiver for her single mother, Dorothy. She was the baby of the family, with two older siblings who lived nearby. For years before her death, Dorothy lived independently but suffered from mental illness. Michelle described her mother's living conditions as worthy of being featured on the television show *Hoarders,* and explained how her mother often spent her free time dressed as a "bag lady," collecting trash on the streets. From the time that she moved out on her own after high school, Michelle felt ashamed of her mother, but felt obligated to check in on her. She stopped by each week to collect the mail, bring some groceries, and check on her physical and mental condition. A year before her death, Dorothy shared with her daughter that she was experiencing pain and vaginal bleeding, so they went to the emergency room. Tests showed a tumor, which could be removed with surgery. Although Michelle encouraged her mother to have the surgery, her mother refused and wanted to go home with hospice care. Reluctantly, Michelle agreed, but convinced her mother to move in to *her* home. Although Michelle had two siblings, she was the one who held a steady job, owned her home, and had savings that could help her support her mother in her final months of life. She wanted to care for her mother financially and medically and wanted time to try repairing her relationship with her mother. However, Michelle worried that her mother's erratic behavior would be a challenge. And, sometimes, providing her care became overwhelming, but she found ways to cope when the costs of care felt too high:

> I went in my room, in my closet, and cried. I never wanted her to see me cry. I would always cry in my closet, which was a great distance from her room. So, I would get in there and I would pray. And then I'd put in eyedrops so she wouldn't see my red eyes and know I was crying.

Michelle persevered in her caregiving. She attributed her willingness to care as creating space for a "Hallmark moment" when she and her mother could reconcile their often strained and argumentative relationship:

> So, we're sitting there and we're eating breakfast at night. My kids have taken baths, and they're getting ready to go to sleep. She says, "I just wanted to tell you that I'm sorry." I said, "What are you apologizing for?" She says, "I just feel like I need to tell you I'm sorry." I said, "No, Mom. You don't owe me an apology." So, she said, "I'm so proud of you. You got your degree. You're working on your masters," (which I had to pause because I had to take care of her). "And, I just want to tell you I love you, and I thank you for it." And, I said, "Well, Mom, I'm showing you how it should have been for you. Your family should have been there for you back when you needed them. Dad should have been there for you when you needed him when you were together. And, funny enough, even though I'm divorced, those eight years I was married showed me an abundance of love. It showed me how families should be. It showed me how families embrace each other, pray for each other, pray over food, travel with each other. . . . We hugged. And, she had to hug me kinda sideways because of the tumor; it was like she was carrying triplets.

Michelle faced challenges as a caregiver, and yet the experience ultimately provided meaning and worth for her and reconciliation with her mother.

In this chapter, we shift our focus from the needs of the care recipient to the needs of the caregiver. We explore how families found support in managing the costs of care, including money, time, and emotion. We first address the financial responsibilities of elder care and contrast those voluntarily assumed obligations with the somewhat-punitive state filial responsibility laws. We then look at the Family and Medical Leave Act (FMLA), which is the primary source of legal recognition for the time involved in caregiving. Last, we explore how best to protect the vulnerability of the caregiver.

Financing Care and the Role of Filial Responsibility Laws

Providing adequate care involves not only accommodating the daily needs of aging or sick parents and advocating for their wishes concerning medical treatment, but also accepting responsibility for managing—and sometimes actually paying for—the costs related to custodial care, shelter, and medical treatments. Most parents and the grown children we interviewed were working class based on education level and current job, although a few were comfortably in the middle class.[1] The expenses of medical treatments were significant to virtually all of the families. Will, who shared caregiving responsibilities with his two brothers for their divorced father, explained how he and his brothers had to convince their father, William Sr., to seek treatment despite the potential cost:

> we really, really pushed him to go to M.D. Anderson Hospital in Houston. We really wanted him to go out there just because they're the best. He'd say, "It costs this and this." And I'm just like, "I really don't give a shit what it costs. That's not an issue. Me and my brothers do very well thanks to you all giving us a good start. Trust me. It ain't a problem."

After their father moved in with Will and his brother, Will created an elaborate spreadsheet with straightforward formulas for splitting the costs of care and, ultimately, the burial costs, among him and his two brothers.

Had Will and his brothers refused to cover the costs of caring for their dad, would they have been punished? Potentially, yes. Filial responsibility statutes impose civil and, sometimes, criminal liability on children who fail to finance the care of their parents at a level deemed acceptable by the state. They are most likely to affect the caregiving child—in part because that is who the state is most likely to have jurisdiction over.

Today, more than half of the states, including Louisiana, have filial responsibility statutes on the books[2]—down from the 1950s, when almost all of them did.[3] Although the statutes are rarely enforced, they have a long history, and there are signs that they may become more prominent.

American adoption of filial responsibility derives from the early seventeenth-century Elizabethan Poor Relief Act,[4] which established reciprocal responsibilities among parents, grandparents, and children of "every poor, blind, lame, and impotent person" to support one another.[5] As the federal government assumed more financial responsibility to care for older people through Social Security in the 1930s and for the health-care needs of low-income people and older people through Medicaid and Medicare in the 1960s, some states repealed their filial responsibility statutes and enforcement rates dropped, but most states retained their laws.[6] Contemporary American statutes vary between states, but, as other scholars have explained, they are often characterized by the following:

- first, "language establishing grounds for financial liability (such as Virginia's grounds, the parent's "necessitous circumstances," or Pennsylvania's undefined "indigent" status);
- second, "a provision prioritizing liability among several children or other obligors (such as Virginia's language providing obligated parties shall "jointly and severally share . . . duty") [along with] a statement of any exceptions to liability (such as a child who was not cared for sufficiently by the parent while a minor);[7]

- third, establishment of liability based on ability to pay (characteristic of slightly more than half of the statutes);[8]
- fourth, lists of who may initiate the suit, ranging from the parents themselves to creditors to a public entity[9] along with the means for enforcement;[10]
- and finally, efforts to reconcile the filial responsibility law with support provided by various welfare programs, such as that available through Medicaid.[11]

Louisiana's laws generally require that children "honor" their parents, and the statutes impose financial obligations on children to support needy parents.[12] The precise amount of support depends on both the needs of the parent and the economic capacity of the child.[13] Although these statutory provisions have been legislatively modified twice over the past fifty years, there are no reported decisions during that time period.

Filial responsibility statutes are controversial legally, pragmatically, and morally.[14] They have, however, repeatedly survived constitutional challenges.[15] Although filial responsibility cases are rare, a 2012 Pennsylvania case resulted in national attention to the laws.[16] Maryann Pittas spent six months in Liberty Nursing Rehabilitation Center after she broke her legs in a car accident. She applied for Medicaid, but it was not approved in time to cover her bills. Although two siblings of her son, John, had moved to Greece—and his mother had joined them as well—Liberty's parent corporation sued John for his mother's outstanding bills. The courts determined that John Pittas was responsible for his mother's outstanding $93,000 nursing home bill under a Pennsylvania law that imposes liability on family members for support of an "indigent person"[17] based on his ability to pay.[18] Critics of the decision noted that the courts did not seek funds from his mother's spouse or other children. Similar to this case, the suits are typically not brought by parents, even though they are entitled to sue their children for support,[19] but by third parties who provide medical or residential care.[20] For example, a 2014 bankruptcy case almost casually mentioned the proceedings of an assisted-living facility to use Pennsylvania's filial responsibility law to collect money owed by a decedent's mother.[21]

The actions of the assisted-living facility prompted one brother to sue the other concerning the debt, an example of how filial responsibility laws can affect intrafamilial relationships. Although reported legal cases remain rare, and recouping costs for caregiving provided to a decedent could be difficult and time consuming, the increasing expense of elder care could make the government, medical, and residential care providers more likely to use these laws.[22]

In terms of the intersection between family structure and elder care, the financial realm may be where we see the full effect of changing family structures. Grown children from single-parent families drew on their own personal finances to a far greater extent than did children in married-parent families. In fact, no study participants from married-parent families mentioned drawing on their own finances to help with care costs, whereas all grown children from single parents did.

With the increasing incidence of "gray" (late-in-life) divorce, there will be more single parents needing care, each with fewer financial resources to contribute to meeting the costs of that care. Researchers have found that older married couples have five times the wealth of older divorced Americans, and even those who have been widowed have twice the wealth of those who have been gray divorced.[23] Although a late-in-life divorce would not include child-support responsibilities, asset division, including pension, retirement, alimony, and so forth, can be costly and put both ex-spouses at risk financially.[24] Moreover, if those gray divorcees remarry, their grown children may balk at providing care for not only two parents but now, potentially, four parent figures. And, their stepchildren may not feel obligated to provide care at all; as observed in Chapter 1, researchers have noted that the level of financial obligations felt by stepchildren to late-in-life parental remarriages remains low and depends heavily on the quality of the new relationship and the financial abilities of the grown children.[25]

The coupling of responsibilities for finances and actual physical and emotional care can complicate relationships and lead to conflicts of interest and emotions those caregivers must seek to resolve. Because the majority of those interviewed were working class and the parents were not yet eligible for Medicare and had not applied for Medicaid, some coordinated collecting money from extended family members to cover medical treatment and others even took on a second job. No one mentioned awareness of Louisiana's filial responsibility laws, although many acted within the spirit of these laws by taking on whatever financial obligations they could.

Finding Time to Provide Care

In addition to the financial costs of providing care, many study participants needed to carve out time on weekends and evenings as well as time off from employments to provide hands-on care or make visits in a care setting. In this section, we address how grown children managed the time cost of providing care.

Geographical proximity to the parent in need played a large role in determining which sibling had time to meet pragmatic care responsibilities. Nationally, the majority of caregivers (72%) live within twenty minutes of the care recipient.[26] Indeed, that was true in our study. Of those interviewed, 40% played either a major or auxiliary role in hands-on care; all of these caregivers either resided with the seriously ill parent or lived nearby. Of those, ten actually lived with the parent during the caregiving window, and six lived in a separate house but on the same property. Close geographical proximity aided in the ability to manage day-to-day crises in person. In the remaining 60% of families, sudden death or estrangement from the dying parent precluded the need for care.

Employment status of the grown child also played a determinative role in who could provide care. The grown child who had acted as a caregiver was often unemployed by choice or chance during the caregiving window, as was true for Brady's family, profiled in the previous chapter. Others had flexibility to respond to the care needs of their parent because they were engaged in freelance work or worked from home. Some found support from their employer, using vacation leave, leaving work early during an emergency, taking "comp time," or working a flexible schedule. For example, Peter explained that was able to take two weeks off from his work to be with his father in the ICU because

> I had so much comp time and leave built up. I work overtime so much that I wind up with an ungodly amount of leave ... and my supervisor said, "Take the time you need. You got it. Do what you need to do." And so I wound up being off for about two weeks, just being at the hospital and being back. I had the time, and they understood. They said, "Don't worry about what's going on here. We got it covered."

No one remembered their employer suggesting that they were entitled to unpaid leave, nor did they report considering that they could use the law to receive time off.

The lack of awareness about legal support for caretaking is not surprising. A 2016 poll reported that 44% of respondents in California had never heard of family leave, which in California is now paid.[27] The FMLA offers the best and most direct form of support to employees in need of time off from their jobs to meet the care needs of a family member, its coverage is limited, and, most problematically, uncompensated.[28] The FMLA, enacted in 1993, allows eligible employees to take up to twelve weeks of unpaid, job-protected leave from work for medical reasons related to care for a close family member.[29] More than half of FMLA leave is taken for an employee's own illness, and it is often used to care for a newborn. Women are one-third more likely to take leave than men, and households with children are more likely to use leave than those without children.[30] Almost as frequently as it is used for parental leave, FMLA leave is also taken to care for a spouse, a parent, or for someone who has acted as a parent.[31] Indeed, the 1993 Senate Report accompanying the act recognized the importance of family caregiving for the increasing number of older people, although the formal findings at the beginning of the actual statute do not explicitly recognize the aging population.[32]

Even if they had considered taking FMLA leave, however, they might not have qualified. Eligibility is limited in several ways. First, the employer must be covered; the Act does not reach private employers with fewer than fifty employees at any one workplace, but does apply to all public agencies. Although comparatively few workplaces (under 20%) are covered by the FMLA because of their size, close to two-thirds of all American workers are employed at one of the covered sites.[33]

Second, the employee must have worked for the employer for at least twelve months, with a minimum of 1250 hours over the previous twelve-month period, and at a location where the company employs fifty or more employees within seventy-five miles. Accessing the FMLA might have given Angela, who was first mentioned in Chapter 2 and whose father moved into the trailer behind her house, more flexibility in her care schedule, especially as her father's condition worsened, when he needed more assistance with transportation to and from medical appointments, and she started to supervise home healthcare providers. However, her own erratic employment history would have most likely excluded her from eligibility.

Third, to qualify for leave, the health condition must be "serious," which means it requires inpatient care or "continuing treatment by a healthcare provider."[34] The parents of 70% of those interviewed would have met this requirement based on the location of their care at the time of their death in a hospital, at home with hospice, or in a hospice inpatient unit. In these families, the FMLA could have afforded study participants much needed short-term or intermittent leave to provide care at home or visit the ICU. The remaining 30% of parents died suddenly, and thus the FMLA would not have applied to their potential caregivers.

Fourth, although the FMLA covers care for a parent or someone who acted *in loco parentis*[35] (acting in the place of a parent by assuming parental rights and obligations), it does not cover grandparents or stepparents or ex-stepparents who may not have parented throughout the employee's childhood.[36] For example, Chantrelle's mother and stepfather married when Chantrelle was in her early twenties. She served as the photographer at their backyard wedding. A year before her stepfather's death, she enrolled in a local beauty school and moved in with them. Living with them helped her cut her expenses so that her earnings from her job at a local gas station could be used toward her education. When her stepfather had a stroke, she described how she helped her mother, who stayed at the hospital with her dying stepfather: "I just washed dishes, cleaned the living room and the bathrooms, cleaning around the yard and stuff, just keeping the house up while my mom and him would be in the hospital." Chantrelle played a behind-the-scenes role supporting her mother as the primary caregiver, a role she could manage alongside a full-time job and school. However, if she had wanted a larger part in providing care for her stepfather, she would not have qualified for leave under the FMLA.

Finally, unpaid leave is unrealistic for many employees. Brady couldn't afford to take time off from work to care for his father; it was his unemployed stepsister, Sally, who volunteered. And, although Michelle, whose story opened this chapter, had flexibility in her job and some vacation time available, as a single mother to three children, she could not afford unpaid leave. Some interviewees could access their paid vacation leave or sick leave to cover short-term absences from work, but most had to be creative or do without. These anecdotes resonate with national statistics related to the economics of unpaid leave. In 2012, more than half of leave takers received partial or no pay, and many covered for lost wages by limiting spending, using savings, delaying bill payments, cutting leave short, or borrowing money.[37]

Protecting Caregivers from Abuse

The mental and emotional costs of caring for an aging and dying parent can also be added to the financial and time costs of care. The weight of caring for a parent in need can put both vulnerable elders and caregivers at risk for abuse. Although (not surprisingly) no study participant described engaging in abuse of an elder, they did sometimes have to protect themselves from the potentially abusive actions of their parents.[38] Abuse laws protect elder parents, but leave a gap in protecting the caregiver as a vulnerable party. Past experiences of less-than-adequate parenting fundamentally affected a grown child's decision to care.[39] Negligent, inappropriate, or unsavory behavior was broadly defined, ranging from parents who had abandoned their children at some point over the life cycle to parents who exhibited other negative or disruptive behaviors often stemming from substance abuse. Some used the experience of nonparenting or disrespectful parenting to refuse care. For example, Jeremy basically washed his hands of his mother whose substance abuse caused erratic behavior:

> At the time of her passing, her and my stepdad had gotten on the bricks. She got kind of tough to handle. I was in a weird spot, trying to figure out who do I back in this fight or whatever, 'cause my mom would act weird sometimes. They were constantly arguing. There may have been some prescription drug abuse. They may have been drinking too much. It was all on her side. We know that there was scrip abuse—having a couple a day and a few glasses of wine, that sort of thing.

However, when she died suddenly, he became the family member to take responsibility and settle her affairs after death. And, even though her behavior had pushed away her ex-husband, Paul, Jeremy would find a reliable source of support in him both the night of her death and in the year following.

Others, like Angela, felt obligated to honor a parent in need despite emotionally difficult behavior, as a response to the physical, financial, emotional needs of the suffering and dying parent. Angela recognized the dangers, however, and struggled to protect herself from potential abuse. The fact that her father lived in a trailer behind her house, rather than in her house, helped create a buffer between them. Her brother, Timothy, refused to have direct contact with their father, but agreed to pay for his care. Her sister, Jackie, lived in Oregon, and during our interview, explained that she felt pressure from her sister, Angela, to come home to Baton Rouge and help care for their frail father. However, the demands of her own family and her conflicted history with her father kept her from coming home:

> I tried to figure out a way, what are my terms to be able to carry on a relationship with him that doesn't transgress against me and

dishonor me, but at the same time maintains an appropriate parent relationship that you can carve out of a family that has the kind of history that we had . . . I would try to be respectful, at the same time I would not allow him to cross my boundaries or revert back to old patterns of treating me with disrespect.

She could not reconcile her history with her father with coming home to help provide day-to-day care for him. Jackie offered emotional support to her sister instead.

Many of those interviewed developed coping mechanisms that allowed them to express an acceptable level of care while remaining tempered by healthy personal boundaries.[40] They differentiated between the person of their parent and the parent's actions or addictions, sometimes honoring the conversion of a parent from substance abuse to sobriety when the sobriety led to repentance and reconciliation; some honored their parent by simply choosing not to be ashamed of them or not speaking poorly about them publicly. Some drew on their personal faith: The grace and love they believed they received from God led them to show grace and love to their parent.[41] As Michelle discovered in coping with her mother's often difficult behavior, finding a quiet place to release her emotions and to pray could help her garner the strength she needed to meet the demands of care.

As with the FMLA and filial responsibility laws, no one mentioned explicitly an awareness of elder abuse laws or legal protection for caregivers. Almost all believed that a parent in need required some level of care response; however, they shared a common sensibility that elder care should be provided respectfully and safely, for both the parent and the family caregiver. Daniel reflected on caring for his beloved father, who died several years before the interview, as well for as his troubled single mother:

I believe that it's our responsibility to take care of our parents. Sometimes, like with my father, it was easier to do that responsibility. With my mother, she had a lot of self-imposed issues, and that made it hard. I had to get away from it to keep myself sound, stress-wise. But still, when she needed us, my sister and I took care of her, because she was family.

CONCLUSION

The costs of care can include money, time, and mental and emotional energy. Society seeks to support caregivers who choose to provide care for an aging or dying loved one through various laws, like the FMLA, and to enforce the financing of care for those who may be reluctant to do so through filial responsibility laws. However, even laws encouraging care can have practical limitations in their ability to provide relief; unpaid leave, for example, is not always realistic, nor are many employees covered by the FMLA. Moreover, many caregivers are unaware of these laws, although they are willing to provide care anyway. That said, the demands of care can expose both elders and caregivers to the risk of being abused. Elder abuse laws seek to protect the ill and aged, but leave caregivers at risk.

Decision-Making with Planning

I went through making a lot of decisions and learning a lot about myself out of the whole [caregiving] process.

—KYLE

Kyle's parents divorced when he was in third grade, and for several decades he lost track of his mother's whereabouts. Raised by his grandparents and father, he knew of his mother mostly through pictures and stories. In adulthood, he learned of her battles with substance abuse, which helped him understand her absence but did not remove the pain of her abandonment. In his early thirties, he decided to seek her out with the hope of repairing their broken relationship, a reconciliation that became fully realized during the caregiving process.

At the time of our interview, Kyle was 42 years old, Caucasian, married, a commercial pilot, and the father of three elementary school–aged children. His single mother, Mary, was diagnosed with cancer several years before her death, and when he learned of her illness, Kyle adjusted his schedule to meet her varying needs. At the start, he served as an advisor and emergency contact, but in her final year of life, he became her primary caregiver and agent under a power of attorney. She died in his home, under his care, and Kyle served as the person who acted on her behalf during her incapacity and after her death.

In this chapter, we explore how family members assumed responsibilities as the primary decision-maker when the parent engaged in formal planning in advance. The primary decision-maker acts as a complement to, and may be the same person as, the primary caregiver, but not always. We catalog the different advance planning resources available and highlight the ones used by study participants. Specifically, we look at the role of the Do Not Resuscitate (DNR) order and the process of appointing an agent under a power of attorney plays in offering guidance to a grown child and in resolving conflicts within different family structures. Few study participants, however, reported that a parent had engaged in such advance planning. As this chapter shows, the parents' efforts provided guidance, although they did not necessarily prevent all conflicts.

BACKGROUND TO SURROGATE DECISION-MAKING

Individuals have the right to make their own decisions when they are mentally competent to do so. The law sets out different standards for when people have the mental capacity to make these decisions; for example, the capacity standard for signing a contract is higher than the standard for signing a will. If someone signs a contract or a will, but lacks the requisite mental capacity to do so, then those documents are void. Issues of mental capacity are critical to medical treatment because informed consent is typically required for any form of medical treatment.[1]

The concept and form of advance directives, through which individuals indicate their wishes in advance of any incapacity to make their own decisions, arose from the basic principles of informed consent, which focus on protecting and preserving the patient's autonomy.[2] Several types of advance directive documents increase the possibility that a person's wishes for treatment will be followed should the individual be rendered unable to speak or decide for themselves.

Beyond the basic right to make healthcare decisions for one's self, the benefits of advance care planning extend to the family and to the healthcare system as a whole. Through advance planning, individuals typically choose not only treatments focused on relieving pain and discomfort over life-extending treatments but also enrollment in hospice earlier, thereby avoiding many physical and psychological stresses.[3] Countless studies find that simply conversing about one's wishes gives patients and families the opportunity to start preparing mentally and emotionally for death and often supports several of the primary concerns of people with life-limiting illnesses: staying involved, clear communication, shared decision-making, and maintaining control.[4] By stating the kind of care they want in advance, patients may alleviate the burden of decision-making on family members.[5] Surveys report that among severely or terminally ill patients, fewer than 50% have an advance directive in their medical record,[6] as do only 28% of home healthcare patients. By contrast, as patients become more involved with healthcare professionals, they become more likely to have an advance directive: 65% of nursing home residents and 88% of hospice-care patients have filled out an advance directive.[7]

End-of-life decision-making raises a set of distinct issues. The parameters of the decisions authorized, including whether individuals can choose to continue or end life-sustaining treatment and what rights their surrogates have to make the choice on their behalf, have been framed by numerous high-profile court cases over the past few decades. What the cases ultimately establish is that a competent person has a constitutionally protected liberty interest in refusing unwanted medical treatment. However, when another seeks to act on an incapacitated person's behalf, both the interests of the state and of the individual must be considered and balanced.[8] In the early twenty-first century, the Florida case of *Bush v. Schiavo* dramatized the issues at stake when an individual does not plan for her own disability and a loved one seeks to end life support. Terri Schiavo went into cardiac arrest at the age of 27, and the ensuing battles over who would make healthcare decisions for her ultimately resulted in appeals to Congress and the president to intervene.[9]

In the next two sections, we address how the law provides mechanisms for different forms of advance planning concerning both financial and healthcare decisions. We analyze how surrogates made decisions when advance planning had been completed by the parent and discussed.

Healthcare Decision-Making

Federal law encourages planning for incapacity. In 1990, Congress enacted the Patient Self-Determination Act, which requires that federally funded healthcare institutions and health maintenance organizations show that their patients have been informed that they have the right to make decisions concerning medical treatment, including through advance health directives.[10] In this section, we define the different types of healthcare advance directives as well as applicable laws and physician orders that can replace, amplify, or color the carrying out of these wishes.

LIVING WILLS

A living will is a written document in which an individual specifies preferences regarding life-sustaining medical care in case of incapacity, and it is limited to end-of-life decisions. It is directed to medical professionals and concerns specific treatment options. State statutes generally allow an individual to indicate a preference either for or against further medical treatment when the person becomes terminally ill, permanently unconscious, or when death is imminent. Through a living will, a person may, for example, state a preference not to receive life-sustaining artificial nutrition and hydration if there is no reasonable expectation of recovery or to receive such treatments for a limited period. Although the execution requirements for a living will vary, states typically require that the document be in writing and be signed, and many also require witnesses and a notary. In Louisiana, a living will can be done either in writing or orally through verbal or nonverbal means, so long as there are two witnesses.[11] A living will becomes effective only once the patient is unable to make his or her own decisions. States generally provide immunity to medical professionals who follow their patient's instructions in a living will, although states may not impose liability if a medical professional fails to comply with a living will.[12]

A Healthcare Power of Attorney

A healthcare power of attorney appoints a surrogate decision-maker and generally allows the individual to include treatment instructions. A healthcare power of attorney (sometimes also called a "healthcare proxy") is a written document that gives legal authority to another adult to make healthcare decisions on behalf of the individual. The healthcare power of attorney is far more comprehensive than a living will and can address the principal's preferences concerning not only continuation or termination of artificial life support but also instructions about any medical treatments that the principal may wish to undergo or to avoid, such as surgery or chemotherapy. Although a healthcare proxy and living will can be completed independently of each other, some advance care planning documents, such as the highly popular *5 Wishes,* combine the medical power of attorney and living will into one document.

The Health Insurance Portability and Accountability Act

The Health Insurance Portability and Accountability Act (HIPAA) is designed to protect against the disclosure of patients' medical records. The act requires that healthcare providers obtain authorization from a patient before they release most health information, although, in an emergency, a healthcare provider may disclose information if doing so is in the patient's best interest. Caregivers may be frustrated at their inability to access important medical records that would help them in their healthcare decision-making. Consequently, an individual can include a HIPAA disclosure authorization as part of an advance medical directive or on a separate form.[13]

HIPAA disclosures can be complicated by family structure if the quality of the relationship between the authorized decision-maker, such as a spouse, and the kin network of grown children and stepchildren, is poor. That negative relationship could determine what information is available to those who feel a claim to it. For example, Delores was the oldest daughter of her father, Lawrence, who had divorced her mother in Delores's infancy. Soon after the divorce, he married Tina, his wife at the time of his death, and had three children with her. Delores always felt estranged from her father and his second family. Her own health issues and blindness often deterred her from making an effort to connect to him, and she resented that neither her father nor her stepmother attempted to stay connected to her over the years. Because she lived with her mother and relied on her for transportation because of being blind, Delores felt that the distance enforced by her stepmother could be attributed to jealousy of her mother who accompanied her on visits. After learning of her father's hospitalization through a family friend, she tried to see him, but her stepmother refused to let her in the room or even to inform her of her father's medical condition. When the doctor found out that the stepmother was trying to exclude the daughter, the doctor exclaimed, "she's trying to keep her out of the room? She can't do that." The doctor then informed Delores of her father's critical condition and of her appropriate demeanor—to speak and to stand in a way that would be calm and quiet—during visits. Delores appreciated that medical professionals honored her position as a daughter in a way that she felt her stepmother tried to deny or negate.

PHYSICIAN ORDERS FOR LIFE-SUSTAINING TREATMENT

Advance care planning can also take the form of Physician Orders for Life-Sustaining Treatment (POLST).[14] The National POLST Paradigm began in Oregon in 1991 as a way to improve consistency in following a patient's wishes for end-of-life care by creating a form that would become a part of the patient's permanent medical record as a physician's order.[15] The POLST Paradigm soon spread to other states, which adapted the model to fit their unique legal, medical, and cultural contexts.

POLST differs from other forms of advance care planning in that the healthcare professional, not the patient, completes the form and, once signed by the physician, it becomes a *physician's* order for treatment that, like HIPAA, is portable across care settings. It is designed for people with a severe illness, it can be less ambiguous than other forms of advance directives, and it appears to be more effective at keeping people away from hospitals.[16]

The Louisiana legislature adopted its version of POLST, the Louisiana Physician Order for Scope of Treatment (LaPOST) in 2010. LaPOST is a brightly colored, standardized form for physicians to complete after conversation with a patient and family regarding a range of life-sustaining treatments and the patient's wishes concerning them.[17] Unlike other state forms, the LaPOST includes space for updates to the order, thereby recognizing the possibility of multiple conversations about life-sustaining treatment during the course of an illness as well as across a healthy life span. The majority of the deaths in our study occurred in 2010 when the LaPOST was just beginning to be used.

DO NOT RESUSCITATE ORDER

A more commonly used physician's order at the end of life or in acute-care settings is the DNR order. Many hospital and hospice patients complete a DNR or "no code" that, once signed, becomes a physician's order not to revive a person should their heart stop beating or they stop breathing. A DNR covers only these two situations, whereas a living will is designed to cover all types of life-sustaining treatments and procedures after a person develops a terminal and irreversible condition. A living will is not a doctor's order, whereas a DNR is.

Three interviewees spoke of a DNR explicitly. One daughter, Chloe, regretted the DNR order because she perceived that the quality of care received by her mother in the hospital changed after the DNR was signed, but improved once they moved to a hospice inpatient unit. Chloe had disagreed with her single mother's choice to sign a DNR, and thus was observing the staff closely to determine whether the choice was for the best. Her religious beliefs told her that

> regardless of any prognosis, diagnosis or whatever, never give up, don't speak death on someone. Let them [your loved one] know that you're still trying, don't throw in the towel on God. We've [her church members] seen people who shouldn't even been living today that's still living.

Simply talking about hospice was "speaking death" on her mother; thus she may have interpreted the medical treatment provided negatively as a way to support her original opinion that aggressive treatment was preferable. She also had to deal with the vocal opposition of her aunts and cousins who disagreed with her mother's choice to enroll in hospice, which may have also influenced her perceptions. Physically changing the care environment to a hospice inpatient unit seemed to help Chloe refocus on the needs of her mother, be fully present to her in her final days, and feel that the staff was doing all they could for her mother.

The second example showed how a daughter, Veronica, was grateful for the DNR order because when her father died in the hospital, the nurse's first response was to call a full code, but the daughter spoke up and said, "No, he's DNR. He's gone. Take your time." As a registered nurse, Veronica was well aware of hospital protocols to default to a full code. Because of her medical experience, her mother and brother trusted her to intervene with staff and speak on their behalf. Working closely with a pulmonary doctor before being admitted to the hospital and with a palliative-care physician while in the hospital also helped Veronica and her family prepare for what she would experience as death neared and to feel that the DNR was the best choice for her father. She remembered the last doctor's visit before his admission to the hospital:

Dr. H_ said, "Okay, this is pretty serious." His oxygen levels were 56, when 98 to 100 is what they're supposed to be. Dad didn't look good. He was shivering in a wheelchair under a blanket. It was hot September, so I kind of had a feeling this was gonna be it. So Dr. H_ explained to us how he was gonna treat everything, that he was gonna go into the hospital. . . . He said, "If the [new medicine] don't work, we're gonna do palliative care, which is hospice in the hospital." At that point, I accepted the fact that death was coming. I think that's kind of what made it easier for me. Dad went to the hospital on a Thursday and he passed away Sunday.

Because Veronica participated in the care decisions with her family and the physicians, she felt confident in advocating for the choices they had made concerning what treatments to try and when to stop them.

The third example showed how the DNR became a legal form that played a critical role in ensuring that a mother's preferences for end-of-life treatment were followed and in mediating ongoing conflicts over authority among her three grown children. In previous chapters, we introduced Michelle's family. She served as the primary caregiver for her single mother. After moving her mother into her home with hospice, conflicts between her and her siblings began to arise over money and decisions about her mother's care:

> I'm the primary caregiver. There was no power of attorney, but hospice knew me as a person to make the decisions. She trusted me, and I was the sole beneficiary of her little bitty life insurance policy that my grandmother—my dad's mom—had on every-body in the family. So, my brother and my sister became resent-ful towards me. First, I was able to take care of her because my brother didn't have a place to stay. She, my sister, had five kids, a man with no job, and an apartment. So, I had the means to take care of her, and in that, they became resentful. So, we were clash-ing a little bit.

Michelle learned about her mother's DNR after Dorothy had a stroke and was taken to a hospital emergency room. Michelle joined her sister in the emergency room, where they learned that their mother had signed a Do Not Resuscitate form while under hospice care. The existence of this form circumvented the ongoing tensions and arguments between the daughters, who competed with each other for authority. As much as they disagreed with each other, they accepted that their mother's wish, as explicitly stated in her DNR, was not to be resuscitated. In Dorothy's final days, the hospital became neutral ground for the siblings to sit vigil at her bedside. Michelle's mother's arrangements show how even relatively simple advance care planning (through the DNR) can play a significant role in patient care and in calming disagreements within a family.

POWER OF ATTORNEY FOR FINANCES

In families in which a grown child assumes the role of next of kin, a power of attorney document can offer valuable role clarity and guidance. Appointing an agent pursuant to a financial power of attorney gives the designee the authority to make legal and financial decisions on behalf of the person. The person designating an agent must have capacity to do so, and the designation continues once capacity has been compromised or lost, hence making the power of attorney durable.[18] An individual can complete a power of attorney for finances as well as one for medical decisions.

Only one interviewee, Kyle, whose story opened the chapter, was designated a mandate (the Louisiana terminology) and given a financial power of attorney by his single mother, Mary. She completed these forms with her son following her admittance to hospice care and moving in to live with him and his family.

In the early stages of her cancer diagnosis, his mother, who lived about an hour away from his home, would call with an emergency and he, or his uncle if Kyle was out of town on a trip, would drive to the hospital to help her in navigating the relevant care decisions. Between these crisis moments, she lived on her own. Kyle mowed her lawn and checked up on her every few days by phone, but that form of care didn't intrude too heavily into his day-to-day life or into hers.

But then his mother's cancer treatments became less effective, the emergency calls came more frequently, and the doctor sat down with Kyle and his mother to explain that she could not live on her own any longer. She was referred to hospice, and she could either be admitted to a long-term-care facility, which would require her to "spend down" her personal savings in order to qualify, eventually, for the Medicaid Room and Board benefit, or move in with Kyle and his family.

As both mother and son contemplated their next steps, Kyle talked with his wife about what they could afford to do. The couple decided that home care would be best, if she would agree to it, and that they "were prepared to ride it out knowing how difficult it might be." The next day, they invited Kyle's mother to live with them, but with one stipulation: that she not smoke cigarettes inside the house, a choice he knew would be hard for her to make as a lifelong smoker. She agreed, but there were new tensions as his mother dealt with the reality of what moving in with them would really mean. Closing out her financial accounts and settling her debts coupled with moving out of her home into one room in Kyle's house made her feel she was losing her self-sufficiency, independence, and privacy.

The initial conversation about money was especially awkward. He was nervous to broach the private subject of finances with his mother. He wanted to respect her autonomy and to reassure her that he would honor her wishes, while recognizing how much her health and her personal privacy were now out of her control. He didn't want her to feel he was taking control of her money too. To cover the cost of her room and board, his mother set up a small payment plan with Kyle so that she could contribute to the family's food and utility costs. In time, Kyle approached his mother about a power of attorney while she was still able to make decisions for herself:

We sat down with her one evening when she was out on the back porch smoking, and just said, "We want to help you with your financial situation, but we need to know what it is. What's going to happen? What do you have? Do you have debts?" She told me that situation, and there were some issues in there that I needed to work on, so I told her, "I think I should have power of attorney." She agreed, so I called the lawyer that just helped us close on our house, and I was like, "My mom is in bad shape. Can you do a power of attorney thing and a living will?" He said, "Yeah, I can do that." So he filled out whatever paperwork there was and came to the house with his secretary to be a witness, and I got our pastor to come to the house. He came and prayed with us again that day. We got through that, and I started having to straighten out some tax issues and all for my mom.

Kyle said that going through the process of becoming her agent gave him "some sense of relief in the situation." He wanted to be able to work on her behalf to settle her financial debts and to follow her wishes to make financial gifts to her grandchildren or friends. Kyle appreciated his mother's ingenuity in finding ways to prepay expenses. For example, several years prior her moving in with Kyle, she had bartered flight lessons with a local mortuary owner for her cremation costs, which reduced the eventual financial burden that Kyle faced after her death. Kyle confirmed this contract with the mortuary and was able to say thank you to his mother for making those types of preparations. Kyle admitted that serving as his mother's next of kin was "not always easy," but was a role he would claim all over again if given the chance:

> You know, it wasn't about me, and what's good for me, and what do I have to gain from this, because there wasn't anything to gain out of it. There definitely wasn't a goldmine of inheritance that I thought I was going to get. So yeah, I went through making a lot of decisions, and confronting a lot of issues, and learning a lot about myself out of the whole process, and one of those lessons was that you just sacrifice and do it. You know? The reality is that my wife and I will be in this situation again. We may be in this situation a couple more times because her parents are divorced and remarried. They remarried late, and they already had kids and stuff, so you have a very complicated dynamic there. My wife and I know that we'll be taking care of somebody again. I wouldn't say I look forward to it, but that's just it—you just do it.

And for Kyle, being able to formally plan with his mother made the doing of care easier.

CONCLUSION

A foundational concept in contemporary healthcare lies in making medical decisions that honor the wishes of the patient, when known. Advance planning documents enable individuals to direct their care even when incapacitated. Accessing legal directives can provide much needed clarity and confidence for those serving in a decision-making capacity. All the examples in this chapter, excluding Veronica, involve single-parent families, in which the grown child would have been in the preferred group of default surrogate decision-makers. Formal planning on the part of the parent made the burden of choice that fell to the adult child we interviewed more manageable.

Part of the reluctance to engage in advance planning may result from confusion about how all the different medical forms and orders interact, work together, or compete with one other. Indeed, regardless of the racial, ethnic, religious, or socioeconomic background or the gender of the interviewee, the common factor among all of the parents who engaged in planning appears to be either their admission to hospice or palliative care, or, more broadly, access to healthcare providers who made those referrals to formal end of life care. Those services tend to introduce and facilitate access to formal planning tools. In the next chapter, we explore how surrogates made decisions in the *absence* of advance planning, when default rules came into play.

Decision-Making without Planning

Looking for Direction

I need to know what you want to do.

—Dr. Johnson

The doctor's words hung in the air as Angela stared at her father lying comatose in the intensive care unit. Her father, Roberto, had not completed any legal documents to name her or anyone else as his medical healthcare proxy. He also had not completed any documents that could provide guidance concerning what treatments or medical interventions he would wish to have or to avoid should he be unable to make those decisions for himself. The decision fell to Angela and her siblings.

Angela was 43 years old, married, raising three teen-aged daughters, and working part time. According to Angela and her sister Jackie, her father had not been a model parent. She described him:

> Dad was very overbearing, temperamental, judgmental. He wasn't always very kind. You either loved him or you hated him, there was really no in-between with Dad. He never would say he loved you or anything like that. He was a hard man.

Both Angela and Jackie had sought counseling and support from faith communities to help process the often erratic and verbally explosive behavior of their father during childhood and in the present. Jackie was Hispanic, 41 years old, and married with four children. She described her strained relationship to her father:

> Somewhere along the way in my late teens I decided I'm not put-
> ting up with his crap anymore and if he wants to have a relationship
> I'm not going to tolerate abusive talk. I told him in a respectful way,
> because I am a Christian and I do believe the command to honor
> your father and mother should they do well with you; it's the only
> commandment that has promise with it. I believe that there is a
> way to honor without allowing yourself to be dishonored. I spent
> a lot of part of my teens, really up until the time that he passed
> way, refining over time what that looks like to be respectful while
> not allowing him to revert back to old patterns of treating me with
> disrespect.

Angela, the second oldest child, had become the primary caregiver and surrogate decision-maker. Before he was diagnosed with an illness, Roberto, 69 years old, exhibited a high level of frailty and forgetfulness, which Angela and Jackie attributed to lifelong alcohol abuse and recent nerve damage. In Chapter 2, Angela described their caregiving arrange-ment, in which he lived in a trailer behind her house. Her experiences caring for him in this way for over a year created a nuanced understanding of his values, which then informed her subsequent choices concerning his care. This arrangement also helped her maintain some physical distance from his negative behaviors.

Angela's father was able to make decisions for himself until his final days, although he did seek her advice concerning treatment options, including his determination to undergo a risky surgery to calm a chronic tremor in his hands. Going against the medical judgment of several physicians and the opinions of Angela, Roberto set a date for the surgery. Angela pleaded with him for weeks, emphasizing that the risks of the surgery outweighed the potential benefits, but she finally "gave up" and acknowledged that it was his choice to make. As Angela feared, the surgery did not go well, and her father never awakened from the anesthesia. Angela stood at his bedside in the intensive care unit, listening to the rhythmic whoosh of the respirator and the constant beep of the heart monitor, and wondered, "What does he want me to do now?"

Advance medical directives were created for just this type of moment, for countless "Angelas" standing in the foreign and stressful environment of a hospital facing a difficult decision on behalf of a loved one. Despite the many reasons for advance care planning, most people, like Roberto, have not done so; they don't have any of their preferences about end-of-life decision-making in writing, and they haven't even spoken with family members or their doctors about their wishes.[1] For most caregivers, like Angela, serving as primary decision-maker began by acting as a trusted advisor to her father and then shifted to making decisions on his behalf as death neared.

In this chapter, we explore the surrogate decision-making experience in the absence of advance directives. We explain the default rules for appointing a decision-maker and the guiding principles for that decision-maker, such as substitutive judgment or best interests. Finally, we explore how decisions were actually made and what role family structure played to complicate or simplify the experience, especially in the decision to "pull the plug."

Becoming a Surrogate Decision-Maker

In this section, we use the interviewee narratives to show how family structure determined who became the surrogate decision-maker in the absence of formal direction. Despite the many planning options available, most people don't have advance medical directives.[2] Consequently, instead of the individual controlling choices through his or her own agent as designated prior to his or her incapacity, default rules establish how those choices will be made and who will make them. States generally have laws that establish a hierarchy of default healthcare decision-makers, often called "surrogates," for any medical decision that must be made while the person is incapacitated. Under these statutes, spouses, sometimes along with recognized domestic partners, are generally listed first.

Louisiana law sets out a list of people who can authorize surgical or medical treatment, with priority given to the individual herself or himself, then a court-appointed guardian, followed by family members: a spouse who is not legally separated from the patient; an adult child; the patient's parents; the patient's siblings; other relatives. If there are no family members who can act, then Louisiana (where all the deaths in our study occurred) authorizes an "adult friend," someone who is familiar with the patient's wishes, to act; followed by, among others, an interdisciplinary team of professionals.[3] Under certain circumstances, then, the treating physician is given discretion on moving forward with the medical procedure.[4] The surrogate is then responsible for making the best decision for the incapacitated person.[5]

In the absence of an advance directive, all fifty states allow a surrogate to make decisions on behalf of an incapacitated individual to decline or terminate life-sustaining treatment. Many states require clear and convincing evidence for end-of-life decision-making, preferring to have the default as prolonging life. The burden of proof in other states might be the lesser one of a preponderance of the evidence.[6]

States differ on the substantive standard for decision-making on the appropriate outcome. Some states mandate that a surrogate be guided by the patient's best interests, others use "substituted judgment,"[7] a standard based on what the patient would choose if he or she could speak on his or her own behalf. Some states have developed a hybrid that allows the surrogate to exercise substituted judgment when the patient's wishes are known but to make a decision in the patient's best interests where these wishes are unknown.[8] States may explicitly require, as part of a substituted judgment standard, that the surrogate act after a review of the patient's moral, religious, and ethical beliefs.[9]

Apart from a DNR and Kyle's mother appointing him as her agent, no participant in our study reported that a parent had completed a healthcare directive; thus default rules came into play. No one referred to the law explicitly when it came to designating a decision-maker, so the de facto surrogate generally assumed responsibility informally, but without challenge. Study participants who were not the decision-makers themselves had varied reactions to the surrogate's exercise of authority; those reactions depended on family structure. One-third of our participants needed to act as surrogates in making healthcare decisions, a statistic that echoes national studies showing that 40% of patients admitted to a medical care facility are unable to direct their own treatment.[10]

Those interviewed told stories of going to extreme measures to interpret their parents' actual wishes, including interpreting a head nod of a father unable to speak because of a breathing tube inserted in his throat or a hand squeeze of a mother in a persistent vegetative state. Surrogate decision-making happened only when the parent or spouse was nonresponsive to oral questions or physical touch, which is when an advance care planning document would have been most helpful. To give a sense of the tenor of these moments, participants described their decision-making experience using phrases such as "it was too much," "I didn't think I could handle it," "I thought I was going to fall apart," and "I almost broke down." The phrases point to a general state of mental and emotional stress that potentially compromised their available mental bandwidth for making logical choices quickly or easily.[11] The timing of the interviews at a year after the death gave the surrogates time to live with the selections made and to assess relatively longer-term implications of what was influential to their choices. And, although most felt that they adequately chose what their loved one would have wanted, the interviews present only one perspective.[12] We do not know the story of the deceased loved one or other family members, except for several instances in which we interviewed siblings (separately), such as Jackie and Angela. The two sisters recalled similar facts concerning their father that were deeply shaped by each sister's unique history, personality, and choices. Even Kyle, who was his mother's power of attorney, confessed, "I can speak for myself. I can't speak for my brother or my dad or my mom."

The surrogates in the study typically remembered anticipating the need for end-of-life decision-making. One-fourth of those whom we interviewed described watching how treatments became increasingly futile in curing the terminal illness or in returning their loved one to a pre-illness state of cognitive and physical ability. They mentally cataloged an intensification of the signs and symptoms of disease leading to death. They used words like, he was "changed" or their parents were "not themselves" to describe their observations of the parent's worsening mental and physical condition. Although they were not relatively surprised that choices needed to be made, they still did not know explicitly what their parent did or did not wish in terms of treatment options. When a decision needed to be made on behalf of the parent, default rules came into play in determining who would make the choices.

In married-parent families—regardless of whether it was a remarriage—the spouse of the patient typically acted as the decision-maker. For study participants whose parents had remained married throughout their lives, this default rule caused little to no verbalized turmoil or conflict. The grown children, and any siblings, followed the lead of the parent making decisions. At the same time, the grown children interviewed saw themselves as fully included in the process of discerning the best medical decision for the incapacitated parent, they expressed their opinions freely, and, even if minor disagreements occurred among family members, they believed that the eventual choices made were collectively owned as a family. They also found that medical professionals spoke freely in their presence. The interviewees used the pronoun "we" to describe choices that legally were only the spouse's to be made. They described this inclusive process as ongoing; it extended to burial and cremation decisions.

In remarried-parent families, the spouse of the parent also assumed the surrogate role, but the grown children felt more distance from the decision-making process, and their reactions took different forms, depending on whether the spouse was the stepparent or the parent. If the stepparent was the surrogate for a study participant's parent, then the grown children expressed strong feelings about their role, feeling either 1) conflict or a lack of confidence in their stepparent's ability to make the best decision on behalf of their parent, or 2) complete exclusion by the stepparent in any discussion related to the choices. On the other hand, if it was their parent making decisions for a stepparent, study participants tended to feel more distance from the situation, but expressed a duty to support their parent, particularly when they faced conflicts or doubt from their stepsiblings.

In single-parent families, without another legal spouse, default laws establish that siblings will share responsibility for surrogate decision-making with a majority rule. Although no interviewee stated awareness of this legal requirement, the grown child who took the lead in making medical choices made a good-faith effort to include other siblings, grandparents, aunts, and uncles. In terms of which sibling took the lead role, in some families, there was an implied understanding that the oldest child would serve as the primary decision-maker, but in others, the sibling living in closest proximity or who was considered the closest to the parent emotionally took on the next-of-kin role. This is how Angela, whose story opened this chapter, became the primary caregiver and locus of decision-making. She was the closest geographically and emotionally to her father; she looked for confirmation and support from her siblings through phone calls and would have welcomed their in-person support had they chosen to be present.

How Decisions Were Made

In the interviews, the common sole decision faced by a surrogate decision-maker was the one to remove their parent from life support—or to use their vernacular: "Pull the plug." Without advance care planning or other definitive direction, surrogates drew on three sources to guide their decisions:

1) understanding of the patient's wishes, based either on recent conversations with the parent related to the current illness or general character assessment;

2) a desire to act in the best interests of their loved one with a focus on the reduction in suffering; and/or

3) the faith beliefs of the surrogate decision-maker.

Medical professionals prompted the decision concerning life support, but did not otherwise influence the particular decision that was made.

Substitute Judgment and Its Influences

When faced with the decision to end life-support measures, the family typically wanted to make a choice that was consistent with what they believed their incapacitated loved one would have made. Conversations about, and during, the illness became a critical guide. The months and weeks prior to the moment of decision-making were filled with many instances when selections were made collaboratively or by the parent with the counsel of other family members. Conversations closer to the moment of decision were more influential.

We introduced Brady in Chapter 2. His father's direction prior to his incapacity provided useful guidance at the end of life. His father, James, had been married three times and was estranged, but not legally separated, from his third wife when he was diagnosed with terminal cancer. Brady's father loved living in the rural swamps of Tangipahoa parish. He built his home and refused to leave it as he faced his final months of living with terminal cancer. He wanted to exert as much control as possible over the illness. Brady described a family meeting convened by their father at the beginning of his illness, "He told us all of his appointments and what needed to be done." Brady's stepsister, Sally, volunteered to move in with his father and served as the primary caregiver, but she did not feel comfortable being the primary decision-maker. When his father had a heart attack, Brady remembered clearly receiving her frantic phone call:

> We had just gotten outta church. My wife and I were heading out to go and eat somewhere. My stepsister called us on the phone and said, "Brady, he's on the floor convulsing. I don't know what to do." And I said, "Call 911. Just call 911. Call emergency; they'll get an ambulance over there." Got the ambulance over there, went to the hospital. But he had already told everybody he didn't want to be revived if something happened.

Brady remembered his father explicitly stating, "he didn't want to be a vegetable, per se. He wanted to live what he could live and let it be done with." Because of these expressed wishes, the siblings decided not to continue life support. They "all lined up around the bed, one at a time, some as a family, and said our goodbyes."

Best Interests Interpreted as Not Wanting the Person to Suffer

Surrogates' beliefs about the patient's best interests served to supplement their determinations of substituted judgment decisions. This assessment was often drawn from years of caregiving during which families had weighed together the goals of countless medical procedures, medications, and therapy regimens with the costs to the loved one's quality of life. At some point, for all the interviewees, the risks and costs of curative efforts outweighed their potential for a full recovery. Once determined that further curative treatments were futile, the goals for care shifted to maximizing the quality of life or best interests of the patient. No one used the phrase "best interests" when weighing proposed treatment options or the choice to remove a loved one from life support. Instead, individuals explained, "I didn't want them to suffer," or "I wanted what would be merciful," or "I just didn't want him to be in pain." "Mercy," an avoidance of or relief from "suffering" translated to the loved one's "best interests" when it was realized that the only outcome of the illness would, in time, lead to death.

For example, Courtney moved in with her mother and father after her mother, Leigh, was admitted to hospice with terminal cancer. Courtney was 34 years old, a single mother to an 8-year-old daughter, a registered nurse, and the youngest of her four siblings, one of whom had died in her teenage years. By the time Courtney moved in with her parents, her mother had already experienced multiple stays in the hospital while undergoing surgeries designed to remove and treat her cancer. At the point when her mother could no longer eat or drink, or stand or ambulate independently, and when she experienced constant pain at high levels when not on a consistent schedule of pain medication, the family opted for palliative care and to move home. Hospice was, Courtney explained, "a change in what they hoped for." They no longer hoped for a cure but for comfort. One decision Courtney remembered making with her father, Carl, on her mother's behalf was discontinuing an IV of fluids. She and her father agreed that her mother did not want to drown in her own fluids, which they feared as her breathing rattled as fluid collected in her lungs and throat and her legs become swollen. Ultimately they believed that the fluids "weren't helping her but hurting her." Their determination of her mother's best interests confirmed their sense of what her mother's wishes might be in the situation.

Although Courtney took the lead in suggesting the removal of fluids, she agonized over whether resuscitation would be in her mother's best interests. Her mother had not signed a DNR order. As a registered nurse, Courtney was trained to conduct cardiac pulmonary resuscitation (CPR) as a default response to death. She worried that she might, out of instinct and grief, try to resuscitate her mom at the time of death even though she knew that prolonging her mother's life by artificial or forced means was not in her mother's best interests. Part of what complicated Courtney's thoughts on resuscitation was that she found purpose and meaning in her role as a caregiver for her mom. Once hospice was able to get her mother's pain under control, Courtney reflected on her daily schedule of tending to her mom's physical needs, and she surmised, "I could live like this." Courtney felt that she could care for mom for years, if that was what was demanded. However, in time, Courtney realized that resuscitating her would be keeping her mother alive for Courtney's sake when her mother's body had already died. She confessed that ultimately she wanted a "miracle" in which her mother would be cured and would return to her former self, but instead she had to accept that her miracle was the gift of pain control in her mother's final days.

Courtney expressed her struggles and confirmed her conclusions with her father and the hospice nurse, and they affirmed that letting her mother's body die on her own timetable and not doing CPR was indeed the most compassionate, least painful choice. Resuscitation efforts would be futile in the hope of curing her mother of terminal cancer. When her mother died, Courtney was outside in the backyard, playing with her daughter and their dog. Her father waited about fifteen minutes after her mother breathed her last, when resuscitation would have been ineffective, to tell her to come in. At first, Courtney was angry that he had waited, but when we spoke to her a year later, she was thankful that he protected her from potentially intervening in a way that was not in her mother's best interests.

FAITH

Religion both influenced the particular decisions that were made and served as a form of support to the surrogates. Participants drew comfort from their religious beliefs and practices as they faced their roles as surrogates. Before the choice was made, participants engaged in personal and collective prayer to fortify them for the decision. Their theological beliefs helped them define what was in their loved one's "best interests" as they approached the end of life. At the moment of the decision, participants believed that God was present, giving them strength to make the choice. And, after committing to a choice, religious beliefs helped reframe the ultimate responsibility for the outcome of the decision.

RELIGION AS DEFINING "BEST INTERESTS"

Surrogate decision-makers often drew on their personal faith beliefs and practice to determine a loved one's best interests related to specific treatment decisions, especially when curative efforts were deemed futile. Overall, suffering was not viewed as holding spiritual merit or as something to be endured for the sake of spiritual purification. Respondents sought to relieve suffering without hastening death. Up until the point of withdrawing life support, respondents spoke of a cure as in the best interests of their loved one. Their prayers and hopes focused on a full recovery from illness or injury. Courtney, from the previous section, described her shift in thinking when her mother entered hospice care; what she hoped for changed from a cure to a merciful, pain-free life until death.

For some, their theological beliefs, especially related to the concept of "mercy," shaped that definition of best interests. For example, Sam's family had to decide whether to insert a feeding tube in his mother, Edith. At the time of the interview, Sam was 45 years old, the owner of a lumber business in a small town to the west of Baton Rouge, and remarried with five children: "She [Sam's wife] came with one, I came with two, and we have two together." He fielded calls to his wife several times during the interview, coordinating school pickups with an impromptu volleyball practice for one of the daughters. As he told his story, he attributed his high level of involvement in the day-to-day care and medical decision-making for his seriously ill mother to the stability of his twenty-two-year marriage, his ability to set his own hours at work, and the close geographical proximity of his parents, who lived about a fifteen-minute drive from his home.

Sam's mother, Edith, had long lived with epilepsy traced to brutal beatings she had received from her parents before being placed in foster care at a young age. Sam's parents met as children, when his mother moved in with a foster family next door to his father, Abe. Sam described his father's tale of love at first sight: "He knew that she was 'the one' in the third or fourth grade." They married the summer after graduating high school. His mother never worked, and his father became a preacher of a Baptist church, a job he still held through her illness and after her death. Sam described his childhood as one shaped by caregiving.

> The epilepsy was always a big part of our relationship, because when I think back on it now, I always had to take care of her. I felt that was my job. We'd be in church, and she would have a seizure in the middle of church while Dad was up there preaching. I knew what to do, and so I would get her out, and just do what we had to do. I remember three different occasions she was bringing us to school, she would just be driving and start having a seizure, and we'd get in a car wreck. When I was in the first grade, we ran off a bridge and went into the Amite River. I managed to get her out of the car and drug her to the bank. I still don't know how I knew how to do that, other than my grandmother teaching us all how to swim from an early age.

Sam's role as caregiver continued until she died. For the six years preceding her death, she had been paralyzed, only able to squeeze a finger as a means of communication. Sam's father, Abe, served as Edith's main live-in caregiver, with Sam and his siblings checking in each week and providing respite visits for their father. Sam spoke with great admiration for the ways that his father transported his mother around town during those years, going to the grocery store or out to a restaurant even though she could only respond with a small squeeze of her hand.

As his mother's ability to swallow waned, the family faced the difficult decision of whether to use the feeding tube to extend her life. They debated what benefit the feeding tube would bring to his mother's quality of life, especially when her one response gesture, the squeeze of a hand, had become sporadic at best. Although Sam remembered his extraordinary efforts to care for her during his childhood, at the end of her life, he valued the quality of his mother's days over their quantity. The family decided the feeding tube would only "prolong the inevitable." Sam's theological belief in the concept of mercy, understood to be an unmerited gift of kindness or compassion, and in a merciful God who would be present to relieve suffering, shaped his response. When his mother came home with hospice care, Sam said that their prayers changed from a cure to mercy. They asked that whether "God healed her or took her, please just show mercy." They gathered around her bed each day. Sam remembered little things like holding her hand and saying, "Momma, I love you." Sam was with her the night she died:

> I was working. Daddy called me and said that he didn't think she was gonna make the night so I went straight over there. I was sitting on the side of her on the bed when she died. And it was not a big dramatic thing. She was having the gurgling breathing when the lungs were filling up with fluid and, she just took that one last breath, and that was it. God granted mercy.

Framing his family's decision theologically, using the term "mercy," helped Sam understand the goals for his mother's care at the end of her life as well as the outcomes. When all medical interventions were deemed futile, they could still seek a peaceful, pain-free death as an act of mercy.

BELIEF AND PRAYER AS FORTIFYING

Keith, the oldest son of Keith Sr., a divorced and single police officer, attributed his faith as giving him the strength to stay at the hospital with his father, accept the role as "next of kin," and make the choice to "pull the plug." Keith was 36 years old, African American, married with two children, and, at the time of his father's death a year prior, had been recently released from prison after serving a sentence for dealing drugs. He described himself as in the process of extricating himself from his past associations on the street while recommitting himself to living with and financially supporting his wife and young son. He confessed that his relationship with his father had always been strained, in part because his father was in law enforcement while he had already served several stints behind bars for drug offences. However, he counted his being free and able to be care for his father in his final week of life as "a real blessing."

After a stroke left his father comatose in the hospital, Keith faced the decision of removing his father from life support. His family collectively looked to him, as the oldest son, to make the determination. He struggled to understand his father's medical condition, and then decided that his father should not be kept alive through additional medical intervention. Rather than take responsibility on his own for making a choice, which resulted in his father's death, he used his Christian faith in God's providence to justify what happened. Keith explained:

> I prayed on it. You know, Lord, 6:00, it's going to be your will. . . . And I did learn death come when God decides—designated it to come, not when we want to. I was talking to [my dad]. I was holding his hand, telling him I love him. That's the main thing. Just told him I loved him and kissed him before the doctor pulled the plug.

Although Keith himself had actually made the decision to end life support, he recast the event as divine intervention on just when his father's life would end. His religious beliefs allowed him to reconcile his very human control of the situation with his father's death, framing his decision as based on a higher power and not solely his own. His faith also gave him a spiritual discipline, private prayer, that structured his preparation for the choice and gave him credibility with other family members. Private prayer was communally understood as a critical step in any major discernment process and as sign of humility that shows that a person is "leaving things in God's hands."

As was true for Keith, after a decision about life support was made, belief in God's providence and control became a comfort. As Sam phrased it, there was a sense that "we put it in God's hands and we said if you kept her here this long, if for some reason you're keeping her here, then you'd better do something." From the perspective of the surrogate decision-maker, beliefs about God's control of life's length tended to predominate in such statements as "it was a God thing," "God's plan," "God took her," "God planned it," "God does things for a reason," or "if God brings you to it, God will bring you through it." A pronounced sense of God's providence gave comfort and justified the decision made to themselves and to any family members who doubted the selected option. Making a choice was easier if it wasn't ultimately theirs to make. More than half of those interviewed described themselves as nondenominational Christian or Baptist Christian, and, although they did not recite any tenets of their faith to support their belief in God's providence, these beliefs may resonate with that unique theological perspective.

While Keith and Sam drew on their own religious beliefs, many of the grown children also called on a clergy person for spiritual help. The presence of a clergy person supported the surrogate's end of life decisions. For Peter, whose family was introduced in Chapter 1, a clergy member was critical in framing the overall experience as well as the specific choices to be made. After a sudden heart attack, Peter's father, Leonard, was initially comatose, but then regained consciousness for a few hours. He was intubated so he couldn't speak, but he could mouth words and nod his head yes or no. They told him the score of the LSU game, and he was able to mouth, "What happened?!?" As they stood around his ICU bed, they took turns rotating closer to his father to speak with him. As Peter waited his turn, he recalled his father saying, "If I die on a golf course, on a racquet ball court—don't worry. I was happy. I just don't wanna be stuck in bed."

Standing at the end of bed, Peter observed his mother quietly say to his father, "You need to fight this," but his father just shook his head, "no"' His father lapsed back into a coma and did not regain consciousness.

A few days later, the doctor sat down with the family and explained, "I'm doing stuff *to* him as opposed to *for* him. It may be the time we'll have to make the decision to pull the plug." Peter and his family wanted their pastor to be present with them in the ICU as they made the decision on life support. Peter recalled Pastor Frank visiting and offering guidance in their steps for saying goodbye. Peter had not realized how close his father was to Pastor Frank, and that knowledge brought him a great deal of comfort. On the day of his father's death, Peter remembered "when Frank walked in and saw him there, he said, 'Boy. If your dad knew he was here, he'd jump off the bed.'" Pastor Frank explained to Peter and the family that sometimes people wait to hear from their loved ones that it is okay to die. He then asked, "Well, Pete, do you wanna go in and just tell your dad it's okay to go?" Giving his father permission to die had not occurred to Peter or his family, and it made them feel less helpless. Peter walked to his father's bedside and said, "Dad, don't fight any more. We're gonna let you go." Pastor Frank then stayed with the family until Leonard died. Peter felt that the pastor's role was critical to allowing his family to sort through all of their complex emotions to make the choice that his father would have wanted.

The Role of Medical Professionals

Medical professionals did not heavily influence the specific choices made by a surrogate beyond presenting the available treatment options. Doctors acted to force the choice; nurses provided information and focus after a decision was made. The doctors offered a diagnosis and presented options for treatment or removing treatment. For example, doctors were the ones who said, "It's time to call hospice." When asked about what advice they might offer physicians, interviewees stressed that they appreciated the doctors who were honest and direct with them about the prognosis and the seriousness of the illness. A year after the death, they spoke highly of those doctors who "didn't sugarcoat things" and "didn't speak over our heads, but told us clearly what to expect."

In contrast to the instigating role of doctors, nurses asked instrumental questions and responded with directive statements related to providing hands-on care. The nurses helped the family members understand what making the decision meant and walked them through the experience. They were the ones who told families that death was near. They encouraged family members to "talk to their" loved one; they taught about the dying process, telling them that "hearing is the last sense to go." Because end-of-life decision-making involved highly emotional stakes, the nurses provided a useful grounding that helped family members focus on what the patient needed. They especially appreciated when the nursing staff allowed a large group of family members to visit, despite being cramped in the room and a little loud, or when a nurse allowed a son to stay after ICU visiting hours the night his father died. Nurses were deemed "people who care."

For Angela, whose story opened the chapter, it was only when the doctor asked her to step out in the hallway that she realized she needed to make a choice. Although the doctor's request was simple and direct, Angela's mind held a jumble of memories and voices ranging from images of her tumultuous childhood with her father's voice barking orders and slurs at her and her siblings, arguing with her father just a week ago about the very surgery that led to this decision she was forced to make on his behalf, to the voices of her sister and her brother who both refused to come to the hospital but who counseled her several times a day by phone. Most of all, she struggled to believe that this moment could really be happening, "He's come out of this so many times. He's going to get up off the bed; he's going to walk out."

Angela weighed what she knew about her father's recent choices concerning his healthcare, especially this recent surgery that he chose as a slim chance at improving his quality of life over a large risk of complete disability and death, her memories of how frustrated he was at losing elements of his independence over the last year leading to his reliance on her and paid help for his day-to-day needs, and her confidence that she was the right person to discern his best interests and wishes because he always came to her first when he needed help. She called her brother and her sister to talk about her choice to remove him from life support, and they stated their full support of her decision. When the physician returned to the room for her answer, she declared, "You make him as comfortable as you can, but don't resuscitate." The staff shifted his care plan to one of comfort. The nurses surrounded her and encouraged her to talk to him and hold his hand. She remembered the sudden silence left when the beeping of his heart monitor and rhythmic whoosh of his respirator stopped followed by the voice of the doctor pronouncing his death:

> I stayed there for a few minutes with him. Then I was asked to leave so that they could prepare him. They asked me where I wanted him, and I told them he was going to be cremated. Then I walked out, stood in the hall and cried, by myself.

CONCLUSION

Barring sudden death, most individuals at the end of life will require at least one healthcare decision to be made on their behalf. Knowing clearly a loved one's wishes about life support, treatment options, and comfort care has become a privilege that relatively few surrogate decision-makers have, but all would value having. Without such clear directives, surrogate decision-makers rely on a range of other influences, including their memories, their imaginations, their understanding of the disease process, a definition of what is in their loved one's best interests, and their faith to make critical decisions about the end of their parent's life.

A Caregiver Becomes a Griever

Everybody grieve a different way.

—CHARLES

When Shannon's father died, her understanding of the world changed. Shannon grew up in a rural Louisiana town north of New Orleans. Following college at LSU in Baton Rouge, she got married and moved back home to build a house on several acres of her family's land. When her father received a diagnosis of early onset dementia, she appreciated that she could jump on a four-wheeler, drive across several fields, and be at her parents' house whenever needed.

Her father was a farmer, teacher, and influential person in their local community; she revered and adored him. But then, over the course of a year, she watched as he lost the ability to control his body and to remember basic pieces of information, including his name. Hard decisions had to be made, like a move to the nursing home. She made sense of his illness and her experiences as a caregiver through writing down everything: her thoughts, poems expressing her emotions, his medication schedule, and even penning an impressive obituary appreciated by her family and community members. She came to the interview carrying a stack of papers. As she recounted her story, she would pause, rifle through the stack, and pull out a poem or journal entry that applied to that point in her narrative.

However, she confessed that she had written almost nothing in the year since her father's death, an occurrence she attributed to her feelings of loss. Her inability to use her preferred coping mechanism, the written word, made her feel even more overwhelmed by the range of emotions she felt in reaction to her father's death. She struggled to reconstruct her sense of self in a world without her father. She found new ways to cope with the support of her mother, her husband and sons, and friends, but initially, grief caused her to question everything she thought she knew about herself, the world, and God: "I thought I had a strong faith and belief, but this last year without my daddy, I didn't know what to believe."

Shannon's experience with grief, difficult and painful as it was for her, is nonetheless typical of what most grieving individuals experience. They are no longer caregivers, but they are survivors, sometimes orphans. The private and personal experiences of grief give shape to how individuals experience the burial, mourning, and wealth transmission process, each of which is discussed in the next set of chapters. Grief begins at the time of death and can last long after the funeral is over and the estate is settled. In contrast to the prescribed rhythms of funerals and mourning practices and the detailed tasks entailed in the inheritance process, the experience of grief can seem to be highly unstructured, private, and distressing. We met study participants at a critical moment in their grief journey, at the year anniversary of their parent or stepparent's death. In the final twenty to thirty minutes of the interview, we heard stories about a year of firsts (first holiday, first birthday) without the deceased parent or stepparent.

Most people, like Shannon at the beginning of the chapter, experience what therapists describe as normal, uncomplicated grief.[1] In preparing to explore the interviewees' stories of coping with loss, it is useful to distinguish between the different terms related to dealing with death:[2]

- *Grief* is the internal experience of one who has lost a loved one to death.
- *Normal or uncomplicated grief* includes acute emotional reactions to the loss, but also includes more positive feelings, and the acute grief typically resolves into a less intense sense of loss as

the individual integrates the death into her life.[3] This form of grief has been institutionalized through services associated with hospice care.[4]

- *"Complicated" grief,* by contrast, occurs when the pain continues and the griever has severe trouble moving forward.[5]
- *Anticipatory grief* is preparing for a death by imagining it before it happens.[6]
- *Mourning* is the external process that one goes through in adapting to the death of the person, which we address in Chapter 7.
- *Bereavement* is "the process of grieving and letting go of a loved one who has died."[7]
- *Resilience* is the adaptation to a loss.[8]

Interviewees' diverse descriptions of feelings, thoughts, and actions since the death accorded with what grief theorists define as the "tasks of grief."[9] These tasks of normal, uncomplicated grief, as articulated by Harvard psychologist William Worden, involve

- absorbing the reality of the loss,
- processing different emotions of grief,
- making adjustments to living in the world without the deceased, and
- finding an enduring connection to the deceased in the midst of embarking on a new understanding of life and family.[10]

Worden's research stresses that engaging in these tasks contributes to a healthy adaptation to loss, also known as resilience. Adaptation to loss incorporates the shifts in the individual's sense of self, family, the holy, and ultimate purpose in life caused by the death of a loved one.

Other frameworks exist for understanding uncomplicated grief. The work of Elisabeth Kübler-Ross, best articulated in *On Death and Dying*,[11] introduced the concept of the "stages of dying," which shaped not only end-of-life care but also grief counseling and the public perception of loss.

The stages theory identified a sequence of steps followed in the dying process that was then applied to grief.[12] Contemporary theorists often critique the stages theory because it can be misinterpreted to be literal and sequential: The person dying or grieving will move seamlessly through the stages of denial to anger to depression to bargaining to acceptance.[13] Variations to the stages approach, such as the "phases of grief" theory, with phases ranging from numbness to anger to despair to reorganization, have also been proposed by other theorists.[14] Worden's grief work doesn't directly quarrel with the stages or phases frameworks, but as a clinician, Worden sees the tasks of grief as providing the mourner with something to do, and thus grief is not experienced passively, as merely passing through stages or phases.[15]

In this chapter, we organize the interviewees' grief experiences using Worden's four tasks of mourning as a framework. The tasks, though numbered in this chapter, were not necessarily experienced chronologically; many interviewees lived these tasks in fits and starts throughout the year. All those interviewed described various experiences of fluctuations in emotion, thought, and behavior, and they cultivated coping skills to help in living with those reactions. Unlike family structure's more direct influence on public mourning rituals and the rubrics of inheritance, family structure tended to affect grief around the edges. The work of moving forward in their own lives involved interviewees remembering key moments in the relationship to the deceased, understanding how the world in which they lived was different, and accepting their own feelings.[16] Even for those who engaged in anticipatory grief, the actual occurrence is something that cannot be anticipated, and the accompanying feelings may similarly be unexpected.[17]

TASK 1: ACCEPTING THAT DEATH HAS REALLY HAPPENED

Accepting the reality of loss is the first task in grief; hearing the official words, watching the machines stop, or making funeral arrangements were mechanical tasks compared with the internal realizations that the parent was truly no longer there. Barbara's mother died after a diagnosis of cancer, spending months in the hospital and a week at home with hospice for her final days. Barbara's job as a church secretary allowed her to work flexible hours, and her husband took over all the family carpooling duties so that she could maximize time spent with her mother. Barbara and her brother moved in with her parents for her mother's final week in hospice care. She sat vigil at her mother's side and observed every decline in her mother's ability to walk, eat, drink, and speak, but she confessed that it was still hard to believe she died, "Sometimes I look at her picture and in the back of my mind, it's like she's gone on vacation and she's coming back. But she's not. It's hard." To the interview, she brought a purse made of vinyl fabric printed with various images of Elvis, her mother's favorite singer. She explained that carrying this purse helped her feel close to her mother in the year since her death.

Many interviewees experienced instances during the first year following the loss when they forgot that their parent had died. These flashes of forgetting were quickly followed by moments of realization that the death had happened. Although the funeral and burial often marked an important first step in acknowledging the reality of death, the truth of the loss often hit the one grieving sporadically throughout the first year after the death, especially during holidays, birthdays, or other personally significant moments.

For example, Sam and his family, introduced in previous chapters, had been preparing for his mother's death for years. He, his father and sister made the difficult decision not to insert a feeding tube and to enroll his mother in hospice care for her final months of life. He sat vigil with his father and sisters the night that she died. Driving home with his father after the funeral and burial, his father, whose life had revolved around caring for Sam's mother for more than six years, asked, "I wonder what your momma wants to eat tonight?" Sam sat quietly for a moment and then replied, "I think she's okay, Dad." Sam remembered how his father's eyes filled with tears, and Sam nodded his head in resigned understanding.

One common experience shared by a tenth of those interviewed was picking up their cell phone to call the parent—only to realize that they could not. Jimmy, a 30-year-old truck driver from Arkansas whose mother suffered a stroke and died, told us,

> I was sitting in my house and it was the Sunday right after she passed. I picked up my cell phone to call her. I was sitting in the living room, and when I looked out I saw my car and her car underneath the carport and I said, "Oh God. Mamma's dead," and I threw the phone.

For the most part, the true finality of their parent's death took much longer to accept than many interviewees thought it would, a realization that the year anniversary served to solidify.

TASK 2: HANDLING EMOTIONS

The death of a loved one causes an individual to experience some level of pain. Within the range of uncomplicated experiences of grief, a wide range of emotions, such as "sadness, guilt, anxiety, helplessness, and loneliness,"[18] can be experienced in isolation or combination as a way to process the pain of loss. For example, 20% of those we interviewed spoke of crying at some point in the year since the death of their loved one, and almost everyone cried at some point during the interview. Tears were both a sign of deep emotion as well as a release, but interviewees also feared that tears were a sign of being out of control. Many interviewees apologized for crying—even though we opened every interview with placing a box of tissue on the table and acknowledging that much of what we might talk about could be emotionally sad.

Certain songs could trigger strong emotions that were then expressed through tears. Veronica told of what happens if she heard any of the songs played at her father's funeral, like "I Can Only Imagine"[19]:

> I just gotta start crying. There were a few times when I had to pull over the car and I was just bawling. They played one song in

worship and my mom and I just grabbed each other and started
boo-hooing.

Veronica's parents were married at the time of her father's death, and
although there was tension with her brother, the family shared a common
understanding that expressing emotion through tears was acceptable and
was a vulnerability that could be witnessed by one another. They were
able to process the pain of loss safely with each other. For the most part, a
high level of norm coherence led to an interpretation of good will on the
part of the grown child or empathy for the widowed parent for emotional
expressions, such as tears.

In families in which the norm coherence was low, emotional expression
by one member, often a steprelative, could be misunderstood or interpreted negatively, a partial disruption of this grief task. Several months
after her father's death, Delores's stepmother brought the family together
to talk about the headstone. Delores tried to be quiet and defer to her
other siblings and her stepmother, who she believed had more authority to
dictate what they wanted, especially because she didn't have funds to contribute to the cost. After the meeting, however, her half-sister told her that
her stepmother said that, "she looked mad." Delores couldn't understand
how her demeanor could be misinterpreted negatively or why her stepmother didn't talk to her about it directly. On the other hand, Delores did
explain during the interview that she didn't trust her stepmother, because
she didn't cry at the funeral. The mistrust isolated *both* the grieving stepmother and daughter.

TASK 3: ADJUSTING ONE'S WORLDVIEW TO LIVE WITH
THE LOSS

Even though Jackie had not had a positive relationship with her father
before his death, had refused to come home to help her sister, Angela, care
for him as his health declined, and had relinquished all claims to his estate,
she still had to make adjustments. On the flight home after the funeral
she said that it hit her: "It's just surreal to realize the person who has been

there since your beginning—win, lose, or draw, positive or negative—is not there anymore. What does that look like in your life?"

As the griever experiences the reality of death and related emotions, the adjustment to a new world without the deceased begins. The death of a parent figure created an empty chair at the family table and a heightened awareness of the unique role the deceased family member played in family events and in defining the family identity. It might also cause ontological questioning.

Changes in Holidays and Anniversaries

Holidays and special anniversaries offered a chance to reinvent family rituals and manage the absence of the deceased. Many interviewees sought simply to survive the holidays or the anniversary of the death. Courtney planned out their family's traditional celebration and meal for Christmas Eve, normally planned by her deceased mother. She followed her mother's recipes, her father and brothers and their families all dressed formally, and they attended the late afternoon Christmas Eve mass together so as to return home and eat together, per their tradition. But when the family arrived home and saw all the fine china set at the table but Courtney's mother not there, they decided to put on their pajamas and eat casually while watching a movie. Courtney grieved the tradition that her mother had spearheaded (and she hoped that in years to come they might reinstate it) but for now, she felt comforted that her family created a new ritual, together. She trusted that future fluctuations in family traditions would happen together as well.

On the anniversary of her father's sudden death after a car accident, Betsy and her mother marked the occasion at their camp on a local river. She drew on her religious beliefs and knowledge of Christian scriptures to assist in her adjustment to a world without her father:

We sat and looked at the water and I was just thinking, "Okay, God, how do I get to the other side of this river, like I don't see the bridge. God, I know, by faith, but like where's the bridge? How am I supposed to cross over into this next year?" And God really spoke to me and said, "Who said you need a bridge? Don't limit me. You think you can't live without your daddy. You can. You didn't think you could breathe again or live and just even get along without having your daddy. You can." So I was just like, "All right, I'll keep my eyes on you, and I'll get there. I'll get to the other side. Sure, I can walk on water. You've done it before."

Betsy was able to process her thoughts with her mother and help her mother cope with how she would move forward without her husband.

Changing Conceptions within the Family

For interviewees with a surviving parent, like Betsy, the presence of that parent supported them in the year since the loss. Greg had moved in with his parents because of his own heart problems several years before his mother died from a brain aneurysm. His mother had always been the emotional one in the family and had served to draw out the thoughts and feelings of Greg and his father. Greg knew that they would need to adjust not only to her absence but also to the role that she used to play in their family. In the year since her death, Greg and his father made a deal with each other to cope with their loss, without annoying each other:

> The deal was: if you're freaking out, you come tell me and if I'm freaking out, I will come tell you, but otherwise we're okay. Otherwise we're going to kill each other asking, "You all right?" "You all right?" and we are going to get on each other's nerves and kill each other. That was the deal. It happened, too. I said, "Hey I am freaking out," and he said, "okay." That was it, but once I felt that wall behind me, I was all right, I was okay.

With the support of his father behind him, Greg could then adjust to a world without his mother and begin negotiating how to compensate for the different roles she had played in his life.

In families with low norm coherence, reorganization as a family unit rarely happened. Some of these families could attribute their low level of reorganization to the substance abuse issues of the deceased parent. But, for others, the marital history of the parent led to weak ties between the grown children and the stepparents. The grown children began a new expression of their family without the deceased parent *and* without the presence of the widowed stepparent. They did not see their stepparent as a source of emotional support. Many of the grown children expressed surprise that they had not talked with their widowed stepparent more than once or twice in the year since the death, whereas most of the grown children with a widowed parent relied heavily on their widowed parent for emotional support.

For those grown children from remarried families, maintaining a family identity that included the stepparent entailed work and intentionality. Rhonda was already planning for Thanksgiving and Christmas at the interview. She wanted to host everyone at her home, but her half-siblings and stepmother wanted to celebrate at her stepmother's home, and her sister, Marti (who was still holding up the settling of the estate), refused to speak to their half-siblings or stepmother, or to Rhonda for signing her rights to the house over to their stepmother. Rhonda was at a loss for how to hold everyone together, "We can't get everybody together anymore. It's really hard—we can't get the family thing going anymore at all." Rhonda did not see how the family would stay together in the future and at a year after her father's death, she was exhausted and discouraged from trying.

Grown children who had undergone the divorce of their parents experienced the death of a parent differently from some of the grown children from married-parent families, for whom the death of the parent was their first experience with loss. Experiencing divorce, grieving the expression of a family that no longer existed as it once did, caused some grown children to develop coping skills that now came to be used again after the death.[20] Some also knew the destructive coping skills they wanted to avoid. Earlier in her life, Rhonda had coped with loss by drinking alcohol and in sexual relationships. Her father had needed to bail her out of two different abusive relationships in her twenties. After her father's death, she recognized the same instincts to drink or take up with men, but she knew she didn't have her father to rescue her now *and* that she didn't want to repeat those mistakes.

Awareness of Mortality Changes the Griever

For many interviewees, the death itself gave them perspective on their own life. Author Joan Didion writes in *The Year of Magical Thinking* of how she learned in the year after her husband's death that "when we mourn our losses we also, mourn, for better or worse, ourselves. As we were. As we are no longer."[21] For example, as Will watched his father die from heart disease, he saw a potential future for himself, one that he wanted to avoid. Will loved his father and though he remembered his father as distant and always working during his childhood, he always relished his memories of being included with the "guys" (his father and uncles) in holiday traditions of cooking and drinking. After his parents' divorce, Will knew that his father was living alone and drinking, eating, and smoking more and more, but because Will was often traveling for work, he didn't pay much attention until the diagnosis of congestive heart failure served as Will's first wake-up call.

After his father moved in with him and his brother for his final months, Will began to realize just how unhealthy his father had become *and* how he himself was becoming a mirror image: a person who works, eats, drinks, and smokes too much. "I looked at my dad in the hospital bed and thought, 'Shit. That's me in twenty years.'" In the year since his father's death, Will lost over one-hundred pounds, changed jobs, ran his first half-marathon, and was preparing for a move to the East Coast the week following our interview, all done in memory of his father. Will was an atheist and noted during the interview that he was quoting Emerson to describe how he imagined grief transforming his life story:

> The death of a dear friend, wife, brother, lover, which seems nothing but privation somewhat later assumes the aspect of a guide

or genus, for it commonly operates revolutions in our way of life, terminates an epic of infancy or youth, which is wanting to be closed ... allows for the formation of new ones more friendly to the growth of character.[22]

Will's identity narrative shifted dramatically with his father's death and resulted in transformations in his physical and vocational life.

Changes in Religious Beliefs and Practices

Living with the loss of a parent often served to shift the individual's existing sense of ultimate meaning as well as routines of worship attendance and spiritual practices. For some, an established routine of worship attendance and membership in a faith community was a source of support. For example, Peter recounted how after his father's death he felt a little uneasy about returning to church. His family and his parents all attended the same church, and his father had played in the worship band. Peter talked with their pastor about his hesitation, and, as they talked about how their faith shaped their definition of hope, Peter realized, "What better place to be when I'm grieving than church with which I have such a strong association to my father?" On Peter's first Sunday in worship after his father's funeral, the worship band placed his father's banjo in an empty chair. But Peter realized as he looked at the banjo that his "dad's offering of music in worship was never intended to point to himself but to a gift he offered to God." So when Peter went forward during the collection of the offer, he picked up the banjo, and placed it on the altar. "Dad and his gifts of music belonged to God and were with God now."

Although Peter found a stable source of support and meaning in his pastor and congregation, many other grown children felt unmoored. As mentioned at the beginning of the chapter, Shannon understood God through words. But then her father died and the words dried up, and she struggled to make sense of the world and God without him and without her words. A connection to the divine and to her sense of ultimate meaning in life needed help from the words of another poet as well as nature.

Shannon recalled how on a visit to her father in the nursing home, he spoke to her through poetry. She sat on his left-hand side, on the bed close to him, and held his hand. His eyes opened and she said, "Daddy, I have to get home to the boys now...I love you, daddy." He grinned slyly, looking at her and asked, "How much?" She replied, reciting a favorite Disney movie of her sons, "To infinity and beyond." And he, with his eyes closed again, quietly said, as if reciting a prayer, "Beyond, beyond, beyond."

At home that night, she told her husband, "I would not doubt that there was some poem or something that he had to memorize way back when with that phrase in it." And, in the year since his death she found the poem in a collection of Tennyson, a discovery she interpreted as God speaking to her when her traditional sources of meaning and hope had failed her. As her quote that opens the chapter says, she always considered herself a faithful person, but the death of her father threw all her beliefs in doubt. However, she believed that she was spoken to through poetry. Several months after her father's death, a friend found a collection of Tennyson's poems in an antique store and brought it to her. When Shannon opened it, she turned directly to *Far, Far Away*, which includes the line, "beyond, beyond, beyond." She described herself reading this line of poetry: "I'm just getting hyper, slapping my leg, crying one minute, laughing the next minute. And, I say to my husband, 'Jim, I am being spoken to through the pages of Tennyson!'" Finding this poem gave her comfort and helped her feel connected to her father after his death.

In addition to those words of Tennyson, her grief forced her to step out of her comfort zone in the written word. She lived in the country and she decided to start walking, to get away from her desk and the empty page and still pen. As she walked, she looked at the trees and began to see pictures—meaningful designs and religious symbols, and she decided she better photograph them to prove that she really saw them. She interpreted these signs as visual words of encouragement to her from God; meant to open her eyes to new ways of seeing the world. She bought a camera, took photos, and shared them with her family, who was amazed at her vision. They found a source of comfort in her photos as well. At the end of our interview, she concluded that the words would come again soon. But for now, God was beyond words, in the trees.

TASK 4: DEFINING A NEW WAY TO BE CONNECTED TO THE DECEASED PARENT

One-fourth of those interviewed mentioned that they missed talking with the deceased parent, and they recognized the irreplaceable role that parent played in their life. Isaac thought about his deceased mother and the unique and supportive role she had played in his recovery from drug addiction and his return to society after jail time. She used to drive him to classes at the local community college, and those drives allowed him to divulge his doubts and worries. Although he found carpool alternatives after her death, he missed his confidant. He wondered, "Now, who do I talk to? Who is going to understand me?" Part of adapting to the world without the loved one entailed finding new connections as well as cultivating an imagination for what the deceased loved ones might say if they were still present. Of those we interviewed, 10% mentioned visiting the grave and talking with their deceased loved one there. The cemetery served a role as a "memorial space"[23] although not everyone finds visiting a grave to be comforting.[24]

Certain activities or experiences contributed to an enduring connection to the deceased. Some interviewees enjoyed engaging in the types of activities that the deceased liked to do, such as making jelly, watching football, sewing, and even "riding the bus and making groceries." For example, Kendra made DVDs of pictures and music that her ex-stepfather loved and distributed them to all the siblings and stepsiblings. Watching the DVD comforted her and helped her feel close to her deceased ex-stepfather. Clay refurbished his mother's old Singer sewing machine, and even though he doesn't know how to sew, he liked how the sound of the machine reminded him of his deceased mother making Halloween costumes for him and his brother; "that sound ... it just kinda sticks in your mind."

Some interviewees had dreams or visions of their deceased loved one that they interpreted as their loved one appearing as a guiding or comforting presence. Six months after Michelle's mother died, Michelle realized that her own bedroom had become a pit. Although she kept the rest of the house clean and in order for her children, her room had become filled with trash and tissues, reminiscent of how her mother had lived. One evening, after tucking her children in bed, she retired to her bedroom to see that all the tissue on the floor had been piled in a corner. She interpreted this pile of tissues as her mother telling her to clean her room because she would not want her death to cause Michelle to fall into disarray. Michelle even asked out loud, "Mom, are you in here?" She confessed that she hadn't told anyone about this experience "because I know people wouldn't believe it," but it served to inspire her to start cleaning her room and to begin thinking about how be at peace with her mother's death.

CONCLUSION

Many interviewees expressed amazement and relief that they survived the first year after the death. Chloe said, "Honestly, I'm surprised with myself. I'm a lot stronger than I thought I was because I'm still here. I haven't broke, you know?" Many study participants explained that the interview served as a critical moment for them to reflect on how they had managed their life after loss. Management entailed engaging in the normal tasks of grief. Regardless of the current structure of their family of origin, interviewees adapted to their changed lives by accepting the reality of the death, developing the ability to express their grief, making adjustments to their family rituals and general worldview, and establishing a continuing relationship with the person who had died. For families with higher norm coherence, that first year was a collective loss, with

shared and harmonious experiences. For families with less norm coherence, the grieving process often served to exacerbate tensions. Although
many study participants acknowledged that grief would be with them
in some form all their lives, they hoped that telling their story at this
moment would help other grown children caring for and grieving a parent or stepparent. We now turn to the next steps following the death of a
parent or stepparent, the more public tasks of mourning and transmitting
an inheritance.

Mourning Rubrics and Burial

Just give me a minute, please.

—MICHELLE

It was Christmas day, and Michelle lay in a hospital bed, next to her mother's body. Michelle and her siblings had sat vigil all morning, experiencing their mother's last surge of energy together. The absence of the heart monitor beeping left a deep silence in the sterile room. Michelle heard her brother and sister in the hallway weeping, but she wanted to stay by her mother's side for a few minutes more. The doctor entered the room, followed by a nurse, and said quietly, "Time of death, 2:32 p.m." The nurse and doctor stepped closer to the bed, and Michelle beseeched tearfully, "Just give me a minute, please." The nurse replied, "You take the time you need, we'll wait right here." Michelle breathed slowly, trying to take in the last of her mother, and she knew, "It's over now." She was no longer a caregiver.

Michelle and her siblings soon left the hospital, and they began the tasks of mourning. Michelle wrote the obituary, paid for its public posting, and met with the funeral home personnel to view her mother's body and make burial arrangements. Although her mother had told Michelle and her siblings that she wanted to be cremated, Michelle learned from the funeral home that this might not be possible: Because her mother had not completed an authorization for cremation, Louisiana law requires that all three siblings agree on cremation.[1] She then spoke with her pastor, who agreed to officiate at the graveside service because her mother did not belong to a faith community.

Michelle's story shows the general progression of public mourning. After death, surviving family members must shift their verb in talking about the deceased loved one from "is" to "was," and similarly shift their focus from caregiving to grief and mourning. Regardless of family structure, all interviewees completed three general tasks of mourning:

1) Publicly announce and acknowledge that death has happened.
2) Properly tend to the dead body of the loved one through burial or cremation.
3) Begin to reorganize and redefine who they are as a family without the physical presence of the deceased member.

Although some families undertook these tasks harmoniously, other families experienced friction or separation, and the disagreements sometimes caused ongoing rifts with long-lasting ramifications related to estate administration and the quality of the kinship relations. Where the shared norms were strong and an expectation of continuing connection existed, the families were able to move forward collectively or to resolve their disagreements amicably. Harmony was strongest in married-parent families in which the grown children honored their surviving mother or father as the primary interpreter of what the deceased parent would want. The child might have offered advice or an opinion concerning the choice of a casket or song for a memorial service, but ultimately deferred to the widowed parent's wishes. In families with competing norms and expectations, whether between the surviving spouse and the grown children or between the grown children themselves, rifts tended to isolate the individuals involved and then reverberate into debates over the deceased's estate and a lack of contact in the year after the death.

In this chapter, we follow the chronology of mourning[2] from the time of death to the burial. The purpose of mourning is "getting the dead where they need to go, and get the living where they need to be."[3] Typically, the first formal step is professional certification of the death. Next is public acknowledgement that death has occurred, traditionally in the form of an obituary posted in the print or on-line edition of the local newspaper. Social media platforms, such as Facebook and Twitter, also now play a role in this step. Then comes a public gathering, often religiously based, where the family and community memorialize the life of the deceased. Next is disposal of the body through cremation or burial. As this chapter shows, each of these moments typically begins with standard legal or religious forms or protocols that can be personalized to various extents. In turn, each step reflects tensions or harmony within family systems.

MEDICAL CERTIFICATION OF DEATH

The first formal step in the shift of a life from present to past tense is medical certification of death. Paula, whose family was introduced in Chapter 2, and her mother, both nurses at a local nursing home, cared for her father, Lawrence, at home under hospice care. Because of her medical background, Paula had a sense for the legality of the moment. She described his time of death, including everyone standing around the hospital bed:

> His head [her father's] was up here. The nurse wasn't there yet. Reverend Charles was there. The aide was there. My mother-in-law was there. My brothers were there. About that time, I said, "He's gone. He's not breathing." I said, "Give me a stethoscope." I put it over his heart and said, "He's gone," which, of course, I can't pronounce. The nurse had to actually get there and pronounce him. Then, we each had our own time. When the nurse got there, we let her do her thing. His time of death was 12:55 p.m.

For most families, like Paula's, this process remained a relatively private matter between them and the hospital or hospice staff, and family structure was irrelevant because of the standardized nature of this process. Only physicians can medically certify death.[4] Hospitals and hospice organizations initiate filling out the death certificate, with the attending or pronouncing physician signing to certify. A coroner (who, in Louisiana, must be a physician) or medical examiner is involved if the death occurs in a nonmedical setting. Legally, the coroner is responsible for certifying most deaths that occur outside of a hospital, including those in home hospice, from accidents, or from something crime related.[5]

The death certificate itself in Louisiana does not become a public document until fifty years after the death. Those authorized to request a copy in that fifty-year window of time include the surviving spouse, parent, adult child, adult grandchild, or beneficiary of an insurance policy of the person named on the document.[6] Stepchildren and ex-stepchildren are not included. The standard certificate of death in the United States includes sections for basic demographic information of the deceased, including marital status, a section to be completed by the person pronouncing or certifying death, which includes the location, date, time, cause of death, and a section to be completed or verified by a funeral director.[7] Although most interviewees had not thought about the legal requirements for certifying death, they did understand that it was the first step toward public acknowledgement that death had occurred.

PUBLIC ANNOUNCEMENT OF DEATH: OBITUARIES AND SOCIAL MEDIA

After the medical certification of death comes public acknowledgment that death has occurred, often through a published obituary, and, today, preceded and followed by social media announcements.

Obituaries

Obituaries are basically paid advertisements. They can range from a terse death notice, which includes simple information such as the name, date of death, and funeral arrangements, to an obituary often penned by a family member or friend that includes extensive biographical data. These obituaries may include nicknames, the date of birth and death, the cause of death, the occupation and education history of the deceased, personal attributes and anecdotes about the deceased, a list of the surviving family members and their spouses, those who preceded the deceased in death, and then close with the funeral arrangements.[8]

Obituaries serve not only as the "final public notice of an existence" but also as the basis on which "survivors begin reconstructing a disrupted relationship"[9] that now, after death, is one sided. Obituaries represent a lens of remembrance based on what the author picks and chooses to share.[10] Indeed, many obituaries are written to project an idealized version of the deceased, combining the facts of death with commemoration written by a loved one. Obituaries are more than personal statements; they are "literary miniatures that chronicle a life and valorize the values associated with it." Historian Janice Hume studied thousands of obituaries from the nineteenth century to early twentieth century as a way to analyze how American values had changed.[11] In studying "four framing categories of obituaries—name and occupation of the deceased, cause of death, personal attributes of the deceased, and funeral arrangements," Hume observed shifts American attitudes toward death, general values in life, and markers of social inclusion and exclusion. As Hume might predict, contemporary obituaries reflect modern family structures; for example, the list of surviving kin might include not just spouses, children, and parents but also significant others, ex-spouses, and stepchildren. The author's choice on whom and what to include can be as revelatory as who and what is excluded.[12]

Obituaries can be long and do carry a literal cost.[13] Historically, that cost covered the journalist who wrote the obituary for the family, but now, the purchaser submits the wording or the funeral director helps the family craft the wording based on a standardized form, and the cost covers the type space as well as printing a photo, if desired.[14] In papers such as the Baton Rouge *Advocate,* where all the deceased's obituaries in this study were published, a lengthy death notice could be included in both the print and digital versions of the paper in a way accessible to all socioeconomic classes. Some families may also choose to have the previously published obituary posted at such sites as www.legacy.com, which can also include an on-line guest book where visitors can comment with memories and words of encouragement. The interactive quality of the digital version of an obituary is a relatively new development.

Overall, the process of drafting the obituary reflected the coherency of family norms. In families with a high level of shared norms and trust, the decision concerning obituary authorship turned on who had the gift for writing or who was willing to serve as a recorder to curate facts and anecdotes from all family members. Although coherent family norms could exist in all family structures, they were more likely to exist in married-parent families. For example, Shannon and her mother served as the main caregivers for her father as he lived in a nursing home with Parkinson's disease in the last months of his life. As covered in Chapter 6, she was also known as the writer in her family. A long-time teacher and amateur author, she brought to the interview a stack of her writings several inches thick that was written testimony to how journaling about her father's illness and her role as a caregiver helped her make sense of her relationship to her dad as illness affected his physical abilities. Shannon's mother and two siblings all knew that she would be the one to pen the obituary and trusted her to represent the family honestly.

In stepfamilies in which norm coherence was high, the person with writing gifts was also chosen and worked cooperatively with other family members. Phillip felt comfortable with his stepmother, Cheryl, writing his father's obituary because "she's the writer." Their decision about the obituary also reflected their team approach to planning the funeral and burial arrangements.

By contrast, most remarried families exhibited a low level of shared norms and trust. The grown children of the deceased tended to be excluded from the writing of the obituary by the surviving spouse, who took the lead in completing this task and paying for it, with the interviewee unaware of the choices made by the stepparent. In those families in which hurt feelings arose concerning who would be given the responsibility for penning the obituary, the anger or sadness could be traced to being excluded from the decision. Not knowing who or how it was written led to a feeling of conspiracy and eventual estrangement from the stepparent. Even in something as seemingly straightforward as writing an obituary, family norms played an important role.

Although we did not learn about authorship until the interviews, the obituary was our first point of contact with all families. For example, we first met Michelle (whose story opened the chapter) through the words of her mother's obituary:

> **Dorothy H_** was called home to rest surrounded by her family on Saturday, Dec. 25, 2010, at 2:32 p.m. at Our Lady of the Lake Regional Medical Center. She was 68, born in Bronx, N.Y., on Aug. 8, 1942. She was a retired nurse and resident of Baton Rouge. She will be greatly missed by her children, Ricky H_, Michelle H_ and Autumn L_; and her seven grandchildren. Preceded in death by her parents, grandparents and grandson, Mark H_. There will be a private family graveside service on Thursday, Dec. 30. Visiting at New Southside Funeral Home on Thursday, Dec. 30, from 10 a.m. until noon. Graveside service at Roselawn Memorial Park at 12:15 p.m.

The thousands of obituaries read as part of this study echo the basic structure seen in Michelle's mother's obituary. In some, a nickname, a funny anecdote, a private joke, a scripture verse, a famous quote, or a list of civic club memberships might be included. Our focus was on the list of survivors, and we contacted those who fell within study parameters.

During the interview, we asked how the list of survivors was compiled. We learned that, when the deceased was in a first marriage at the time of death, regardless of who authored the obituary, there was little thought given to the list of surviving kin. Who was considered family, and who was not, was tacitly agreed on by all family members. The list of surviving family members portrayed a harmonious picture in the obituary and that harmony continued throughout the mourning process.

In families in which the parent had remarried, grown children described the harmonious picture presented in the obituary as masking tensions over who was, and was not, considered kin. For example, Delores was the oldest daughter of her divorced and remarried father. Her stepmother wrote the obituary, and, although she listed Delores as a daughter, she excluded her from the attached photo, which included Delores's three half-brothers. Delores interpreted this oversight as a decision made by her stepmother that was intended to slight her and make her feel that she was not a legitimate member of her father's true family. (As we'll see later, children from second families interpreted the obituary lists differently.) In Winifred's family, the author of her mother's obituary explicitly labeled the children as either "biological" or "step." (Because Winifred was estranged from her family, she did not know who had authored the obituary.) As a "biological" daughter, she had no problem with the distinction, but she wondered how her stepsiblings felt.

In families with complicated kinship structures, grown children struggled with how to present the various connections to the deceased. Keith explained that his family included "inside" versus "outside" kids because his father had married twice and had a long-time girlfriend at the time of death. He saw his father as having three families: "me, my two sisters . . . then those two from that marriage, and then you've got the other ("step" children of his girlfriend.)" In the obituary, he decided not to distinguish who were siblings by different mothers. He put in print what he hoped he would experience in reality: to feel "like we was actually one family."

"I know (that) my redeemer liveth, and that he shall stand at the latter (day) upon the earth." Job 19:25. **Keith S_, Sr.,** a captain with the Department of Corrections at Jetson Correctional Center for Youth, returned to the joy of our Lord at 6:37 p.m. Sunday. Those cherishing his memory include four daughters, Avril H_, Sheila S_ , Deborah S_, and Donna S_; three sons, Keith S_, Jr., Larry L_, Payton K_, and Michael S_ ; two sisters and brothers-in-law; six brothers; **longtime companion, Beatrice P_;** 11 grandchildren; two stepchildren, Sonny and Clifton P_; goddaughter; and a host of nephews, nieces, cousins, other relatives and friends.

The obituary of Keith's father also shows how in single-parent families, the grown children experienced uncertainty concerning where to list the name of the parent's significant other. In contrast to married (or remarried) parents, in which the surviving spouse was always listed first, the name of the boyfriend or girlfriend was lower in the list of kin connections, after the children.

Determining whom to include and to exclude became more complicated with ex-stepchildren, resulting from the complex dynamics between the deceased's families as well as with their own families of origin. For example, we found Kendra through the obituary for Arthur. The obituary listed her mother as Arthur's wife, and Kendra as one of his four daughters. During the interview, however, we learned that Arthur was actually Kendra's ex-stepfather and that Kendra's mother was his ex-wife; it was Kendra and her mother, however, who had cared for him during his last year of life and were with him the night he died. The obituary (which they drafted) reflected the definition of kin that they had experienced. On the other hand, listing themselves as kin in the obituary exacerbated tensions with Arthur's three daughters, who were estranged from him at the time of his death.

Some grown children experienced anger from their biological families for being included as stepchildren in the obituary of an ex-stepparent. Destiny considered Albert, her ex-stepfather, a father figure. She treasured childhood memories of Albert walking her and her siblings home from elementary school and attending her softball games, all things her biological father never did. Those childhood memories of care and attention translated to Destiny's sense of obligation to visit and offer care to her ex-stepfather on his deathbed. After Albert's death, Destiny contributed funds to help pay for the obituary. She was proud to be included as a stepdaughter in the obituary; however, her biological father felt that this public recognition of Albert's role usurped his own role. He was not mollified when Destiny explained to him that Albert had been more of a father to her than he had been in her childhood, and she was honored to be listed in the obituary.

Social Media

In a major change to mourning practices over the past two decades, the actual public awareness of death commemorated in a formal obituary may be superseded by—or at least happen concurrently with—status updates and notices through social media sites, such as Facebook. The ubiquity of social media proved challenging for all families regardless of structure or level of shared norms. All families believed there was a proper order in which people should be informed of the death, with immediate and extended family learning first, followed by close friends, and then the general public. Because an obituary takes at least a day to write and then have published, that practice has historically given the family time to begin the mourning process, contact the first tier of relatives, and tell others at a more gradual pace. In our digital age, the shift to death becoming public knowledge via social media is changing that sequence, so the knowledge of a death can be spread to many people almost instantaneously with the death itself. This new sequence requires adjustments, and can, for some people, result in the sending out of the news too quickly, truncating the time buffer between the private experience of death and the public experience of mourning.

Those interviewed took offense at friends and acquaintances sharing family information but the risk of offense also applies to families without coherent norms concerning the desired privacy level or hierarchy of how and with whom family knowledge should be spread. Married-parent families tended to "circle the wagons," so to speak, and wanted to process the immediate days after the death together, without outside interference or interpretation. Single-parent and remarried-parent families tended to scatter more, and thus social media sharing could replace private sharing, causing further rifts and competition over who is defining the family story of the loss. Conversely, we found that choosing a "digital proxy," a person who is close to the grieving family but not directly impacted by the death, could be helpful in the immediate days after death. Courtney described her feelings and choices concerning a digital proxy after learning that her mother's death was announced on Facebook without her knowing:

My mom's best friend's put it out on Facebook within 30 minutes of her death. Whereas, my family, we're all very private. It upset me because then everyone found out and the phone starts blowing up. We had a plan: first phone call is my brother, then my dad's brothers, and so on. I felt like the world needed to stop. How dare an hour pass without her in it, without the whole world knowing? My best friend was already there, and I gave her my phone. I said, "Deal with people, I'm going to sleep."

Rather than this unplanned, unanticipated posting, had Courtney and her mother considered digital planning, they might have chosen a trusted best friend as a digital proxy and discussed their wishes in advance. In some families, because of the objective distance maintained by many of the stepchildren interviewed, a stepchild could have served as the digital proxy for the family, who could write status updates and distributes news concerning the funeral services, memorial donations, and so forth.

These experiences related to grief and social media serve as keen reminders that mourning practices allow for a semblance of control and order during a chaotic time. Walking away from other mourners is more difficult when those mourners are on your digital device.

FUNERALS AND MEMORIAL SERVICES

After the public announcement of death, the family, along with the community, gathers for a funeral or memorial service, often religiously based, that celebrates the life of the deceased and begins to make formal sense of the loss. In *The Good Funeral*, theologian Thomas Long and funeral director Thomas Lynch remind the reader that "those who bury the dead are performing a piece of theater in which they act out the deepest truths they know about life and death."[15] They explain that "any human's death is a tear in the social fabric, and it invokes two great needs, both of them very public: first, the body must be cared for and given disposition. Second, the community needs to tell once more the story of the life of the one who has died."[16] Although the interviewees' narratives of the time of death were highly detailed, the narratives about the funerals were told in broad sweeps with snapshot memories of specific moments during the wakes and services. Unless they brought the service bulletin or remembrance card with them to the interview, they struggled to recall what scriptures were read, who spoke (unless they gave the eulogy), or what songs were played or sung. What they remembered most clearly was their own sense of exhaustion, the faces of those who attended the ritual, and the family seating arrangement for the service.[17]

Both family structure and norm coherence played a determinative role most clearly in the funeral seating arrangement, which often foreshadowed the family's level of adaptation and reorganization after the ritual. We've given extensive space to analyzing the seating positions at the funeral because spatial arrangements assumed great importance for all respondents. Most respondents had not anticipated being upset by the seating arrangement. Yet they traced subsequent disputes over the deceased's estate and a general fraying of connections to tensions over where they sat (or didn't sit) at the funeral.

Married-Parent Families: "We Sat Together"

In married-parent families, role clarity within the family system continued from before death to after. The absence of the deceased loved one caused pain and sadness, but mothers remained mothers, children remained children, and siblings remained siblings. Although death may have affected their connections, no member risked losing his or her place in the family. Similar to how they made decisions about withdrawing life support, members of the married-parent family planned the funeral service collectively, with the surviving parent and any grown children who wanted to participate making decisions. The story told, using the pronoun "we," reflected relative harmony as well as creative conflict resolution involving compromise among all members when disagreements occurred.

Spatial arrangements reflected that coherence. Most grown children stood next to their widowed parent during the wake to greet visitors who came to offer their condolences. At the funeral, grown children sat with the surviving spouse in the front row for the service. Minus the deceased, the family was a coherent unit.

Married-parent families were not without conflict, but the cohesive history of the family helped them resolve disputes, invariably showing their respect for the surviving parent. For Sam, some steps were easy: "Momma loved roses so we picked a rose-colored casket and the lining had roses on it. It was beautiful." But disagreement then arose concerning whether to have an open casket during the visitation. Sam and the family knew that his mother didn't want an open casket because

> she was always self-conscious about her looks. Daddy said her dad and her mom would always tell her she was ugly and then beat her— she had a rough childhood. . . . She even said, after the stroke when she was coherent for about the first month or so, she would joke about dying and said, "Abe, I will haunt you to the day you die if you have an open casket funeral."

As they planned the funeral, Sam reminded the family of his mother's wishes, but their father insisted on an open casket. A year after her death, Sam wonders if she is indeed haunting their father because they acquiesced to the wishes of their widowed father for an open casket.

Single-Parent Families: "It Was All Me"

As was true for children of married parents, children of deceased single parents maintained their role clarity as siblings and children. But without the mediating and often calming presence of a surviving parent, one sibling often stepped up and acted as the parent. Typically, the one who took the lead in caregiving also took the lead in planning and coordinating the funeral or memorial service. The loneliness of that role persisted in the narratives, symbolized by the use of the pronoun "I." For example, Jimmy's single mother suffered a stroke following surgery. As an only child, he called together his grandparents and extended family to surround his mother when they "pulled the plug." He also made the decisions about the funeral. He even chuckled as he remembered his mother's outfit:

> She loved sports so I put her in a real nice Alabama shirt and some jogging pants. Mamma didn't hardly put on no dressy-dress clothes. "Lord," *(he chuckled)* "Here's mamma in a football shirt and jogging pants. We gotta redneck funeral."

No one challenged his decision not to use "dressy-dress clothes," but he also didn't tell his humorous observations to anyone gathered at the funeral, which could have been a point of intimacy and shared memory between family members and friends.

He felt similarly alone at the funeral: "I sat on the front bench, looked, and I stayed to myself. A lot of her friends were there, but I just wanted some time to myself. . . ." As people gathered, he remembered seeing familiar faces, including his pastor, who had traveled from Natchitoches, more than an hour away. Seeing familiar faces reduced his sense of loneliness.

Even if the grown children of single parents were physically surrounded by the current and ex-partners of their parent as well as siblings, half-siblings, and stepsiblings, they continued to use the pronoun "I" to tell their story. As was true for obituary drafting, grown children of single parents struggled to clarify what role, if any, a boyfriend or girlfriend of their parent should play in the public acknowledgement of death. In each of these moments, the significant other began moving away and out of the family, both physically and emotionally.

Grown children of single parents understood that they would sit in the front row with any siblings for the funeral. For example, Keith, whose father's obituary can be read earlier, had listed all the siblings in the obituary, but the lines of insiders and outsiders amongst the potential kin became apparent at the funeral. Keith sat in the front row of the church with all of his sisters and brothers, and they each wore blue to match the color of the casket lining. He hoped that the siblings' togetherness at the funeral would continue, but it didn't: "all kinds of chaos" broke out after the funeral as they settled his father's estate and the siblings divided into groups by mother.

The presence and placement of ex-spouses also proved challenging. Although Keith sat with his siblings, he was aware of where his mother, his father's current "long-time companion," and other previous partners of his father sat scattered throughout the worship space. He felt anxious about how they would interact with one another. For some, an ex-spouse seemed out of place to the grown children who now considered them familial outsiders. Angela and Jackie were offended that their single father's fourth ex-wife took a prominent place during the visitation. Jackie recalled how she and her sister united in coping with her unwelcome presence.

> Our brazen, awful, ex-stepmother actually positioned herself next to the memorial. They'd been divorced ten years! That's just the way she is; she likes to be the center of attention. My sister [Angela] was freaking out. I said to Angela, "Don't give her the satisfaction. She's making a fool of herself. We're not going to cheapen ourselves by walking over there and causing a scene. Let her look stupid. Just ignore her."

Not everyone was uncomfortable when an ex-spouse attended the visitation or service. For some, it was important for the ex-spouse to stay in the background. Others, however, expressed gratitude when an ex-spouse attended to show support for them, rather than as a public act of mourning. Brady's mother, though long divorced from his father, attended the funeral and sat in the back. She prayed with Brady in a side room during the wake and reassured him that his father had been "saved" when they were married. This knowledge gave Brady comfort. For Jeremy, it was his ex-stepfather, Paul, who provided him with support. Jeremy felt emotionally challenged by his mother's turbulent, drug-addicted life, sudden death, and lack of planning. Paul's support for his ex-stepson stemmed from the warm relationship they'd had during his marriage to Jeremy's mother. He was the first person Jeremy called when he discovered his mother's dead body, and there was no one else Jeremy wanted to sit next to during the services other than Paul.

Remarried-Parent Families: "She Sat in Front"

The remarried-parent families in our study included those in which either a biological parent or a stepparent had died. As in the married-parent families, the surviving spouse took the lead in planning the funeral and in paying for the funeral arrangements. Instead of using the collective pronoun "we" to describe the experience, however, grown children used the pronoun "she" or "he" to explain how the surviving spouse made choices. Seating arrangements at the funeral reflected these tensions. For grown children whose biological parent died, they came to the funeral expecting to sit in the front row. For grown children whose stepparent died, they expected to sit with family members, but in the second or third row. However, all grown children expected that their family would sit *together*, a reality that often failed to happen. For example, Candace recalled arriving at the funeral services and reaching out to her stepmother. The two had historically had a negative relationship marked by ill will, but Candace wanted to try to connect over the death of her father. As a gesture of compassion, she asked her stepmother, "Do you want us to sit with you, like, as a family?" And her stepmother replied, "Yeah, that would be nice because I really feel like an outsider with your family." However, as soon as other people started to arrive, her stepmother "never talked to us again. Never asked us to come sit up there with her—nuthin.'" In defiance, Candace stood in the back.

Overall, for most remarried families, the death of the parent seems to mark the death of that expression of their family. The stepparent, and what his or role could or should be as a parent, became fuzzy or conflicted without the mediating presence of the deceased. Grown children wondered, "Am I still a stepdaughter? What does that mean?" Then, when they felt the stepparent had not appropriately reached out to them, by inviting them to sit together in the front row or stand next to them during the visitation, they took offense and began to put distance between themselves and the stepparent. Similar to that of single-parent families, the absence of the parent who provided clarity and purpose for being that expression of the family caused turmoil, confusion, and, ultimately, disownment.

Even in families who had worked smoothly together during the illness of the parent, the kin relationship began fraying during the funeral. Rhonda and her siblings, half-siblings, and stepmother of thirty years, Judith, became a caregiving team in her father's final months of life in hospice home care. However, the funeral service began to dredge up past hurts. Rhonda's stepmother's extended family attended the funeral but, according to Rhonda, "Judith's family never accepted us, because our dad was divorced, and Judith's family didn't like that. We were the stepchildren." When they sat down for the service, she believed that she and her siblings belonged in the front row, with Judith. Instead,

> Judith's family and her sisters sat in the front row, and pushed us to the back, and that really upset me.... And you know, I'm sure Judith didn't think about it, but why? It's huge—it pushed me back, it pushed my children back. And we're his first family. My dad had five children. It made me feel so divided because we were shoved to the back.

In the year after her father's death, Rhonda tried to overcome her hurt feelings. She had given her father her word that she would check in on her stepmother, and despite her hard feelings about the funeral, she did so once a month. But her sister, Marti, continued to hold on to her hurt feelings.

In the few instances in which stepfamilies worked well together, a history of warmth in the relationship between the surviving stepparent and the grown child set the stage for subsequent interactions. The stepfamilies in which shared norms developed hold in common several traits:

- geographic proximity,
- specific personality traits and faith background shared between the stepparent and grown child,
- the stepparent's deliberate inclusion of the grown child in information sharing and decision-making, and
- the ability of the grown child to appreciate the stepparent as an individual and as someone who benefits the life of his or her parent.

We defined positive stepfamily relations as those who, a year after the death, still considered each other "family," as evidenced by continuing to celebrate holidays and significant events together, including the anniversary of the parent's death. For example, Phillip's parents divorced when he was in elementary school, and his parents were able to foster a good relationship with each other, even though his father quickly remarried. His father even left part of his inheritance to his first wife. Over the years, Phillip grew to appreciate his stepmother, Cheryl, and described how she was the one he turned to for advice on his finances. When his father was diagnosed with congestive heart failure, Cheryl kept Phillip in the loop through text, e-mail, and phone calls concerning different treatment options. They were both with his father in the ER after his heart attack when a blood clot killed him. Cheryl included Phillip in making decisions at the funeral home about the service and the burial. They sat together at the funeral services and remained in touch in the year since his father's death. Phillip attributed his successful relationship with his stepmother to their having similar personalities and a shared connection in faith.

In the families in which the stepparent died, the grown stepchildren attended the funeral but with no expectations of sitting in the front row or in a place of honor. They considered themselves a part of the family but they marked their placement based on where their biological parent sat, echoing that their main concern was supporting their widowed parent.

Deborah, the youngest of six children, considered herself close to her deceased stepfather. She was the one stepchild who still lived at home while attending community college, and she had taken the lead in helping keep up the house while her mother spent time at the hospital with her stepfather. She held fond memories of his giving her advice about life and about spending time with him outdoors fishing or tending to their chickens. At the funeral, she "sat on the second row with his grandchildren. I sat behind my mom." She expressed no hurt feelings related to seating arrangements.

BURIAL OR CREMATION

Often at the same time as they made choices about the funeral services, families made decisions concerning the disposition of the body. If the body was to be embalmed, a short service at the graveside followed the funeral in order to inter the casket and body. In surveys, cost is often cited as the prime reason for choosing cremation over embalming and burial; the median cost of cremation is $3190, far lower than the median cost of $8343 for a funeral plus burial.[18] Cost was a concern for many of the families in our study. Most interviewees expressed surprise at the high cost of embalmment, burial, caskets, and so forth. Many of the respondents did not realize that the headstone would be a separate cost, and, a year after the death, they were still saving up for that expense. If there was life insurance, most of that money went to the funeral and burial costs. Often, the family did not have much money, and they believed that their parent would not have wanted them to spend exorbitantly either. For some, their church community helped cover the cremation costs. Daniel's mother did not have life insurance so he needed to be "as cheap as possible. We had a cremation and the church stepped in and helped. My pastor and everybody were just right there."

Of those interviewed, 75% of the deceased parents were embalmed and then buried, and 25% of the deceased were cremated. This cremation rate is lower than the national rate, which was 48.2% in 2015, slightly higher than the 45.8% of people who were buried, but reflects the rates of the

Louisiana, Mississippi, and other southern states.[19] The trend toward cremation has grown continually since the 1950s, and the National Funeral Director's Association projects that by 2030, 71% of Americans will choose cremation.[20] Research shows that cremation is almost twice as common in the US west as in the south; Louisiana is in the 20%–29% range, consistent with the numbers in our study. Like the rest of the funeral industry, cremation is a regulated practice,[21] and Louisiana law imposes various legal requirements.

In Louisiana, if the deceased has *not* completed a notarized authorization for cremation, then default rules give the authority first to a surviving spouse, then to *all* surviving grown children, next to *all* surviving siblings, and so on.[22] All grown children or siblings must be in agreement. Conflicts arose in those families whose decedent had not completed the form, as was true for Michelle, whose story opened the chapter. Although Michelle's mother had not written down her wishes, she explained, "we all knew. Mom said it to all of us, 'Cremation, cremation.'" Then she died, and Michelle's siblings said, "No, we want my mom buried." Their lack of consensus meant that Michelle's mom had to be embalmed and buried. That choice imposed additional financial costs, which Michelle paid by emptying her savings account and receiving a generous gift from her brother's employer. Michelle regretted that she did not know in advance that the law would require *all* her siblings to agree for cremation.

Cremation required decisions concerning the ashes. National statistics show that one-third of survivors bury the ashes of their loved one, one-third scatter them, and one-third keep them.[23] These national statistics were echoed in our study, although a slightly higher number of interviewees opted to keep the loved one's ashes.[24] Some families disagreed about what to do with the ashes, and a shared history and expectation for ongoing connection helped in resolving these conflicts. In married-parent families, grown children deferred to the wishes of their widowed parent. For example, Peter and his sisters wanted to honor their father's expressed choice to be scattered in northern Louisiana, but their mother refused. Peter and his siblings acquiesced to her wishes. But, when Peter and his wife retrieved the ashes from the funeral home, they learned that there were excess ashes beyond what could be contained in the ornamental urn they had purchased. When they gave the ornamental urn to his mother, he asked, "Well, mom, could we go spread those ashes up on grandma and grandpa's grave?" His mother agreed.

Conflict could also happen over the disposition of a stepparent's ashes, with the grown child siding with the widowed parent and no collective resolution being found. For example, Theresa considered herself to have a warm and respectful relationship to her stepfather, Bruce, although she did not consider him a "stepfather" in part because they were near in age and because she was already middle aged, married with two children of her own, when he and her mother married. After Bruce's sudden death, she acted as the primary support for her mother, who knew that her husband's wishes were to be cremated and put in a mausoleum. However, Bruce's ex-wife, parents, and two biological children were Catholic and vehemently disagreed with the choice, even wanting to dig up his ashes from the mausoleum to be properly "laid to rest." They did not consider her mother to be legitimate kin. A year after his death, the debate over burial remained unresolved. Theresa's defense of her mother against Bruce's children and first wife shows children's loyalty to their parents in remarried families.

Ultimately, the relationship to the deceased often affected the relationship the survivors had to the ashes themselves. For example, Angela and Jackie, along with their brother and sister, had few kind words to say about their father in life and after death (or ex-stepmothers who show up to mourn at the memorial service!). Jackie admitted that a year after their father's death, his ashes were still in a plain box sitting on a shelf in the garage, "because nobody wants them." Their history of estrangement with their father continued in their relationship to his remains.

CONCLUSION

For all families, the tasks of mourning accomplished two critical goals. First, they served as public acknowledgement of the death of the parent. Lynch and Long summarize well the purpose of the grave and the public funeral ritual to proclaim: "Our kind was here. They lived. They died. They made their difference. We did right by them. They were not forgotten."[25] The tasks of mourning help the community at large as well as the private family begin to understand that death has truly happened. Regardless of family structure, medical certification of death, writing an obituary, cremation or burial, and a memorial service of some kind, helped to solidify the knowledge that a loved one died.

Second, the tasks of mourning helped the surviving family members begin to reorganize as a system with one critical member no longer present. Here is where family structure played a role in determining the potential for a high or low level of family reorganization after the death. In all married-parent families, the grown children used the term "we," but there was a recognition that reorganization would be challenging and new but handled communally. Grown children in single-parent families struggled to hold siblings, extended family members, ex-spouses, and significant others together, and their personal character and their own immediate family of spouse and children guided them as they navigated the tasks of mourning as an "I." Grown children from remarried families remained loyal to their biological parent, which meant that if the biological parent died, they struggled to remain connected to the stepparent, and if the stepparent died, they sided with the perspective of their parent over the views of the surviving stepsiblings or stepfamily. The potential for reorganization among stepkin was low, which was reflected in the interviewee's use of the pronoun "she" or "he" to refer to their stepparent and in sitting apart from the stepfamily during the funeral ritual.

With the burial or disposition of the ashes, the formal tasks of mourning came to a close. As relatives and friends began to return to their homes, family members then turned to sorting through the belongings of their deceased loved one and settling the estate. Moments of connection and disconnection that began during the tasks of mourning often set the stage for harmony or discontent in settling the estate. As in each moment of the care and grief journey, family structure played a role in shaping the experience as they sought to make things fair with the inheritance.

The Intricacies of Wealth Transfer

We had to make things fair.

—LARISSA

The heart attack of Peter's father set in motion a well-orchestrated family response. Peter, his mother, and two siblings took turns sitting vigil with him in the ICU, they were all present when his father was removed from life support, and they worked together to plan his father's funeral services. Although each of those moments had been experienced in quick succession, with decisions being made under pressure, settling his father's estate took more time, stretching out over the first year following his death. And, in the same way they deferred to their widowed mother's decision concerning scattering their father's ashes, they deferred to her wishes concerning distribution of their father's belongings:

So we were basically leaving it for mom to disburse as she would. There were a few things that we knew, "I'd like," and, "I'd like that." I got his moccasins. I'm not a moccasin person. I don't use them that often, but it's still nice to know that I have dad's moccasins. And his cigars. If anything, that's probably the closest tie. We had smoked some cigars together. . . . And he was big wine drinker, and so he had some really good wines. We've been parsing it out. . . . For Christmas that year mom gave to each one of us a present that would have been his. So, little things like that probably meant more than the whole because there's a lot of stuff that is still there.

The distribution of his father's belongings happened intermittently over time, and Peter and his siblings did not feel any claim over his dad's property or financial assets. However, Peter believed that his mother would make things fair between them and so he "tried to be fair as well."

Dying people have the right to dispose of their property however they wish, although it is up to the living to make the actual dispositions. Tensions about inheritance are the stuff of great drama from novels like George Eliot's *Middlemarch* to Jane Smiley's *A Thousand Acres*, a retelling of the King Lear story. Interest in a parent's inheritance explains will contests throughout history.[1] Today's more complex families have only heightened the tensions, spreading the pool of heirs among a greater number of potential claimants. Money—whether there is a lot or a little— can complicate and intensify the emotions around loss.

But, although emotional claims might be powerful, most transfers in our study occurred without dispute, even amicably, with little consciousness of what the law actually provides, much less direct intervention by the law. To be sure, without in-depth studies of formal probate property transfers and informal transfers that occur outside of court, it is impossible to determine whether most wealth transfers are, indeed, amicable. Nonetheless, in our joint experiences, this is true; even studies of probate court have found relatively little litigation,[2] and they probably occur in a manner similar to how Peter's family arranged matters. Peter's father was an attorney, but even he had not used any legal tools, such as a will or trust, to formalize his intent. Indeed, most of the deceased died without a will, leaving the families to sort through, on their own, what remained.[3] The lack of formal planning, in turn, mirrors the experience of most people, who typically have not drafted wills because the death happens suddenly, or because of assumptions that surviving family members will just do the right thing, or because people believe they don't have any assets that anyone would fight over, or because they believe that hiring a lawyer will be too expensive, or because people just do not like to acknowledge their own mortality.[4]

When addressing just how property was distributed, those interviewed articulated quite different experiences. There were comparatively few tensions in married-parent and many single-parent families; in other families, when conflicts occurred, they involved resentments between stepsiblings and half-siblings and stepparents and girlfriends or boyfriends who received sharply different debts, bequests, or treasured items from a parent's estate, and they often interfered with the inheritance process.

Two critical, albeit overlapping, factors fundamentally affected their perceptions of the wealth transmission process: the existence of planning and their family structure. First, when there had been advance planning—of any type—those interviewed reacted with appreciation. Even when they disagreed with the proposed outcome, they acknowledged that formal planning, whether it affected disposition of bodily remains or money, provided important literal guidance and emotional understanding of the next steps.[5] David's father died from a heart attack. As the family members sat in the ER after his father had been pronounced dead, David began worrying about all the arrangements that would need to be made in the following few days. He said, with deep relief and gratitude, about the funeral and burial of his father, "Oh, we didn't have to do anything. Everything was already done. We just had to show up." Sadly, his father had learned the importance of planning after burying David's mother and older brother. His father's planning and prepayment circumvented any potential conflicts between his second wife and David and his siblings. However, formal planning eased the transition process, regardless of family type.

By contrast, when there was inadequate planning, such as oral statements of intention without formalized documentation, or when there was no planning, grown children were more likely to feel not just confusion but also, sometimes, conflict. Jeremy's mother, who had been divorced twice, died suddenly after what appeared to be a drug overdose. He and his sister were left to try to settle her estate. He explained that she had money in a retirement fund but had failed to designate any beneficiaries:

> That money has been sitting in her account for the past year and a half, frozen, until I am assigned the executor of her estate ... I've had to get [an] attorney to assign me as executor of the estate, but we can't do that until we go to the probate court ... every time I speak to the lawyer, [it] costs me money.

Jeremy expressed gratitude for his grandparents and his ex-stepfather, Paul, who offered him financial support to help with the legal costs and moral support during the probate process:

> I sent Paul an email saying, "Look, man, thank you for everything. I'd like to hang out with you guys more." He said, "Man, I feel the same way." So Paul and I probably talk, say, once every two weeks. His son and I have started to get together quite a bit now. I'll pick him up, bring him to my house for the weekend, and we'll play video games and can play golf. It's a positive out of all this.

Second, regardless of whether their parents had planned, perceptions of the distribution process were integrally shaped by the marital status of their parents. As we've seen throughout the book, familial norms affected recourse to formal tools.

In the same way that shared norms helped unite family members facing a difficult healthcare decision or choices about funeral and burial, the critical differences between families' experiences in the inheritance process turned on whether there was more than one set of familial norms at issue. That is, families that had developed common ways of approaching problems, and that could draw on memories and experiences derived from years of growing together, tended to manage the inheritance process differently from families that did not have those shared values, or that had two (or more) sets of familial norms combined in a remarried family. Familial norms serve to create a core family identity based on a common definition of insiders and outsiders, shared and recognized patterns of communication, acceptable expressions of emotion, and mutual understandings of a family's identity and priorities. Consequently, the experiences in married-parent and one-parent families were similar and generally involved fewer resentments and conflicts, unless the single parent was involved in a long-term relationship. By contrast, in the remarried-parent and stepparent families, regardless of who had died, the conflicting family norms profoundly affected experiences and emotions surrounding wealth transmission. As they discussed their parent's death, their feelings about their parent's marital situation affected their perspectives on the law.

This chapter sets out how the inheritance process was handled, showing how those interviewed sorted through and allocated the deceased parent's probate and nonprobate assets. As the chapter explores the relationship between these formal and informal structures, it compares and contrasts the outcomes—and tensions—in the different family structures. First, we discuss what grown children valued and wanted to retain after the parent's death. Although lawyers often speak of the "wealth transfer" process, those interviewed treasured many objects that had little economic worth but great sentimental value; consequently, we use the term "inheritance" as well as wealth transfer. The second part of the chapter turns to the actual distribution process, exploring how items were, or were not, transferred from the deceased parent to other family members.

WHAT THEY VALUED

During the interviews, the stories of inheritance flowed naturally out of the death and funeral narrative. As they talked about what their parent had left behind, they identified differing categories of assets that they had inherited or wanted to inherit. Their thoughts of inheritance included potentially valuable financial assets, of course, but also covered personal property that often had little monetary worth; moreover, inheritance might take a less tangible form, as they mentioned the moral values and psychological attributes they had inherited. Many grown children expressed sentiments similar to those of Brady. When his father told him he wanted to bequeath his gun collection to him and his half-brother, he responded, "Dad, I don't really want or have to have anything. I just want my time with you." Brady's father included this wish in his will, but, as discussed later in the chapter, his will did not settle all other intrafamilial disputes.

Almost all of those interviewed mentioned an emotional inheritance, such as a personality characteristic they saw in themselves or their children. More tangibly, for some, it was treasured photos or clothing. Georgia, who received nothing formally in the will of her father, surmised,

> Well, I do have something of sentimental value. My daddy left a jacket at my house, one of his work jackets. It has patches of cement. It has holes in it and whatever, but I wear it. That's the only thing that I have of him outside of pictures, but I have that jacket and I'll have that jacket till the day I die. It's raggedy, but it's from my daddy.

Sometimes, it was jewelry, a particularly important necklace or an unimportant watch. It might also include a truck or a car. The most valuable asset inherited was the house.[6] In the financial realm, respondents frequently commented on life insurance proceeds, and occasionally on stocks, bonds, or retirement plan proceeds. Even if they knew that a life insurance policy existed, which many did, they could not always find the policy or they later learned that the decedent had already borrowed against the policy.[7]

THE DISTRIBUTION PROCESS

For property left at death, American law specifies that disposition is subject to the decedent's intent expressed in a valid will or distributed based on the default laws of intestacy.[8] Regardless of the existence of a will, a surviving spouse is typically protected against complete disinheritance, and Louisiana is the only state that protects children from disinheritance (and even in Louisiana, this is only for children 23 years old and younger.)[9]

Family structure significantly affected the existence of a will or other strong statement of intent, with the nonmarried-parent families less likely to have such formal or informal indications.

Most decedents died intestate,[10] as is true more generally for Americans.[11] More than half of Americans do not have a will, even among those between the ages of 55 and 64.[12] These numbers are even higher for black and Latino adults. All of the parents who died testate were in remarried or stepparent families. Some interviewed noted that their parents did not have wills; each of the people who mentioned the absence of a will came from a remarried-parent, stepparent, or single-parent family. In none of the families of children with married parents were wills even mentioned.

Grown children only occasionally indicated familiarity with the law or legal terminology, and they were more likely to do so outside of the married- or single-parent families. In those situations, there was a general understanding that Louisiana's system of community property meant that a surviving spouse inherited one-half of marital property, but only two people mentioned the technical right of the spouse under Louisiana law to use the decedent's intestate property, "usufruct."[13] The right of usufruct is, indeed, complicated; when the decedent has descendants and dies without a will, Louisiana law grants the surviving spouse a right to use the decedent's share of their jointly held property until the second spouse dies or remarries.[14] For example, Brady, whose stepsister moved in to provide care for his dad, explained, "It's written up in the will that his wife, everybody called her Tiger, that she has—I don't know how to say this properly, but it's usifer or useavidge of the place until either she gets remarried or she passes or moves." Other than Brady, only Carlos, whose mother is granted usufruct of his stepfather's home, uses the legal term, in part, because there is conflict over what actual use and ownership of the property will mean both financially and pragmatically for the widowed spouse and for the grown children.

The scarcity of discussion of wills or more formal processes of inheritance reflected not just a lack of familiarity with the applicable law but also the lack of planning by the parents and the grown child's socioeconomic status. Indeed, many of those interviewed failed to understand what they might receive through inheritance, and levels of awareness differed by family structure and by income. For example, all those from single-parent families understood that they were entitled to share their parent's property. Grown children outside of married- and single-parent families typically experienced some form of friction with the surviving spouse and with half-siblings that led to a break in the filial relationship or required legal intervention. Although cultural images suggest that inheritance is a relatively peaceful process, these families showed a contrary result; of course, probate courts themselves are filled with litigation over inheritance rights and creditors' claims,[15] so the results in these families are not unusual.

This section first discusses their general approach to inheritance before turning to issues surrounding planning (or the lack thereof) and the rights of various family members.

THE MEANING OF FAIRNESS

In all families, there were often postmortem tensions as family members moved forward. Despite conflict and failed planning, most interviewed believed that families should try to make things fair. In marital families, when friction was experienced, it was resolved privately, and, in their interviews one year later, they rarely expressed feelings of frustrated entitlement or ongoing bitterness. In single-parent families, the task of "making things fair" usually fell to one sibling, who then divided the estate (including debt) among the siblings, taking into consideration each sibling's financial ability, financial need, functional ties to the family and to the estate itself, and the expressed or presumed wishes of the deceased. Children in married-parent families rarely discussed inheritance, typically deferring to their surviving parent, who they presumed would informally "make things fair" now or in their future inheritance. They believed that claiming a portion of the deceased parent's estate would not "be fair" to the surviving parent or reflect the wishes of the deceased.

Asset distribution became more complicated in remarried families. The task of equitably dividing the estate involved multiple, nuanced understandings of a spouse's or child's biological ties and formal and informal claims to the deceased's estate, the functional role played by each family member in instrumentally, financially, and/or emotionally caring for the deceased parent prior to death, and an interpretation of the deceased's expressed or understood wishes. In families with remarried parents, inheritance was often a painful topic. For them, making things fair did not necessarily mean justice to a surviving spouse or second family, even when the decedent's wishes were known. Rhonda's father wanted to protect Judith, his second wife of more than thirty years, by moving her into a condo, closer to her sister. He had already purchased the condo, and his wife had moved in—but he died before settling all the paperwork involved with selling their previous home. When he realized that he would be unable to finalize his plans, he asked Rhonda and her two sisters from his first marriage to honor their stepmother by relinquishing any rights to their previous home. They verbally agreed to do so. However, at the funeral services, fissures appeared in the stepfamily relationship. When the stepmother sat in the front with her grown children, Rhonda's two half-siblings, and pushed the three daughters of the deceased back several rows, they felt hurt and disrespected. Subsequently, two of the sisters gracefully sought to carry out their father's wishes by signing away their ownership rights to the property, but the third sister refused to do so, and stubbornly stuck to her position, even a year after the death.

Keith, whose father had a significant other, explained the confusion and tension that arose when no will could be found, and several girlfriends of his father had to be dealt with along with six grown children from different mothers. "I could only give my advice to split everything up. But as far as any will he had, we couldn't find that. We'll probably never find that." Yet he also expressed bitterness, complaining that

[t]hey probably tore that [the will] up because, like I said, the house he was living in was his house, and he left the woman [the current girlfriend] there, so we—I don't know. [There are] a lot of things we could have done to try to get the house and all the stuff that he left still there. We haven't come to an agreement as to who should get

what. And that's been over a year. So we're trying to work that out now. But yeah, I couldn't take charge because my name wasn't on anything to really take charge of as far as money wise.

Even though Keith had informally been given the responsibility of deciding whether to remove his father from life support, he had no power over his father's property. In remarried families, making things fair might also justify accessing the law in order to resolve intrafamilial conflict. Even in remarried families, however, property distribution often happened without contention.

PLANNING—OR NOT

Children noted the formal and informal methods that their parents had used to indicate intent. Even though the interviews were not focused on end-of-life or estate planning issues explicitly, study participants repeatedly addressed the actions that their parents had taken—or not taken. In a few cases, the parents had executed formal wills that offered guidance as to the distribution wishes of the deceased parent. However, managing to apply the terms of the will, or accepting the actual operation of the default rules in the absence of a will, proved challenging to remarried families. In this section, we highlight the role that formal and informal planning played in making things fair in terms of inheritance.

Wills

Among the few who mentioned wills, two, Candace and Delores, believed that they had been cut out of the deceased's wills; they could not be sure, however, because tensions continued to run high between them and their widowed stepmothers, with the daughters rarely speaking to the widows in the year since the death. The other two wills involved usufruct issues, indicating a fairly sophisticated understanding of inheritance law. Brady's deceased father expressed to him and several of his siblings that usufruct of his home should be granted to their stepsister, who was out of work at the time and had moved in with him to help with caregiving duties. After the death, the grown children read the will and learned that he had not included that wish. Brady advocated for honoring the verbal wish of his dad and convinced the other siblings to allow the stepsister to remain in the house, but other family members disagreed. A year after his father's death, both the stepsister and the estranged stepmother were living in the house, although they did not own it. Carlos, who was African American, 31 years old, and married with a young son reported that his mother, the widow, had been granted usufruct of his deceased stepfather's home. Payments remained on the property, which would ultimately be an asset of the deceased's grown children, and so Carlos advised his mother not to make payments on an asset that she would be able to use only during her lifetime or until she remarried or moved. In the year since the death, his mother had moved out of the house she had shared with her husband and now lived with Carlos's family. This decision frustrated her step-son, who was upset because she was not making payments on the house; although she had a life interest in the property, the stepson would inherit it after her death, and he did not want to lose the value of the house.

Then consider what happened to Nancy from a single-parent family; her account shows how, even with an incomplete understanding of formal law, people act in accord with it. After her mother's death, Nancy was cleaning out her mother's house, and, as she explains: "I found a letter that my mom had written and signed concerning her wishes to be cremated and that she wanted her boyfriend to have 2,000 dollars from her 10,000-dollar life insurance policy." Louisiana accepts holographic wills—"olographic testaments"[16] or wills that are entirely in the testator's handwriting, signed, and dated—but Nancy seems not to have recognized the document as formally binding. Instead, she described it as, "more informal because actually, it was only signed by her and I don't even think anybody else signed it. But she did make four copies of it." In addition to this writing, a life insurance policy existed, but Nancy and her brothers didn't find it immediately so she paid for the funeral on a credit card. Once the siblings found the policy, they learned that their mother had borrowed against it, leaving $7000 to be distributed among the three of them. They then distributed the asset:

> I told them [her brothers], you know, Mama's wishes were that William [her mother's longtime boyfriend] would have 2,000 dollars. So I just want to get covered for the funeral expenses and I will give William 2,000 dollars and then you all split the rest....I told 'em that's all I wanted because both of my brothers—one of 'em's in and out of school and one of 'em's got five kids at home and he works at a restaurant, so they needed the money more than I did.

For Nancy, it was fair to honor her mother's wishes for her boyfriend, despite the fact that she didn't realize she was legally bound to do so because of her mother's written statement of intent, and it was fair to excuse her brothers from giving to the boyfriend based on their current financial needs. The law might have mandated a different outcome, however. Although the boyfriend would have had no rights in the absence of the document written by Nancy's mother, a court might have granted him rights based on what Nancy characterized as the "letter" from her mother.

Wills are, of course, legally binding, but, where norms did not conflict and the probate court was not involved in inheritance, the wills might serve as informal guidance. As David, whose father was remarried and had preplanned and prepaid for his funeral, explained,

> We went through some things and they all asked me before I took anything in the house, "Would you mind if I?" "No, y'all can have whatever you want," and if I had something to say, you know, "I don't know about that," but for the most part, yeah, we all went through stuff together and "You mind if I take it?" "No, go ahead," you know.

Although there was actually a lawyer involved, David noted, "even the *lawyer* made the comment, 'Wow, I wish everybody was agreeing and smooth going as y'all.' But you know, for the most part, everything; we agreed 100 percent on everything." The amicable process could be attributed to the hands-off approach of David's stepmother, who had been married to his widowed father for only a few years. She did not compete with the family norms and expectations of her husband's grown children. After settling the estate, she moved closer to her own family in another state and left David to live in his father's house. Although legally entitled to usufruct, she did not choose to stay in the home. David had not spoken to her in the year since his father's death, beyond forwarding some mail to her.

In general, given the size of the estates, little formal legal intervention was needed because the primary assets typically consisted of personal property. The lack of urgency to settle title or debts also meant that, at least in some families, there was a reluctance to handle postdeath property issues at all. Many interviewees expressed an inability to "go through with it" because settling the estate would require facing the finality of death.

Several grown children explicitly noted the absence of a will and the consequences of the lack of formal declaration of the parent's wishes. Sisters Angela and Jackie told of how their deceased single father had not prepared a will and thus the four siblings were left to settle distribution of his property without his guidance. Each assumed a complementary role— or nonrole. Their brother, Timothy, who had handled the financial aspects of their father's care during his illness, took the lead in coordinating all financial and legal matters. Angela, who had served as primary caregiver and surrogate decision-maker for her deceased father, remained on the property and helped with cleaning the home. Their sister, Ginger, who had long been estranged from the family, showed up unexpectedly at the funeral services. Because she was out of work, she decided to stay on the property as well and clean the outbuildings and land itself to prepare it for sale. By contrast, Jackie, who lived several states away, chose to excuse herself from the process and claimed that she wanted no share in the rights or responsibilities of inheritance.

On the other hand, the lack of planning could cause bitterness and resentment toward the deceased. Latikka explained how filial relationships are broken because of friction over wealth transfer. Latikka's stepfather raised her from the age of 2. Because she did have a relationship with her birth father, her stepfather never adopted her, but he was her in-home father, and she called him "dad" throughout her childhood. At her wedding, he was the one who walked her down the aisle. Yet she was angry that in the year after her mother's death; he had let the note on his and her mother's house lapse, leading to its foreclosure and the loss of all the belongings within it. She resentfully explained, "Now I call him by his first name . . . he doesn't deserve the title of dad."

Informal Planning

In some families, when there was an absence of planning, children expressed their powerlessness. As generations of disappointed beneficiaries have learned, intent that has not been translated into the requisite formality is not legally binding, and such expressions of testamentary disposition in this manner are not given effect.[17] For some, the language surrounding the proposed inheritance was precatory, wishful thinking that resulted only in a moral, rather than a legal, obligation.[18] One daughter, Candace, explained that her father had always reassured her that she would be taken care of, and had left her

> what the lawyer said, like a pretend trust. It's called a trust, but they don't actually exist. In other words, if [his second wife] was a decent human being she could say, "Okay. We're gonna take everything that was your dad's—property, business, assets, whatever—and I'll give you and your brother a fair amount." . . . but she doesn't have to and she's not gonna.

The relationship between this stepmother and Candace was still sour a year after her father's death.

So-called precatory trusts are, as Candace recognized, not legally enforceable.[19] The stepmother tried to give her and her brothers a few sentimental jewelry items in lieu of property or money, but they rejected her efforts, angry that she had, literally and figuratively, locked them out of their father's inheritance. Although these were not new tensions, the lack of formal planning exacerbated them.

Spouses' Rights

In married-parent families, there were few tensions between the surviving spouse and children when property was distributed. In remarried families, however, grown children often expressed anger that they were left out of final visits, burial arrangements, and wealth transmission. Particularly when a biological parent had died, the stepfamily relationship quickly became strained; unlike in marital families, there were no legal ties to bind the unit, nor to serve as a background structure to interactions. Stepparents are not, of course, legal parents.[20] Indeed, sociologists find that biological parents exert a mediating role in the stepparent relationship; after that parent's death, contact between children and stepparents becomes more sporadic.[21] Typical is the experience of Georgia, who explained how the situation among herself, her siblings, and their father's wife began to splinter during the meal following the funeral.

> They pulled me in the bedroom and they said, "I didn't like that casket he was in. What are we gonna do about the house and all? What about the trucks in the yard? She don't need all of them vehicles." I said, "Y'all should just let it go. Those are material things. If she wants you to have 'em, she'll give 'em to you, but I doubt if she will, because she's that type of person. Just let it go."

Grown children felt territorial toward their parent's possessions and anger that they had no control over their disposition. They often seemed to feel left out by their parent's new partner, and they responded by displaying a strong sense of territoriality toward property.

In contrast, Phillip was surprised and pleased as he recounted that his father, who had remarried, had "left" money to his mother, the first wife. At the same time, he also felt warmth toward his stepmother; indeed, she was the one, rather than his father, from whom he had sought financial help. They planned the funeral together and grieved his loss together in the year after his death.

CHILDREN LEFT OUTSIDE

In addition to tensions with surviving spouses, interviewees often experienced conflicts with half-siblings. Of the sixty-two interviewees, almost half had full siblings, one-third had half-siblings, and one-fourth had stepsiblings (with overlap within the categories). In virtually every family, one of the siblings tended to move into the main mediator role between the siblings, regardless of whether full-, half-, or step- were involved, and often that same sibling acted as next of kin and primary caregiver during the deceased's illness or hospitalization; this person was often the one being interviewed.

Conversely, most interviewees labeled one surviving sibling a "problem." In other words, one sibling refused to agree with the others over property ownership, even contesting a will. The mediator sibling generally wanted to revert to private ordering for the sake of civility and family harmony, but the private bonds and shared family norms between a stepparent and surviving stepchildren proved to be too weak, conflicted, or marked by suspicion to withstand the empathic compromises intrinsic to private ordering. Brady explained that part of the resistance from some of his siblings to honoring the verbal wishes of his father to give usufruct of his house to a stepsister could be traced to her earlier actions. On the day of his father's death, the stepsister and her mother, his father's estranged third wife, went to the bank, where the stepsister claimed "to be his daughter, and signed off on the account and withdrew all the cash he had in that checking account," causing the legal children to become quite angry.

Several of the respondents used the term "outside child" to refer to themselves or to half-siblings. Although the term appears in Caribbean culture,[22] some scholars have used it to refer to any type of multipartner fertility.[23] When study participants used the term, it might have meant a parent's nonmarital child or a child from another relationship. Even though Louisiana has a high rate of nonmarital parenthood, the law surrounding the rights of nonmarital children were not well known by those interviewed. Many did not seem to understand that, legally, so long as the parent has acknowledged the parent–child relationship, then a nonmarital child stands on an equal inheritance basis with a marital child, even though a nonmarital parent does not have the same rights as a legally recognized spouse.[24]

Although their appreciation of the legal implications of being a marital or nonmarital child varied, their status as an "inside"[25] or "outside" child affected their relationships with the rest of the family. Those who identified as "outside" were less likely to seek an inheritance (regardless of their legal entitlement to do so) and seemed to feel some distance from the rest of the family. Georgia explained that the house her father left is "ours ... [But] my brother and I, the outside brother, we decided just to stay out of it. Let them handle whatever they want to handle." Her sense of entitlement was based on her father's informal acknowledgement of their relationship, although he had never taken the requisite, formal legal steps to do so.[26] Shernetta, who had been raised by the man she called "dad" from the age of 3, self-identified as an outside child, but did not join her siblings in taking steps to inherit some of her father's property. Indeed, in the absence of proof of an actual or equitable adoption, she had no legal claim to his property; in terms of "entitlement" as a child whom he had raised; however, her claims were morally equivalent to those of his other children.

Inside children, however, felt entitled to inherit because of their status. As Keith, who explicitly identified the outside children from his father's three relationships (two marital, one not) explained, even though the insurance policy was in another brother's name and even in the absence of a will, he thought his father's property should be split evenly among all of the children. Keith had listed all siblings as equal in the obituary and he hoped that they could act "like a real family" at not only the funeral but following. Exacerbating the problems in these families among half-siblings were tensions with the stepparent and frustration with the decedent's lack of explicit advance planning. Life insurance policies typically ask for a primary and a secondary beneficiary, without providing space for more than one or two names.[27] A policyholder may intend familial sharing or believe that the proceeds will be distributed through an estate, without a complete understanding that the designee is under no legal compulsion to share the money realized.

CONCLUSION

Ultimately, we found, first, that most people do not make plans on how to transmit property, whether real or personal, at death. They neither draft a will nor update nonprobate beneficiary designations. And this system works for most families, as long as there is a high level of shared norms. Second, lack of planning leads to emotional conflicts within a family without its own coherent norms. Finally, the failure to plan can have unanticipated emotional, as well as financial, consequences.

Twenty-First-Century Caregiving

Have a plan. That's my biggest thing to tell people. Have a plan. Don't be left standing there holding the bag and not know what to do with it.

—KENDRA

Toward the close of each interview, the questioning shifted from drawing out the subjective narrative describing the illness and death of the interviewee's parent or stepparent to asking the interviewee what advice they would give to a son, daughter, or stepchild going through a similar caregiving and loss experience. Beyond the particulars of their situations, most hesitated to extrapolate the details of their experience into specific "dos" and "don'ts," but three themes emerged in their suggestions. First, they expressed a sense of urgency in encouraging parents to plan and prepare *now*. Second, they emphasized the need for support throughout their caregiving and mourning process, whether that support was from family members, friends, clergy, medical professionals, or funeral home personnel. Last, despite any regrets or hardship or family drama, they advised others to care for and support their parent, noting that they would make the same choices all over again.

They are, of course, not alone in this advice to look ahead. Numerous other sources, ranging from the AARP to Aging with Dignity to the Conversation Project, also urge our aging population to plan. However, changing family structures increase the urgency for planning ahead; although intrafamilial disputes at death are the stuff of literature and movies, the potential exists for even more disputes with the increasing number of people who define themselves as core family members but who otherwise share few beliefs. And the silver tsunami means there will be even more demands placed on caregivers.

In this final chapter, accordingly, we offer recommendations for how family members, faith communities, legal and medical professionals, and society as a whole can better support caregiving. In the first section, we address how families can better prepare before a crisis happens. We then look at what reforms could be made to government policies to encourage planning and to support caregiving. Next, we offer suggestions on how legal, healthcare, and religious professionals can help families. As we emphasize, formal and informal planning methods can increase the ability of caregivers, family members, health professionals, and spiritual leaders to know and contribute to honoring the wishes and values of the seriously ill and dying parent. Finally, we return to the complexities of the growing need for twenty-first-century caregivers.

FAMILY WORK BEFORE A CRISIS HAPPENS

Jackie remembered telling her single father:

> I do not want to have a fight with anybody about stuff, especially when I have two siblings who live below the poverty level. . . . I told my dad over and over, "Don't leave things a mess." What did he do? He left things a mess. He didn't have a will.[1]

Family preparation begins with an acknowledgement of the aging process and the corresponding need to plan, whether the process is started by a parent, spouse, or child. As planning occurs, family members should understand both the backstory and the intended aims of any care or estate planning choices. A consistent theme throughout our interviews was participants' disappointment that their parents had engaged in relatively little formal end-of-life planning on issues ranging from healthcare to wills to burial. This lack of planning may have been partially due to their age and to their economic circumstances, but it also seemed to result from other factors, such as a lack of appreciation as to why such planning might be important to surviving family members, an expectation that everything would just work out, and a reluctance to make choices that might have consequences even if not known during the person's lifetime. Contrary to conventional explanations, it did not appear to result from a fear of death. Instead, the parents simply had not thought about it or just wanted to avoid conflict.

Carlos's stepfather had done no planning, and Carlos came to the interview with the express purpose of giving advice to families like his that include parents, stepparents, half-siblings, and stepsiblings:

> Have the conversation. Have a very extensive conversation of what is to come and what your wishes are. What's the reasoning behind your wishes? If I don't understand completely why you want it to happen, it might not turn out the way you wanted. Talk to a funeral parlor, a funeral director about what things should go on. Talk to a lawyer, and not just a regular one, an estate lawyer who knows the legality behind your wants because you may not fully understand all the other things.

Almost all study participants repeated this guidance.

Formal *and* informal conversation holds value. For many families with a high level of shared norms, a common memory of an informal conversation with the parent at an aunt's funeral or when a friend of the parent was diagnosed with cancer, proved invaluable guidance in the midst of a crisis. Remarried families may not have the luxury of these informal memories, thus adding to formal tools the story behind the choices becomes more critical.

In families of parents in their first marriage as well as with one surviving, unpartnered parent, family norms can compensate for a lack of

planning. For other families, as Carlos's advice makes clear, advance planning combined with clarifying conversations could have helped balance
a low level of shared norms within a family system. Family norms help
members know how to interpret the wishes of the loved one. Lifelong connection to the parent in need provides a basis to inform managing each
moment in the care and grief process, and that connection is often disrupted in blended families.

Planning ahead in remarried families can increase caregivers' knowledge about their loved one's wishes as well as the intentions and history
that informs those choices. That knowledge then makes honoring those
wishes manageable and ultimately more meaningful for the caregiver.
Kendra, whose quote opens the chapter, found that her stepfather's lack
of communication with his biological daughters meant that her stepsisters
were unable to understand his choices, unable to be present at the time
of his death, and unable to feel like family with Kendra or her mother in
the year after his death. Carlos's stepfather's lack of communicating why
he bequeathed property as he did led to a rift between Carlos's mother
and her grieving stepchildren. Virtually all study participants concluded
that the caregiving and grief experiences would have been easier if their
parents had explicitly named a healthcare agent and explained how the
rights and responsibilities of that role could be shared among various family members, and engaged in some estate planning.

Healthcare Planning

When it comes to healthcare decision-making, the designation of default
surrogate decision-makers needs to balance family dynamics with expe-
diency. A better solution involves more support for advance medical
planning so that the individual indicates her preferences before she is
incapacitated to ensure that she opts out of the default rules.[2] Few people, even those who are terminally ill, have completed advance medical
directives.[3] Regardless of how they assume their responsibilities, whether
as designated or default decision-makers, family members need better

information about their roles, as well as guidance on how to make medically appropriate decisions. Rather than forcing caregivers into this role at a time of stress in the midst of providing care, advance-care planning could, more appropriately, draw from recommendations made by the Institute of Medicine for "a life-cycle model of planning to normalize the process and to avoid the emotional burden sometimes experienced by patients, families, and loved ones who have not adequately prepared for making end-of-life decisions."[4] Informal conversations in a blended family can clarify who should be an insider and entitled to information and/ or decision-making authority. Numerous websites also offer helpful tools for legally establishing one's wishes for the end of life and then communicating those wishes.[5]

Estate Planning

After death, the assets of the parent, of both monetary and sentimental value, become one meaningful form of connection to the deceased loved one in the future. In popular culture, "last wills and testaments" are formal, indeed formulaic, documents, more appropriate for the inhabitants of Downton Abbey than for those of Baton Rouge. A will's purpose is to distribute property;[6] personal connections are recognized only to the extent that assets may be bequeathed to "my partner" or "my children," and sentimental descriptions of property are rare.[7] Yet incorporating more individualized and personal language may encourage more people to use wills and might result in improved interpretation and fewer will contests.[8]

To be sure, there are good reasons to protect the formality of testamentary intent: Ensuring that decisions with respect to final dispositions have actually been done with adequate contemplation and without others' undue influence.[9] And, certainly, expressive wills will not serve the interest of all decedents. Yet telling stories can be an important source of comfort for families and can create cohesion in blended ones. For the remarried families in our study that worked well together to make things fair, their level of interpersonal warmth, intentional inclusion of each other in their life stories, and their willingness to write a family story together—one that includes not only financial issues but also words of appreciation—were the primary differences setting them apart from stepfamilies that fractured, experienced legal conflicts, or terminated relationships with one another. Those who defined why they are a family became a family.

Using more personalized language also means that individuals may actually talk to their loved ones before death about their wishes. Moreover, as our respondents' stories showed, what they valued in what they inherited was sentimental: a work shirt from Sears, a teddy bear made out of the shirts of a stepdad, a football-shaped beer koozie that a parent used when they watched Monday night football. They fought over asset distribution not because they really wanted the assets (and the socioeconomic status of most of our respondents indicated a need for assets) but because they felt that they were not being respected and honored in their role in the family and their relationship to the parent.

Overall, the most important step that families, especially blended ones, can take to prepare for elder care and loss is to *talk*. Although formal planning can help guide grieving family members, it is not sufficient to prevent confusion and family dissolution. Kendra's ex-stepfather completed an authorization for cremation and Carlos's stepfather had a will. However, the various family members did not know the history or reasoning behind the formal planning; the lack of communication with the deceased parent, together with an inability to fall back on a shared familial tradition, made the interpretation and carrying out of those formal wishes divisive. Knowledge can empower loved ones to serve, find deeper meaning in the experience, and strengthen their connections to all those called kin.

REFORMS TO GOVERNMENT POLICIES

Recommended reforms to government policies fall into three categories: nudges to encourage advance planning, reconsideration of certain default rules related to who is considered family, and expanding support and protection for family caregivers.

Opt-In Mechanisms for Advance Planning

The law could provide more support for advance planning.[10] Few people, even those who are terminally ill, have completed advance medical directives or wills.[11] And there is no public inducement to engage in planning for the elder care or for probate assets. Rather than introducing to patients and their loved ones the stress of end-of-life planning in the midst of providing care, the Institute of Medicine recommends a life-cycle model of planning, in which these multifaceted topics about life values and wishes for treatment options become a normal part of the healthcare experience.[12]

Formal and Informal Prompts to Healthcare and Estate Planning

The government might provide information about advance planning at certain key points, such as in standard interactions with government processes.

- *State income tax returns*: A statutory form will could be appended to the state's form for filing annual tax returns.[13]
- *Voting/Driver's Licenses*: Statutory form wills and other advance planning documents could be made available when an individual renews a driver's license or registers to vote. The back of a driver's license[14] could even indicate whether an individual has filled out an advance medical directive, just as many states' licenses now do for organ donation.[15] Also, making an authorization for cremation form available at the time of opting to be an organ donor when renewing a driver's license could be an easy solution for states. A check mark on the license could alert healthcare

providers, family, and funeral directors that an authorization has been completed. Finally, a public service announcement poster featuring basic questions related to healthcare planning could be posted in secretary of state offices. As citizens wait, this poster could inspire individuals to think about their own wishes or nudge them to talk with their loved ones about theirs.

- *Marriage License/Divorce Process*: Getting married requires obtaining a state license.[16] Legal divorce requires filing in court and a subsequent court order.[17] Having a child leads to a birth certificate. Each of those moments provides an opportunity for the state to encourage planning based on the assumption that significant family changes should serve as an inducement for individuals to reconsider existing disposition plans. No such formal prompting exists. Consider that, although pro se divorce packet filings ask litigants about property, they do not otherwise suggest that divorcing parties may need to take additional actions to ensure that divorce severs various financial arrangements (such as life insurance beneficiary designations).

- *Federal benefits:* A final critical opening occurs when people sign up for Medicare or Social Security or Medicaid; discussing these issues would be particularly appropriate because these are points at which an individual is thinking about age and health. Each of these interactions occurs at times when an individual is considering his or her financial role[18] or his or her obligations as a citizen.

Although these nudges may not lead to formal planning, they may, at the least, help prompt informal conversations among family members.

RECONSIDERATION OF DEFAULT RULES

Many of the laws and regulations surrounding caregiving and death assume an intact marital family with shared norms, wherein agreement is routine. Yet the majority of American families no longer take that form, and numerous laws have not yet adjusted to that demographic reality.

- *Cremation:* As the number of single elders increases in future years, revisiting the default rule requiring *all* grown children, or when no children, *all* siblings of the deceased to agree on cremation when an authorization for cremation has not been completed, could be warranted. Most grown children of single parents noted that one grown child takes the lead, and even, like Kyle, becomes the power of attorney for the parent. Allowing one grown child to make the decision for cremation would have reflected the wishes of the deceased in our study.

- *Intestacy:* In married-parent families, the default rules of intestacy give the surviving spouse much of the property, and that matches the family norm. Moreover, the default rules and family expectations seem to match in single-parent families, with children dividing the decedent's property. In both stepparent and remarried families, however, default rules may not reflect the nuances of who is considered kin, broadly defined. For example, children are entitled to inherit based on their relational status.[19] For children raised by stepparents whom they consider to be their legal parents, the inability to inherit through intestacy[20] may not reflect actual familial expectations. Also, revisions to contemporary intestacy law might include permitting outside children to establish paternity without blood tests, based on holding out (presenting the child to the world as his own child) for a substantial period of time.[21] This would ratify functional rather than solely legal (adoptive/marital) or biological relationships.

- *Earlier Spouses and Inheritance:* We also recommend revisiting the presumption against earlier spouses inheriting: In many states, statutes specify that divorce revokes any disposition in a will to the ex-spouse.[22] Yet the actions in many of the families

we studied belied this presumption. In addition to ex-spouses
receiving bequests, they also entered back into the caregiving
equation to reduce the burden on their grown children. It may
be that revocation upon divorce presumptions should apply only
to "stale" designations that are dated at least ten years prior to
death or divorce. Those dying may want to say thank you[23] or
acknowledge the parental role played by the ex-spouse for their
shared children, and there may even be a role for ex-spouses in
intestacy provisions.

Expanding Support and Protection for Family Caregivers

This section focuses on recommendations for improving the legal land-
scape for caregiving by addressing state filial responsibility statutes;
FMLA; and federal and state elder abuse laws, with the recognition that
there are numerous other areas to address.[24]

Filial Responsibility Laws: Supporting the Impulse to Care

Can we force families to be a "we?" Filial responsibility laws may try to do
so. We recommend reforming filial responsibility laws, at least those that
allow parents to sue children. The few filial responsibility cases brought
in recent years do not involve parents suing grown children to care for
them,[25] but if such cases were to be brought, they would serve as a sym-
bol of a severely dysfunctional relationship. Lawsuits occur when relationships break down, and they are likely to exacerbate tensions rather
than produce the desired funding. In terms of our sample set, even after
dramatic incidents of estrangement, respondents undertook some level
of personal and financial responsibility for the aging parent without legal
compulsion.

Although there are persuasive economic justifications for allowing private institutions and the state to sue a grown child for financial

reimbursement, actual implementation and enforcement of this law is quite onerous. In these cases, as in so many other areas of where the law affects families, the law is a really blunt instrument that does not take into account fine-tuned family dynamics and needs.

Filial responsibility laws reflect that caregiving costs, especially at the end of life, are expensive.[26] But other means can affect the same goals. Reducing costs system-wide as well as supporting informal care would entail a greater level of civil education as well as expanding current programs that are working well.[27]

At a time when kin connections could be multiplying, placing limits on filial responsibility laws that impose financial obligations on children could reduce intrafamilial tensions and stresses. Indeed, this is a compelling testament to the way in which reliance on ethical principles rather than use of the law might be more productive. No respondent mentioned filial responsibility laws; participants voluntarily undertook caregiving, even as it added complexity to their already full schedules and limited budgets. Even respondents who had been abandoned or treated dishonorably as children generally chose to accept the financial and practical responsibility for caring for a mother or father, although they tried to establish strong boundaries to protect themselves. The best way to incentivize elder care lies in increasing ways to reward the voluntary care of grown children.[28]

Support for Caregivers

Caregivers need care as well, and there are a number of different reforms that could serve their needs.

The FMLA should be expanded to better serve all caregivers and to reflect the often long-term demands of elder care. For caregivers who work outside of the home and provide care, we offer several suggestions:

- Paying for FMLA leave, so that taking time away from work to provide care does not affect income.[29] Such a benefit would have supported many of the grown children we interviewed, whom

we considered lower middle class to poor based on employment
history and observation. Statistics from the US Labor
Department show that those making less than $35,000 annually
are less likely to take leave, when that leave is unpaid.[30] Allowing
up to twelve weeks of paid leave for the serious illness of a family
member offers different kinds of benefits. First, home-based care
has shown to be more cost effective than institutional care, both
for recipients and taxpayers.[31] Second, it would provide concrete
support to the 41.6 million caregivers, two-thirds of whom are
women. In 2014, 80% of adults providing elder care for someone
over the age of 65 were working, and 60% of those people were
working full time.[32] Most family caregivers report that they have
had to make some accommodations in their work schedule,
such as by leaving early—or quitting—in response to their elder-
care responsibilities.[33] Finally, paid leave might foster gender
neutrality by encouraging men and women to divide the work of
caregiving more equitably, so neither would risk losing necessary
income.[34] In California, the percentage of men taking Family
Medical Leave nearly doubled once paid.[35] Creative options for
funding paid leave have been recommended including taking
the lead from the international community where leave is paid
through programs similar to public insurance.[36]

- Expanding the definition of eligible relationships to include
relevant family care networks so that the law would cover not just
parents and de facto parents, but also stepparents, ex-stepparents,
and grandparents who could show that they are receiving
a specified portion of care. Just as the Labor Department
recognizes people with no legal or biological ties to a child as
potential parents entitled to take leave if they provide daily care,[37]
so too should it recognize adults providing filial-type daily care to
an older quasi-family member. In addition to expanding the list
of kin, those eligible might even be expanded to include anyone
legally serving as the medical power of attorney for an individual
who is incapacitated to be eligible for the FMLA. This expansion

would allow informal care to be provided to neighbors, friends, and faith community members who are single or whose immediate family does not live in close proximity. Third, the list of conditions for eligibility under federal law does not recognize much of the caregiving that older people require or the needs of those providing the care.[38] Leave to attend medical and legal appointments, as well as bereavement leave, are potential additional expansions for covered leave.

In addition to the FMLA, a Social Security Caregiver Credit could offset lost contributions during periods of unpaid caregiving.[39] Other countries, such as France, Germany, Canada, and Sweden, already do so.[40] The level of Social Security benefits is based on the recipient's highest earning years; those years may include part-time work or unemployment that is due to caregiving. Recognizing the costs of caregiving might result in employment credit for a year in which the employee was not in the workforce full time.[41] As a way to compensate for gaps in privately provided care, a national "Caregiver Corps," structured like Americorps or the Peace Corps, could simultaneously incentivize young adult volunteers by offering college scholarships or student loan debt amelioration for caregiving service, raise public awareness of the virtue of elder care, and create a standardized elder-care training program that benefits those people served in the program as well as create a foundation for the volunteer's potential private caregiving in the future. These efforts would allow all citizens to honor local elders in a safe and organized fashion.[42] Increasing financial incentives for co-housing could help benefit family members who make this choice, especially when the choice may be made for a stepparent, ex-stepparent, neighbor, or friend.[43] Elder-care advocate Ai-jen Poo describes "the Care Grid," a matrix in which public, private, and professional resources intersect to provide dignified aging care to all.[44] Poo doesn't address modern kin constellations, but her recommendations for finding creative combinations for each elder and family would meet the needs of modern families well.

Support for caregivers also includes protecting them from abuse. Our sample illustrates the expanding contexts for caregiver abuse, as the circle of kin caregivers expands. Some respondents chose to care for parents who continued to exhibit verbally abusive or destructive behavior toward them, with much of that behavior likely stemming from mental illness. Establishing healthy boundaries was very challenging and often failed. Indeed, family caregivers themselves are also a vulnerable class who are making financial and physical sacrifices, making stressful decisions, and are often invisible.[45] Grown children who have spent a lifetime extricating themselves from patterns of abuse from a parent may be pulled back in, as several of our respondents were, in the name of mercy and duty. But there were few means to guard them from further injury.[46]

As the number of families with elder stepparents increases in the future, so too may the risk for abuse. Stepchildren are at greater risk for abuse, so the converse may also be true: stepparents will be at greater risk for elder abuse.[47] This may mean developing new programs within both secular and religious communities that support caregivers' and carereceivers' mental health.[48]

SUGGESTIONS FOR HEALTHCARE, RELIGIOUS, FUNERAL, AND LEGAL PROFESSIONALS

Along with private and public support for care and mourning, professional sources of support are needed as well. In this section we offer recommendations to healthcare, religious, funeral service, and legal professionals.

Medical professionals. Medical professionals must develop greater sensitivity to changing family structures, especially when completing a POLST form with a patient or in discussing a HIPAA release of information form.[49] Our interviewees felt validated as family when a medical provider acknowledged that they should have access to their parent and his or her medical information, especially in situations in which they felt invalidated by a stepparent or a parent's significant other. Although Medicare began funding end-of-life conversations in 2016, Medicare benefits do not, for most people, start until they reach the age of 65; many interviewees' parents, however, were under that age. Funding is needed for medical professionals to conduct these highly sensitive end-of-life conversations; they are time consuming, especially as family forms grow in complexity; indeed, as our interviews showed and as is true in elder law more generally, medical professionals face greater risk of lawsuit as conflicting family members face the death of a parent in confusion and look to place blame. Videos and training resources should be offered to help coach healthcare providers in leading these conversations.[50]

In terms of the medical community, expanding the category of medical professional who can serve as a primary care provider to include registered nurses could also expand the ability of families to keep an elder at home affordably.[51] Increasing the number of patients in concurrent care projects[52] that allow for hospice care as well as aggressive treatment could also benefit modern families. Many of our interviewees accessed hospice care and the interdisciplinary model empowered them to provide the hands-on care for their loved one, the memory of which was comforting after the death.

Overall, we saw with interviewees and their families that advance-care planning must happen over the life cycle. People marry and divorce; new kin enter the picture; beliefs and goals change over time. Healthcare providers should return to preferences related to serious illness, end of life, and death at critical moments across the life span.

Faith communities. Clergy members can offer critical support for family caregiving and healthcare decision-making. Faith beliefs and practices played an important role in medical decision-making. Our interviewees often thought about the values and hopes of their loved ones as well as their own as they made decisions about entering hospice care or removing life support. During sermons, counseling, and pastoral care visits, clergy can talk with parishioners about how faith frames their choices concerning withholding nutrition or hydration, CPR, last rites, and handling the body after death. For example, clergy members can counsel couples preparing for marriage to consider who will serve as next of kin and what advising role they would like other family members to play.

Coordinating these conversations in remarried families is particularly important, because differences in faith beliefs can become stumbling blocks when second or third spouses and stepchildren are given authority or included in the decision-making. Faith communities can also bring together multiple families and intentionally create space to hear the stories of others, which can be a motivator for planning and conversation. Because clergy often provide pastoral care in the hospital and hospice setting, having knowledge of the individual or couple's wishes in hand could provide authoritative guidance to family members.

Clergy members and faith communities tend not to be involved directly in matters of inheritance. However, because clergy members offer critical support immediately after and in the months after a death, they can encourage conversations about how remarried couples will settle their estate, plan for supporting the surviving widow or widower, and honor the grown children from previous spouses or partners. During premarital counseling with couples who have adult children, clergy members can begin the conversation, advising couples to consider how they will combine or keep separate their households and assets and how they will distribute those assets, including sentimental items, after death.

Lawyers: Family law attorneys who handle divorce should ensure that they counsel their clients on the impact of divorce on inheritance. Second, estate planning attorneys should emphasize to their clients the importance of updating wills and beneficiary designations based on family changes.

Funeral home personnel: Our key recommendations for funeral and burial support relate to spatial relations at the service itself and then laws related to cremation. Funeral directors and clergy have become increasingly accustomed to the varying forms of modern families. That said, few utilize a seating chart when guiding families in planning for their memorial or funeral service. Our interviews highlight that the family members present when planning the service may not include all the family members who should have a place of honor at the service. Funeral directors as well as clergy can help prepare family members to think about who would like to sit where and why, especially for spouses of the deceased.

CONCLUSION

A year after his mom's death, Kyle admitted that balancing all the emotional and financial costs of caring for his mother were challenging, but
that he would make the caregiving choice all over again. He encouraged
other grown children to overcome their anxiety or discomfort in talking about illness, money, and death with their parents. Having had those
conversations, he felt at peace, because he knew that he and his mother
worked as a team in her final months of life. Of course, "Being prepared is
not the same thing as being ready."[53] None of those interviewed felt ready
for the death of his or her loved one, but prior preparation helped carry
them through the grief and mourning and, ultimately, find resilience as a
family system.

As a society, we have time, right now, to listen and to prepare a supportive
framework for future caregivers—and for their parents and stepfamilies.
Such a framework must encourage more intentional advanced planning
on the part of future care recipients and caregivers while expanding society's programmatic efforts that encourage and reward acts of loving kindness shown to all those we consider kin. This requires expanding support
for caregivers and establishing stronger systems to promote planning on
the private level, the faith-based level, and the societal level. Although we
have moved forward in medical care, we have yet to figure out how to
adapt cultural, legal, and religious mechanisms to promote better quality
of life as we age. Different family structures require awareness of, easier
access to, and increased utilization of formal tools that acknowledge the
complexities of family norms and that encourage more open discussion of
how to age, and die, gracefully.

Project investigators included Amy Ziettlow, Elizabeth Marquardt, and Naomi Cahn. The first phase of the project began in the summer of 2011. We[1] selected a seven-month period in the racially diverse, mid-size American city of Baton Rouge, Louisiana.[2] We read every obituary appearing in its leading newspaper, *The Advocate*, which serves the greater Baton Rouge and New Orleans area. It publishes obituaries in its daily print version, normally running the obituary about three to six days after the death. A brief death notice, free of charge, often preceded a full obituary appearing on the next day. Lengthy obituaries tend to be written (thirty to thirty-five lines) and even death notices for the indigent are included. Almost everyone has a nickname, included in quotation marks. Obituaries are also published online at legacy.com.

We researched deaths using NewsBank to filter by date and newspaper. The paper edition includes a photo of the deceased. Death notices are free and include the deceased's name, age, date of death, place of residence, and service information. Obituaries are not limited in length but cost $2.40 per line/per day with adding pictures or an icon an additional cost.[3] Sample obituary:

NAME

A retired LSU employee and resident of Baton Rouge, she departed this life Friday, Oct. 22, 2010. She was 65 and a graduate of McKinley High School. She leaves to cherish her memory her children and their spouses, NAMES; sister, NAME; 11 grandchildren and two great-grandchildren. Preceded in death by her parents, and son, NAME. Viewing at New Southside Funeral Home, 924 S. 14th St., Thursday, Oct. 28, from 9 a.m. until service at 11 a.m. Interment in Winnfield Memorial Park.

From that seven-month sample of deaths, we made a list of every grown child or stepchild named in the obituary of a deceased person age 70 or younger. We recorded on average of fifty variables on an Excel spreadsheet for each applicable decedent, including the decedent's name, date of death, if the decedent was in a first and only marriage, single, or remarried at the time of death, date of birth, spouse's name or significant other's name and ex-spouse's name (if applicable), all children and stepchildren survivors, birth order, spouse of the grown child or stepchild (which assisted in researching correct contact information), name of the faith community, and clergy member(s) when named. In this way, we compiled a list of more than 2700 names of persons whose Baby Boom generation parent had died approximately one year previously. Decedents were organized by month of death in order to time invitations near the one-year anniversary of the death.

Using information available in publicly accessible databases, we added variables to the spreadsheet, including birthdate of the grown child or stepchild, mailing address, phone number, and e-mail address. We used all available means of contact—regular mail, e-mail, and telephone—to invite these grown children and stepchildren to be participants in our study. From the initial 2700 names, we found correct contact information for a random sample of over 1500. From that sample, we recruited sixty-two participants located in Louisiana, California, Texas, Missouri, and Florida. As interviews were conducted, additional variables were added, such as race, education level, occupation, marital status of interviewee, children of interviewee, number of times the interview was cancelled or rescheduled, and incidence of incarceration or substance abuse mentioned during the interview. Field notes on each interview were made, and the family drawings and consent forms were scanned and filed.

We began conducting interviews in October 2011. The structure of the qualitative interview tool was modeled after the interview instrument Elizabeth Marquardt used in the *National Survey on the Moral and Spiritual Lives of Children of Divorce*.[4] Before their respective deaths, Judith Wallerstein, Don Browning, and Norval Glenn, advisors for *Between Two Worlds*, also served to guide the construction of the research methodology. To guide the overall vision for constructing the methodology, we consulted Loren Marks, a member of the project's advisory group and established social scientist at Louisiana State University who conducts qualitative research in religion, family, and marriage, for guidance in constructing the interview instrument. We held a one-day consultation with Marks prior to finalizing the semistructured tool and beginning interviews. Ziettlow met for a half-day consultation with Marks after the interviews had been conducted to process the interview experience and to construct the coding and analysis methodology.[5]

Interviews were conducted in congregations, public libraries, by telephone, and one by e-mail. Respondents received $50 for their time. After obtaining informed consent, the interviewers used a semistructured interview of open-ended questions. Discussion topics included:

- creating a drawing of their family when they were a child,
- describing their home and family rituals as a child,
- relating the story of divorce/remarriage/cohabitation, if applicable,
- describing their church/faith home growing up,
- describing the time before, during, and immediately after the death of their parent or parent figure,
- describing the funeral and burial,
- describing sorting through the belongings of their parent and the inheritance,
- and, last, describing coping in the past year, how private and public rituals have changed, what spiritual beliefs have been helpful, and their reflections on the commandment "Honor your mother and father."

Interviews began with small talk and a drawing of their family during childhood as a way to build rapport. Sample drawings include these, given in Figures 1–5:

Figure 1 Greg's family drawing: a married-parent family, his mother is deceased

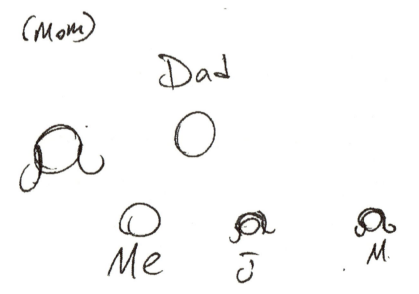

Figure 2 Peter's family drawing: a married-parent family, his father is deceased

Figure 3 Michelle's family drawing: a single-parent family, her mother is widowed from a second husband and is now deceased

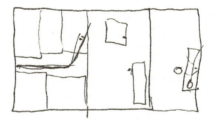

Figure 4 David's family drawing: a remarried-parent family, his father is widowed from David's mother and is now deceased. David includes his father, mother, and siblings, but not his stepmother. He also drew an abbreviated floorplan of his father's house, where he now lives after his father's death.

Figure 5 Candace's family drawing: a remarried-parent family, her father is deceased. She clearly delineates among her family with her parents, her mother's remarriage, and her father's remarriage. She draws three separate families with her in each one.

As the interview intensified near the parent's or parent figure's time of death, it was not uncommon for respondents to begin crying or to experience strong emotions. Interviewers brought tissues and bottled water that were placed on a table between the respondent and interviewee at the beginning of the interview and were available throughout the time. Many of the questions led to multiple subparts. Interviewers loosely followed the basic chronology of questions but also asked relevant follow-up questions and probes, and we skipped questions that were irrelevant to the specific respondent.

Interview demographics (Figures 6, 7, and 8) reflect the gender and race diversity of Baton Rouge and the surrounding area: thirty-eight females, twenty-four males; three Hispanics, twenty-four African Americans, and thirty-five Caucasians. All interviewees were middle aged, with ages ranging from 28 to 48 years old. In terms of birth order, nineteen were the oldest child, sixteen the middle child, thirteen the youngest child, six the only child, and one adopted. The seven remaining were stepchildren. Regarding family structure, twenty-one were from first and only married families, twenty-two from single-parent families, and nineteen from remarried-parent families, seven of whom were a stepchild to the deceased. In terms of religious identification, twenty-six identified as nondenominational Christian, ten as mainline Christian, eight as Baptist Christian, six as Catholic Christian, seven as none, four as spiritual or Christian but non-practicing, and one as atheist. The numbers in the "marital status of parent" and "economic class of parent" column reflect a total of fifty-six to account for the six sets of siblings we interviewed.

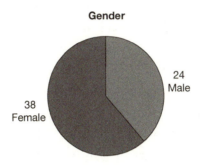

Figure 6

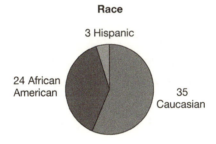

Figure 7

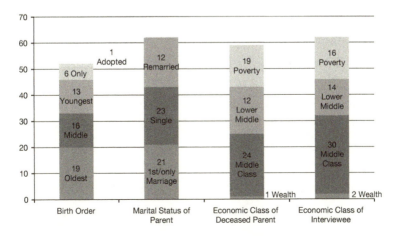

Figure 8

Following transcription of each interview, transcripts were read once and coded for salient themes, such as advice, alcohol, anniversaries/holidays, caregiving, church, divorce, grandparents, burial, grief, honor commandment, inheritance, money/stuff, last memory, prison, names for parents, siblings, ritual, social media, spiritual beliefs, and time of death. Each theme was then coded for subthemes and discussed by investigators. We began with numeric content analysis of the open-coding concepts. To that list of concepts, we added specific themes that may not have occurred in numerical significance but were powerful and salient to produce the list of themes or quote documents previously noted. We then isolated each theme and created a data audit of supporting, primary data from the interviews. We then created "key quote" files for the themes. Counterexamples were included in separate files. At this point, files were shared with other project investigators for further analysis and debate over the processes and insights gained within each theme.[6] All quotes were taken from the transcripts and lightly edited for grammar and repetitive words such as "er" or "um." We used Don Braman's methodology in *Doing Time on the Outside* when addressing quotations.

As with all research, there are limitations. The interviewees were, obviously, a self-selected group, and do not necessarily represent a national cross section of children of Baby Boomer parents. Instead, the interviews were qualitative and designed to offer rich description and point to further points of study. We did not formally survey specific demographic data but drew general observations based on autobiographical information shared in the interview, such as education history and current vocation, and family information published in the obituary, including date of birth, spouse, and siblings. We also used interviewer observation to draw broad generalizations about income level, although we did not ask about an individual's economic status. The interviewers had no prior connection to the respondents. However, Ziettlow, an ordained clergy person, a fact that was noted in the invitation letter, conducted the majority of the interviews. Many of the interviews were conducted in local congregations. That being said, the interviewers did not specifically recruit respondents who had honored a parent or were overly religious. The sample size of our study is larger than many qualitative studies but was necessary to reach an equal variability in family structure divided among respondents whose parents were in their first and only marriage at the time of caregiving and death, respondents whose deceased parent was single, and respondents whose parent was remarried or a stepparent.

We also acknowledge that our findings may not be generalizable because of the nature of self-reporting as well as the unique structure of Louisiana law. However, our aim was to glean the cultural, moral, and spiritual understandings respondents brought to the experience of elder care and grief. Qualitative interviews allowed us to build rapport and trust with respondents during the interview, which increased the chances of obtaining sensitive, sometimes shameful, sometimes highly emotional, information about their family and their experience of death.[7] Moreover, the stories that participants shared reflect the perspective of the person telling the story. Another family member might have a very different perspective on the facts. The deceased might have had a very different perspective as well.

During the *Homeward Bound* project, we drew on countless helpful books, websites, and organizations we'd accessed over the course of serving in hospice care, parish ministry, and writing and teaching family and elder law, respectively. The following resources may be of assistance on either a professional or personal level.

For a catalog of academic and popular writing related to the *Homeward Bound* Project, visit http://www.americanvalues.org/homeward-bound/.

FAMILY SYSTEMS

Naomi Cahn, The New Kinship: Constructing Donor-Conceived Families (2013).

Evon O. Flesberg, The Switching Hour: Kids of Divorce Say Good-bye Again (2008).

Judith Wallerstein & Julia M. Lewis, The Unexpected Legacy of Divorce (2000).

Froma Walsh, Strengthening Family Resilience (2006).

Online Resources

Council on Contemporary Families blog, contemporaryfamilies.org/

Institute for Family Studies Blog, ifstudies.org

CAREGIVING

ALEXIS ABRAMSON, THE CAREGIVER'S SURVIVAL HANDBOOK
(REVISED): CARING FOR YOUR PARENTS WITHOUT LOSING
YOURSELF (2011).

CLARE BERMAN, CARING FOR YOURSELF WHILE CARING FOR YOUR
AGING PARENTS, 3RD EDITION: HOW TO HELP, HOW TO SURVIVE
(2005).

ROZ CHAST, CAN'T WE TALK ABOUT SOMETHING MORE
PLEASANT? A MEMOIR (2014).

HUGH DELEHANTY & ELINOR GINZLER, CARING FOR YOUR
PARENTS: THE COMPLETE FAMILY GUIDE (AARP) (2008).

JANE GROSS, A BITTERSWEET SEASON: CARING FOR OUR AGING
PARENTS—AND OURSELVES (2012).

KENNETH C. HAUGK, CHRISTIAN CAREGIVING: A WAY OF LIFE
(1984).

STELLA HENRY & ANN CONVERY, THE ELDERCARE
HANDBOOK: DIFFICULT CHOICES, COMPASSIONATE SOLUTIONS
(2006).

BARRY J. JACOBS, THE EMOTIONAL SURVIVAL GUIDE FOR
CAREGIVERS: LOOKING AFTER YOURSELF AND YOUR FAMILY
WHILE HELPING AN AGING PARENT (2006).

ROBERT L. KANE, THE GOOD CAREGIVER: A ONE-OF-A-KIND
COMPASSIONATE RESOURCE FOR ANYONE CARING FOR AN
AGING LOVED ONE (2011).

JOY LAVERDE, THE COMPLETE ELDER CARE PLANNER (2009).

GRACE LEBOW & BARBARA KANE, COPING WITH YOUR DIFFICULT
OLDER PARENT: A GUIDE FOR STRESSED-OUT CHILDREN (1999).

CAROLE LECINE (ED.), ALWAYS ON CALL: WHEN ILLNESS TURNS
FAMILIES INTO CAREGIVERS (2004).

JOANNE LYNN, HANDBOOK FOR MORTALS: GUIDANCE FOR PEOPLE
FACING SERIOUS ILLNESS (1999);

VIRGINIA MORRIS & JENNIE CHIN-HANSEN, HOW TO CARE FOR
AGING PARENTS, 3RD EDITION: A ONE-STOP RESOURCE FOR ALL

YOUR MEDICAL, FINANCIAL, HOUSING, AND EMOTIONAL ISSUES (2014).

AI-JEN POO, THE AGE OF DIGNITY: PREPARING FOR THE ELDER BOOM IN A CHANGING AMERICA (2014).

GAIL SHEEHY, PASSAGES IN CAREGIVING: TURNING CHAOS INTO CONFIDENCE (2010).

PAULA SPAN, WHEN THE TIME COMES: FAMILIES WITH AGING PARENTS SHARE THEIR STRUGGLES AND SOLUTIONS (2009).

PAUL TAYLOR, THE NEXT AMERICA: BOOMERS, MILLENNIALS, AND THE LOOMING GENERATIONAL SHOWDOWN (2014).

BETH WITROGEN MCLEOD, CAREGIVING: THE SPIRITUAL JOURNEY OF LOVE, LOSS AND RENEWAL (1999).

Online Resources

AARP, aarp.org

ADMINISTRATION ON AGING, aoa.gov

AGINGCARE, agingcare.com

AMERICAN SOCIETY ON AGING, asaging.org

CATECHISM OF THE CATHOLIC CHURCH ON HEALING AND SICKNESS, vatican.va/archive/ccc_css/archive/catechism/p2s2c2a5.htm

CHANGINGAGING, changingaging.org

DAUGHTERHOOD, daughterhood.org/

GERIPAL, geripal.org/

HEALTH AGENDA (hosted by the Hartford Foundation), jhartfound.org/blog/

END-OF-LIFE CARE

ANATOLE BROYARD, INTOXICATED BY MY ILLNESS AND OTHER WRITINGS ON LIFE AND DEATH (1993).

Ira Byrock, Dying Well (1997).

Ira Byrock, The Four Things That Matter Most (2014).

Daniel Callahan, The Troubled Dream of Life: In Search of a Peaceful Death (1993).

Maggie Callanan & Patrick Kelley, Final Gifts: Understanding the Special Awareness, Needs, and Communications of the Dying (2012).

David J. Casarett, Last Acts (2010).

Camille Pavy Clairbourne, Dying in God's Hands (2009).

J. Fiorito, The Closer We Are to Dying (1999).

Kathleen Foley, When the Focus is on Care: Palliative Care and Cancer (2005).

Atul Gawande, Being Mortal (2014).

Stephen Jay Gould, The Median Is Not the Message (2002).

J. Groopman, The Anatomy of Hope: How People Prevail in the Face of Illness (2003).

Constance Jones, R.I.P.: The Complete Book of Death and Dying (1997).

Christopher Jay Johnson, How Different Religions View Death & Afterlife (1986).

Kathy Kalina, Midwife for Souls (2007).

Elisabeth Kubler-Ross, On Death and Dying (1969).

Joanne Lynn, Sick to Death and Not Going to Take it Anymore: Reforming Healthcare for the Last Years of Life (2004).

Joseph Matthews, Long-Term Care: How to Plan & Pay for It (2012).

Deborah M. Merrill, Caring for Elderly Parents: Juggling Work, Family, and Caregiving in Middle and Working Class Families (1997).

James Miller & Susan Cutshall, The Art of Being a Healing Presence (2001).

Sherwin Nuland, How We Die (1993).

Online Resources

HFA (Hospice Foundation of America),
hospicefoundation.org

Bill Moyers, On Our Own Terms, billmoyers.com/series/
on-our-own-terms-moyers-on-dying/

NHPCO (National Hospice and Palliative Care
Organization), nhpco.org

Pallimed Blog, pallimed.org/

Center to Advance Palliative Care, capc.org

American Academy of Hospice and Palliative Medicine,
aahpm.org

How We Die, how-we-die.org/HowWeDie/home

PASTORAL CARE

David W. Augsburger, Pastoral Counseling Across
Cultures (1986).

Howard Clinebell, Basic Types of Pastoral Care and
counselling: Resources for the Ministry of Healing and
Growth (1984).

Richard Eyer, Pastoral Care Under the Cross: God in the
Midst of Suffering (1994).

Scott Floyd, Crisis Counseling: A Guide for Pastors and
Professionals (2008).

Gene Fowler, Caring Through the Funeral: A Pastor's
Guide (2004).

Edwin H. Friedman, Generation to Generation: Family
Process in Church and Synagogue (1985).

Ruth Hetzendorfer, The Pastoral Counseling
Handbook: A Guide to Helping the Hurting (2009).

William G. Hoy, Road to Emmaus: Pastoral Care with the
Dying and Bereaved (2008).

ELIZABETH JOHNSTON-TAYLOR, WHAT DO I SAY?: TALKING WITH
    PATIENTS ABOUT SPIRITUALITY (2007).
HAROLD KOENIG & JUNIETTA McCALL, BEREAVEMENT
    COUNSELING: PASTORAL CARE FOR COMPLICATED GRIEF
    (2004).
MARGARET KORNFELD, CULTIVATING WHOLENESS: A GUIDE TO
    CARE AND COUNSELING IN FAITH COMMUNITIES (1998).
JOHN PATTON, PASTORAL CARE: AN ESSENTIAL GUIDE (2005).
JEAN STAIRS, LISTENING FOR THE SOUL: PASTORAL CARE AND
    SPIRITUAL DIRECTION (2000).
MARY TOOLE, HANDBOOK FOR CHAPLAINS: COMFORT MY PEOPLE
    (2006).
EDWARD P. WIMBERLY, AFRICAN-AMERICAN PASTORAL CARE
    (1991).

ADVANCE-CARE PLANNING

Online Resources

CARING INFO, caringinfo.org/i4a/pages/index.cfm?pageid=3289
THE CONVERSATION PROJECT, theconversationproject.org
FIVE WISHES, agingwithdignity.org/five-wishes/about-five-wishes
NEXT AVENUE, FORBES, forbes.com/sites/nextavenue/2016/02/
    25/how-to-get-your-boss-to-allow-you-a-phased-retirement/
    #797609b52972
NATIONAL POLST, polst.org

Burial Practices

GEORGE ANDERSON & EDWARD FOLEY, MIGHTY STORIES,
    DANGEROUS RITUALS (2001).

Lucy Bregman, Religion, Death, and Dying, Vol. 3: Bereavement and Death Rituals (2009).

Anne Brener, Mourning & Mitzvah: A Guided Journal for Walking the Mourner's Path Through Grief to Healing (2001).

Michelle Cromer, Exit Strategy: Thinking Outside the Box (2006).

Anita Diamant, Saying Kaddish: How to Comfort the Dying, Bury the Dead, and Mourn as a Jew (1999).

Patricia Fosarelli, Prayers and Rituals at a Time of Illness and Dying: The Practices of the Five World Religions (2008).

Charles Gusmer, And You Visited Me: Sacramental Ministry to the Sick and Dying (Studies in the Reformed Rites of the Church) (1990).

Leor Halevi, Muhammad's Grave: Death Rites and the Making of Islamic Society (2007).

Paul E. Irion, The Funeral and the Mourners: Pastoral Care for the Bereaved (1954).

Marilyn Johnson, The Dead Beat: Lost Souls, Lucky Stiffs, and the Perverse Pleasure of Obituaries (2006).

Harold Kushner, The Lord Is My Shepherd: Healing Wisdom of the Twenty-Third Psalm (2004).

Maurice Lamm, Consolation: The Spiritual Journey Beyond Grief (2004).

Maurice Lamm, The Jewish Way in Death and Mourning (2000).

Thomas Long, Accompany Them with Singing: The Christian Funeral (2009).

Thomas Long & Thomas Lynch, The Good Funeral (2013).

Thomas Lynch, An Undertaking: Life Studies from a Dismal Trade (2009).

Kodo Matsunami, The International Book of Funeral Customs (1998).

Peter Metcalf & Richard Huntington, Celebrations of
Death: The Anthropology of Mortuary Ritual (1991).

Jessica Mitford, The American Way of Death (1963).

Jim Perlman, Deborah Cooper, Mara Hart & Pamela
Mittlefehldt, (eds.), Beloved on the Earth: 150 Poems of
Grief & Gratitude (2009).

Mary Roach, Stiff: The Curious Lives of Human Cadavers
(2003).

Paul Sheppy, In Sure and Certain Hope: Liturgies, Prayers,
and Readings for Funerals and Memorials (2003).

Lisa Takeuchi, Remember Me: A Lively Tour of the New
American Way of Death (2006).

Online Resources

Reform Judaism Funeral Guide, reformjudaism.org/
preparing-jewish-funeral-guide; reformjudaism.org/
preparing-jewish-funeral-checklist

United Synagogue of Conservative Judaism, uscj.org/
JewishLivingandLearning/Lifecycle/JewishFuneralPractice/
GuidetoJewishFuneralPractice.aspx

GRIEF

George A. Bonanno, The Other Side of Sadness: What the
New Science of Bereavement Tells Us About Life After
Loss (2009).

Allan Hugh Cole Jr., Good Mourning: Getting Through
Your Grief (2008).

Deborah Morris Coryell, Good Grief: Healing Through
the Shadow of Loss (1997).

Kenneth J. Doak & Joyce D. Davidson (eds.), Living with
Grief: Who We Are, How We Grieve (1998).

Lorene Hanley Duquin, Grieving With the Help of Your
Catholic Faith (2006).

Geoffrey Gorer, The Pornography of Death (1955).

Elisabeth Kübler-Ross & David Kessler, On Grief and
Grieving: Finding the Meaning of Grief Through the
Five Stages of Loss (2005).

Ruth Davis Konigsberg, The Truth About Grief: The Myth
of Its Five Stages and the New Science of Loss (2011).

C.S. Lewis, A Grief Observed (1961).

Froma Walsh & Monica McGoldrick, (eds.), Living Beyond
Loss: Death in the Family (2004).

Alan D. Wolfelt, Living in the Shadows of the Ghosts of
Grief (2007).

Alan D. Wolfelt, Understanding Your Grief: Ten Essential
Touchstones for Finding Hope and Healing Your Heart
(2004).

William Worden, Grief Counseling and Grief therapy (1982).

H. Norman Wright, Experiencing Grief (2004).

ESTATE PLANNING

N. Brian Caverly & Jordan S. Simon, Estate Planning for
Dummies (2003).

Charles Dickens, Bleak House (1853).

George Eliot, Middlemarch (1871).

Jane Smiley, A Thousand Acres (1991).

DIGITAL ASSETS

Evan Carroll, How to Manage Your Digital Assets (2014).

There are numerous websites that provide advice on digital assets;
we have not included any because there is such change in
the area.

ELDER LAW/TRUSTS & ESTATES

ACTEC, ACTEC.ORG

ELDER LAW PROF. BLOG, lawprofessors.typepad.com/elder_law/

A Bereavement Interview Tool for Clergy and Congregations

Grieving allows us to heal, to remember with love rather than pain.
It is a sorting process. One by one you let go of things that are gone
and you mourn for them. One by one you take hold of the things
that have become a part of who you are and build again.[1]

—RACHAEL NAOMI REMEN, MD

This appendix offers a Bereavement Interview Tool based on Ziettlow's professional experience in hospice care and parish ministry.[2] The background and Bereavement Interview Tool could be used as the basis of a hospice staff in-service, a one-hour breakout session at a clergy conference or chaplain conference, or as an education lesson at a faith community.

BACKGROUND TO THE BEREAVEMENT INTERVIEW TOOL

After spending a year using our qualitative interview tool for research purposes, Ziettlow observed that it could fill a gap in bereavement resources available to clergy, congregations, and hospice bereavement programs. Making the interview tool available could give members of faith communities, hospice bereavement coordinators, and volunteers a structured response to offer those who are grieving. The tool gives grieving persons an opportunity to reframe their lives on their own terms and in their own words. Researcher George Bonanno studies patterns of resilience after loss, and he stresses the importance of sharing stories, especially the processing of the person's perceptions of the deceased:

> The quality of the relationship is less important than expected in a grief reaction because we don't grieve the facts. We don't grieve the actual details of the relationship. We grieve only what we remember of the relationship. And the accuracy of our memories does not determine how we grieve; that is determined by what we do with our memories, how we experience them, and what we take from them during bereavement.[3]

In addition to the clinical background that informs the Bereavement Interview Tool, there is theological framing for the tool as well. In scripture, faithful individuals often mark a liminal moment as holy by building an altar. The stones they place at a particular spot enable them to reflect on where they've been and thus incorporate the lessons learned into how they will live in the future. The individual often feels his or her identity shifting, and building an altar acknowledges that God is with them through the transition.

After the flood Noah builds an altar to God (Genesis 8:20). Abram builds an altar where God appears to him and promises to make a great nation from his offspring (Genesis 12:7). As Jacob runs from his father-in-law and fears facing his long estranged brother, Esau, he builds an altar to mark his wrestling with God and his name change to Israel. Moses, Joshua, Gideon, Samuel, Saul, and David all build altars at liminal moments in their personal faith and the faith of the people they serve.[4]

At first glance we may presume that the primary goal of the Bereavement Interview Tool is to facilitate therapy within the context of pastoral care. And although the tool is based on sound concepts from grief counseling and therapy, having a clergy member or trained congregational volunteer conduct these interviews within a faith community is not only therapeutic but also an opportunity for the individual and the interviewer to collectively build an altar to God through story that acknowledges the liminal time that has been experienced after the death of a loved one.

Why build an altar at a year after a death? The year anniversary of a death marks a moment of having survived the first year of "firsts" without a loved one physically present: the first holidays, first birthday, and so forth. The year anniversary is often the first time that individuals are actually ready to start to formally make sense of the loss in the light of their faith and begin to imagine how to carry that loss with them into the future. The interview, like biblical altar building, is both a way to mark the past as sacred but also as a way to mark the beginning of a new journey. The interview allows for an intentional moment to be shared that proclaims, my life has been, is, and will be marked as holy and sacred by God.

In local faith communities, pastoral care after a death often happens informally over time in the normal course of a pastor's checking in on parishioners. If greater attention is demanded of the pastor or congregation, intervention comes as a response to a cry for help or a crisis, but those rarely happen. The Bereavement Interview Tool is not intended to be used to intervene in a crisis, but to guide discussion with a parishioner who is making sense of his or her life, identity, and faith a year after the death of a loved one. The Bereavement Interview Tool is designed to provide a programmatic option for those clergy and congregations who would like to offer more systematic and scheduled support to those who are grieving beyond the more informal and communal support already provided. The Bereavement Interview Tool could also be used in hospice bereavement programs for communities at large. In addition to clergy, chaplains, social workers, and volunteers trained in active listening and boundaries would be appropriate people to conduct these interviews in both the congregational and hospice-care settings. This tool is intended to be used with individuals experiencing normal, uncomplicated grief, which for most congregations (and hospice settings) comprises the vast majority of loss. We trust that clergy and hospice professionals reading this section have completed an initial assessment of the grieving individual and will refer the person to psychological intervention, if needed.

The initial questions in the Bereavement Interview Tool that address how parents met, their family home, their faith life as a child, holiday celebrations, and how they left home are intended to allow for the defining of family communication patterns, values, and myths as well as defining the roles played by each parent, stepparent, siblings, and the individual being interviewed.[5] The questions in the Bereavement Interview Tool that ask about learning of the illness or sudden event that begins a time of caregiving, the process of being a caregiver, and the experience of the time of death enable the individual to create the baseline definition of what it means to be family, to care, and broadly what it means to be alive. The heart of the interview lies at when the time of death and time immediately after the death are revisited. For many interviewees, these moments were spoken with a fixed stare as though they were watching a movie of the events unfolding. A high level of detail was remembered. Most of our interviewees had not gone back to revisit that moment in story since the death. Walking through that timeline enabled the interviewee to tell the story for her or himself. As we moved away from the event into the time of the funeral, burial, settling the loved one's estate, and the year of "firsts" without their parent, they gained perspective on how that seminal moment shaped their thoughts and feelings in the year since.

As we now introduce the Bereavement Interview Tool, we harken back to its ultimate goal: to empower those who are grieving to give words to their sorrow.

PREPARATION

Before the interview:

1) Establish an invitation schedule. Interviews should happen at approximately the one-year anniversary of the death so that reflections can be made on how the anniversary was marked. The invitation should come from the interviewer.

2) Prepare the interview space. A small-size to midsize office or classroom in the congregation or a public space, such as a library, works well. Ensure that others in the building know that you are meeting for around two hours. Although the conversation will

be vulnerable, you can keep the door ajar to maintain proper boundaries. Before you meet your interviewee, you can prepare by saying a prayer, such as, "Dear Lord, thank you for the life of (the deceased). May I be an open vessel to receive the life story of (the name of your interviewee). May this time be one of peace and renewal for (name of interviewee). Amen."

3) Bring to the interview tissue, water bottle, a copy of your interview questions, and a digital recorder.

4) Begin the interview by explaining that everything spoken today will be kept confidential and that you will burn a CD recording of the interview or e-mail an audio file that can be kept and shared as they wish. The point of today is for them to tell their life story and talk about the death of their mother, father, stepparent, husband, or wife. Make eye contact and sit calmly.

5) For the most part, the interviewer will only ask questions and actively listen. The interviewer may ask for details or further explanation, but should not offer examples from personal experience. This interview is a rare opportunity for the person to process his or her story within a sacred and confidential space. Insights and "aha!" moments may happen but they should come from the person telling the story and not the interviewer.

After the Interview:

Self-care for the interviewer: Remember that listening to a highly vulnerable and potentially emotional story for two hours is physically, emotionally, and mentally exhausting. Don't plan major projects, deadlines, or meetings immediately following an interview. The interviews are fatiguing. Take time afterward to journal any personal insights.

The Bereavement Interview Tool (to be copied and used during the interview)

These interview questions are inspired by questions use in the *Homeward Bound* project. Depending on the relationship between the interviewer and interviewee, the interviewer may omit certain questions, focus on two or three, or choose to follow the chronology closely.

Some of those interviewed will need to be prompted by a question and will answer each question asked as in a typical interview. However, many others will just need to talk and will answer many questions as they talk. The main goals are to assist in allowing the person to revisit the time right before and at the time of death, to remember how they marked the anniversary of the death, how they have survived the previous year, and how their sense of self, family, and God has changed and stayed the same.

Interview Questions:

1) Tell me about your family when you were five years old.
2) How did your parents meet?
3) Where is the first place you called home? What was your house like? Did you have your own room?
4) If you moved, where else did you call home?
5) If your parents divorced, when and how did that transpire? Have there been remarriages? Other significant adults?
6) What role did your grandparents play in your childhood?
7) Where did you go to be alone?
8) When were you expected to come together as a family?
9) What were holidays like? Do you have a favorite holiday memory? Favorite foods or traditions?
10) Did your family have a church or faith home? What did that look like?
11) When did you leave home?
12) When did you realize that your mother's/father's health was failing? (You will know how the person died—so adapt this question appropriately.) When did you get the call about the accident? When did you learn of the cancer? And so forth.
13) What role did you play as a caregiver? What role did your siblings play? Your other parent or stepparent?

14) Did you know when death was near?

15) Where were you at the time of death? What were you thinking? What were you feeling?

16) What did you do next? Whom did you talk to?

17) What role did you play in the funeral planning? Was there something special you wanted to do?

18) What happened at the burial?

19) Did it seem that death was real?

20) What happened next? What did you do concerning your loved one's belongings?

21) Has there been a time this past year when you have felt especially close to your mother/father?

22) Have you felt that God is near or far away?

23) Has there been a scripture that has been helpful?

24) How has worship changed?

25) Has there been a meaningful song?

26) Is there any advice you would give to someone who will experience what you have?

27) Is there anything else you'd like to share?

Funeral Seating Chart

This appendix is intended not only for families but also for funeral home directors and clergy to use when planning a funeral or memorial service.

Our interviews highlighted the heightened importance of seating arrangements at the funeral for today's modern families, which often include a spouse, ex-spouses, a stepparent, a significant other of the deceased, and full children, half-children, and stepchildren. The time immediately following a death tended to be a stressful time for all those grieving. These mourning rituals tended to be remembered in broad strokes, with a gloss, or in snapshot memory. Study participants remembered spatially where they sat during the ritual, who sat next to them, and where other members of the family, broadly defined, sat. The memory of the seating arrangement brought some interviewees comfort and a sense of familial solidarity. However, for many interviewees from remarried families, the seating arrangement at the funeral service sowed seeds of conflict if a grown child did not sit in a place of honor or if the family sat divided. Battles over inheritance could start when a grown child felt snubbed when a stepparent pushed him or her back a row at the service.

This form can be used to help blended families plan for where each member will sit.

Funeral or Memorial Service Seating Chart:

Instructions:

1) On a blank piece of paper, begin by establishing the parameters of the space in which the service will take place.

    a) Draw in the placement of the casket, urn, or memorial photo.

    b) Draw an estimated number of rows of seating.

    c) Draw in any aisles.

    d) Determine how many seats are available in the first row.

    e) Who is sitting in the second or third rows? Will they be offended by this placement?

2) List all family members who will attend the service. For each name listed, note on the drawing where they will sit.

    A) Spouse

        I) Current spouse

        II) Ex-spouses

        III) Significant other

        IV) If widowed, is there a way to honor the widowed spouse through pictures, flowers, or music?

    B) Children

        I) Biological

            a) Spouses?

        II) Step

            a) Spouses?

    C) Other Significant Family Members

        I) Parents of the deceased

        II) Siblings of the deceased

            a) Spouses?

        III) Aunts, uncles, and cousins of the deceased

            a) Spouses?

        IV) Grandchildren of the deceased

            a) Spouses?

            b) Do they want to sit with their parents?

3) Before the service, communicate to all family members where and when they enter to take their seats.

INTRODUCTION

1. All names have been changed to protect the privacy of study respondents as well as that of our friends and colleagues who shared personal stories.
2. Kelvin Pollard & Paola Scommegna, *Just How Many Baby Boomers Are There?* POPULATION REFERENCE BUREAU (Apr., 2014), http://www.prb.org/Publications/Articles/2002/JustHowManyBabyBoomersAreThere.aspx.
3. *Marriage and Divorce Rates Among Baby Boomers Vary by Educational Attainment*, BUREAU OF LABOR STATISTICS: THE ECONOMICS DAILY (Nov. 8, 2013,) http://www.bls.gov/opub/ted/2013/ted_20131108.htm.
4. Ben Steverman, *Boomers are Making Sure the Divorces Keep Coming*, BLOOMBERG NEWS (July 17, 2016), http://www.bloomberg.com/news/articles/2016-06-17/boomers-are-making-sure-the-divorces-keep-coming; Philip Cohen, *Life Table Says Divorce Rate is 52.7%*, June 8, 2016, https://familyinequality.wordpress.com/2016/06/08/life-table-says-divorce-rate-is-52-7/.
5. Susan L. Brown & I-Fen Lin, *The Gray Divorce Revolution: Rising Divorce Among Middle-Aged and Older Adults, 1990–2010* (2013), https://www.bgsu.edu/content/dam/BGSU/college-of-arts-and-sciences/NCFMR/documents/Lin/The-Gray-Divorce.pd; Susan L. Brown, *A "Gray Divorce" Boom*, L.A. TIMES (Mar. 31, 2013), http://articles.latimes.com/2013/mar/31/opinion/la-oe-brown-gray-divorce-20130331; Susan Gregory Thomas, *The Gray Divorcés*, WALL ST. J. (Mar. 3, 2012), http://online.wsj.com/news/articles/SB10001424052970203753704577255230471480276.
6. Ben Steverman, *Boomers are Making Sure the Divorces Keep Coming*, BLOOMBERG NEWS (July 17, 2016), http://www.bloomberg.com/news/articles/2016-06-17/boomers-are-making-sure-the-divorces-keep-coming; Philip Cohen, Life Table Says Divorce Rate is 52.7% (June 8, 2016), https://familyinequality.wordpress.com/2016/06/08/life-table-says-divorce-rate-is-52-7/.
7. Sam Roberts, *Divorce After 50 Grows More Common*, N.Y. TIMES (Sep. 20, 2013), http://www.nytimes.com/2013/09/22/fashion/weddings/divorce-after-50-grows-more-common.html

8. Emily M. Agree & Mary Elizabeth Hughes, *Demographic Trends and Later Life Families in the 21st Century, in* HANDBOOK OF FAMILIES AND AGING 9, 18, Fig. 2.6 (Rosemary Blieszner & Victoria Hilkevitch Bedford eds., 2d ed., 2012).

9. Lori M. Hunter, *Unmarried Baby Boomers Face Disadvantages as They Grow Older,* POPULATION REFERENCE BUREAU (Feb. 2014), http://www.prb.org/Publications/Articles/2014/baby-boomers-and-disability.aspx.

10. Cohen, *supra* note 4.

11. SHARON E. KIRMEYER & BRADY E. HAMILTON, CTRS. FOR DISEASE CONTROL & PREVENTION, NCHS DATA BRIEF NO. 68 CHILDBEARING DIFFERENCES AMONG THREE GENERATIONS OF U.S. WOMEN (2011), http://www.cdc.gov/nchs/data/databriefs/db68.pdf.

12. North Shore-Long Island Jewish Health System, *Aging Baby Boomers, Childless and Unmarried, at Risk of Becoming 'Elder Orphans,'* EUREKALERT! (May 15, 2015), http://www.eurekalert.org/pub_releases/2015-05/nsij-abb051315.php; Carina Storrs, *The 'Elder Orphans' of the Baby Boom Generation,* CNN (May 18, 2015), http://www.cnn.com/2015/05/18/health/elder-orphans; *see also* SANDRA L. COLBY & JENNIFER M. ORTMAN, U.S. CENSUS BUREAU, P25–1141, CURRENT POPULATION REPORTS, THE BABY BOOM COHORT IN THE UNITED STATES: 2012 TO 2060 (2014), http://www.census.gov/prod/2014pubs/p25-1141.pdf.

13. Jennifer M. Ortman, Victoria A. Velkoff, and Howard Hogan, *An Aging Nation: The Older Population in the United States,* Current Population Reports, P25–1140. U.S. Census Bureau, Washington, DC, 2014, https://www.census.gov/prod/2014pubs/p25-1140.pdf

14. *Family Caregiving,* 33 TODAY'S RES. ON AGING 1 (2016), http://www.prb.org/pdf16/TodaysResearchAging33.pdf.

15. Federal Interagency Forum on Aging-Related Statistics, *Older Americans 2016: Key Indicators of Well-Being,* U.S. Government Printing Office, Washington DC, 2016 http://www.agingstats.gov/docs/LatestReport/OA2016.pdf and Renee Stepler, "Smaller Share of Women Ages Sixty-Five and Older Are Living Alone: More Are Living with Spouse or Children," PEW RES. CTR. (Feb. 2016). http://www.pewsocialtrends.org/files/2016/02/ST_2016-02-18_older-adult-FINAL.pdf.

16. ROBERT D. PUTNAM, BOWLING ALONE: THE COLLAPSE AND REVIVAL OF AMERICAN COMMUNITY (2000). His research on Baby Boomer trends in family structure, employment, women's roles, religious practice, and technology use led him to describe boomers as people who "bowl alone."

17. For a complete description of the methodology see Appendix A. Visit HOMEWARD BOUND, http://www.americanvalues.org/homeward-bound/ for a full description of the project. (May 6, 2016, 9:58 a.m.).

18. Baton Rouge is the state capital and one of the fastest growing metropolitan areas in the United States.

19. U.S. Census Bureau statistics on East Baton Rouge parish accessed at *East Baton Rouge Parish, Louisiana,* U.S. CENSUS BUREAU: STATE & COUNTY QUICKFACTS (Dec. 2, 2015, 9:56 a.m.), http://quickfacts.census.gov/qfd/states/22/22033.html.

20. The relationship among family structure, race, and class is complex. "[Black] family ties have traditionally reached beyond the bounds of the nuclear family to include

extended kin and non-kin relationships." Dorothy E. Roberts, *Race and the New Reproduction*, 47 HASTINGS L.J. 935, 942 (1996); see ROBERTA COLES, RACE AND FAMILY: A STRUCTURAL APPROACH 93 (2d ed., 2016)("extended family households are twice as common in black, Hispanics, and other racial minorities as in white households"); JUNE CARBONE & NAOMI CAHN, MARRIAGE MARKETS (2014)(the relationship between class and family structure in the United States).

21. Judith A. Seltzer & Suzanne M. Bianchi, *Demographic Change and Parent-Child Relationships in Adulthood*, 39 ANN. REV. SOCIOLOGY 275, 284 (2013).

22. The term and concept of norm coherence was introduced and developed by Aaron Antonovsky in HEALTH, STRESS AND COPING (1979) and UNRAVELING THE MYSTERIES OF HEALTH (1987). This is his definition of norm coherence: "a global orientation that expresses the extent to which one has a pervasive, enduring though dynamic, feeling of confidence that 1) the stimuli deriving from one's internal and external environments in the course of living are structured, predictable, and explicable, 2) the resources (money, ego-strength, social support, religious beliefs/practices) are available to one to meet the demands posed by these stimuli and 3) these demands are challenges worthy of investment and engagement." UNRAVELING THE MYSTERIES at 19 (with Ziettlow's and Cahn's additions in parentheses).

23. These are also general clinical goals Ziettlow used in in her work as a hospice chaplain. Each hospice team creates a personalized care plan so that each patient and family can understand what is happening, be equipped to manage pain and symptoms, to find meaning in the experience, and through bereavement support, remain connected to each other in the thirteen months after a death.

24. Fifteen come from married-parent families, seven from single-parent families, and three from remarried-parent families.

25. Gretchen Livingston, *Fewer Than Half of U.S. Kids Today Live in a "Traditional" Family* (Dec. 22, 2014), http://www.pewresearch.org/fact-tank/2014/12/22/less-than-half-of-u-s-kids-today-live-in-a-traditional-family/.

CHAPTER 1

1. SANDRA L. COLBY & JENNIFER M. ORTMAN, U.S. CENSUS BUREAU, P25–1141, CURRENT POPULATION REPORTS, THE BABY BOOM COHORT IN THE UNITED STATES: 2012 TO 2060 (2014), http://www.census.gov/prod/2014pubs/p25-1141.pdf.

2. *Id.* at 2 (in 1999, the peak year, the Baby Boomer population consisted of 72.5 million who were born in the United States and another 8 million—including Naomi—who arrived through immigration); see Kelvin Pollard & Paola Scommegna, *Just How Many Baby Boomers Are There?* POPULATION REFERENCE BUREAU (Apr. 2014), http://www.prb.org/Publications/Articles/2002/JustHowManyBabyBoomersAreThere.aspx.

3. Nat'l Acad. Sciences, Engineering, & Med., FAMILIES CARING FOR AN AGING AMERICA 2-17, S-1, 2-13 (2016), http://nationalacademies.org/hmd/Reports/2016/families-caring-for-an-aging-america.aspx.

4. I-Fen Lin & Susan L. Brown, *Unmarried Boomers Confront Old Age: A National Portrait*, 52 GERONTOLOGIST 153 (2012).

5. Susan L. Brown & I-Fen Lin, *The Gray Divorce Revolution: Rising Divorce Among Middle-Aged and Older Adults, 1990–2010* 3 (Natl Ctr. for Family & Marriage

Research, Working Paper No. WP-13-03, 2013), https://www.bgsu.edu/content/dam/BGSU/college-of-arts-and-sciences/NCFMR/documents/Lin/The-Gray-Divorce.pdf.

6. Loraine A. West et al., U.S. Census Bureau, P23–212, Current Population Reports, 65+ in the United States: 2010 (2014), https://www.census.gov/content/dam/Census/library/publications/2014/demo/p23-212.pdf

7. North Shore-Long Island Jewish Health System, *Aging Baby Boomers, Childless and Unmarried, at Risk of Becoming 'Elder Orphans,'* EurekAlert! (May 15, 2015), http://www.eurekalert.org/pub_releases/2015-05/nsij-abb051315.php; Carina Storrs, *The 'Elder Orphans' of the Baby Boom Generation*, CNN (May 18, 2015), http://www.cnn.com/2015/05/18/health/elder-orphans; *see also* Colby &. Ortman, *supra* note 21.

8. Naomi Cahn, *The New Kinship*, 100 Geo. L.J. 367 (2012); Nancy Kingsbury & John Scanzoni, *Structural-Functionalism*, in Sourcebook of Family Theories and Methods: A Contextual Approach 95 (Pauline Boss et al. eds., 1993).

9. David M. Schneider, American Kinship: A Cultural Account 30 (2nd. ed. 1980).

10. *Portrait of Stepfamilies*, Pew Res. Ctr. Soc. & Demographic Trends (Jan. 13, 2011), http://www.pewsocialtrends.org/2011/01/13/a-portrait-of-stepfamilies.

11. Naomi R. Cahn, The New Kinship: Constructing Donor-Conceived Families 30 (2013); *cf.* Jill Elaine Hasday, *Siblings in Law*, 65 Vand. L. Rev. 897 (2012); Maria Schmeekle et al., *What Makes Someone Family? Adult Children's Perceptions of Current and Former Stepparents*, 68 J. Marriage & Fam. 595 (2006).

12. Natl. Ctr. for Health Statistics, Ctrs. for Disease Control and Prevention, Health, United States 101, Table 16 (2014), www.cdc.gov/nchs/data/hus/hus14.pdf.

13. Div. of Vital Statistics, Ctrs. for Disease Control & Prevention, Detailed Tables for the National Vital Statistics Report "Deaths: Final Data for 2013," 12, Table 7 (2013), http://www.cdc.gov/nchs/data/nvsr/nvsr64/nvsr64_02.pdf.

14. Richard Fry, *Millennials Overtake Baby Boomers as America's Largest Generation*, Pew Res. Ctr. (Apr. 25, 2016), http://www.pewresearch.org/fact-tank/2016/04/25/millennials-overtake-baby-boomers/.

15. Natl. All. for Caregiving & AARP Pub. Policy Inst., Caregiving in the U.S. 15 (2015), http://www.aarp.org/content/dam/aarp/ppi/2015/caregiving-in-the-united-states-2015-executive-summary-revised.pdf.

     AARP retired (sorry, for the pun!) the name The American Association of Retired Persons in 1999 because membership is open to anyone over age 50 regardless of whether they are retired. A name change aimed to entice baby boomers to join. http://www.nytimes.com/1999/08/08/weekinreview/ideas-trends-aarp-and-the-new-old-the-retirement-lobby-goes-va-va-boom.html?_r=0.

16. Natl. Hospice and Palliative Care Organization, Hospice Care in America, 4 (2015), http://www.nhpco.org/sites/default/files/public/Statistics_Research/2015_Facts_Figures.pdf.

17. The classic study is from 1997: Joanne Lynn et al., *Prognoses of Seriously Ill Hospitalized Patients on the Days Before Death: Implications for Patient Care and*

Public Policy, 5 New Horizons 56–61 (1997). More recently, Amber E. Barnato et al., *Hospital End-of-Life Treatment Intensity Among Cancer and Non-Cancer Cohorts*, J. Pain Symptom Mgmt. (Aug. 15, 2014), http://www.jpsmjournal.com/article/S0885-3924%2814%2900411-4/fulltext.

18. AARP, *Providing Palliative Care*, http://www.aarp.org/relationships/caregiving-resource-center/info-08-2010/elc_facts_about_hospice.html (last visited Feb. 14, 2016). Note that terms sometimes have slightly different meanings. *See* Diane E. Meier, *Increased Access to Palliative Care and Hospice Services: Opportunities to Improve Value in Health Care*, 89 Milbank Q. 343 (2011).

19. Nancy Altman & Eric Kingson, Social Security Works!: Why Social Security Isn't Going Broke and How Expanding It Will Help Us All, 42–43 (2015).

20. Drew Desilver, *As Population Ages, More Americans Becoming Caregivers*, Pew Res. Ctr. (July 18, 2013), http://www.pewresearch.org/fact-tank/2013/07/18/as-population-ages-more-americans-becoming-caregivers/.

21. *Senior Care Cost Index*, Caring.com (Sep. 2014), https://www.caring.com/research/senior-care-cost-index-2014.

22. Richard Schulz & Paula R. Sherwood, *Physical and Mental Health Effects of Family Caregiving*, 108 Am. J. Nursing 4 (2008).

23. MetLife Mature Market Institute et al., The MetLife Juggling Act Study: Balancing Caregiving with Work and the Costs Involved, 6 (1999), http://www.caregiving.org/data/jugglingstudy.pdf.

24. *Id.* at 2.

25. Amalavoyal V. Chari et al., *The Opportunity Costs of Informal Elder-Care in the United States: New Estimates from the American Time Use Survey*, 50 Health Servs. Res. 871 (2014).

26. *Selected Long-Term Care Statistics*, Family Caregiver Alliance, https://caregiver.org/selected-long-term-care-statistics (last visited Feb. 15, 2016); Janet Viveiros & Maya Brennan, *Aging in Every Place*, Natl. Housing Conf. (Mar. 2014), http://www.nhc.org/#!2014-aging-in-every-place/f1tk2.

27. *End of Life Care: A Challenge in Terms of Costs and Quality*, in KHN Morning Briefing (June 4, 2013), http://khn.org/morning-breakout/end-of-life-care-17/ (last accessed May 6, 2016).

28. David C. Goodman et al., Trends and Variations in End-of-Life Care for Medicare Beneficiaries for Severe Chronic Illness, Dartmouth Inst. for Health Policy & Clinical Prac. (2011); Joan M. Teno et al., *Change in End-of-Life Care for Medicare Beneficiaries: Site of Death, Place of Care, and Health Care Transitions in 2000, 2005, and 2009*, J. Am. Med. Assn. 309 (5) 470–477 (Feb. 6, 2013), http://jama.jamanetwork.com/article.aspx?articleid=1568250. http://www.dartmouthatlas.org/downloads/reports/EOL_Trend_Report_0411.pdf.

29. Inst. Med. Natl. Acads., Dying in America: Improving Quality and Honoring Individual Preferences Near the End of Life (2014), http://iom.nationalacademies.org/~/media/Files/Report%20Files/2014/EOL/Report%20Brief.pdf; Stephen Brill, *Bitter Pill: Why Medical Bills Are Killing Us*, Time (Apr. 4, 2013), http://time.com/198/bitter-pill-why-medical-bills-are-killing-us; Sarah Kliff,

Steven Brill'teven Brill zine articler-pill-why-medical-bills, WASH. POST: WONKBLOG (Feb. 23, 2013), http://www.washingtonpost.com/blogs/wonkblog/wp/2013/02/23/steven-brills-26000-word-health-care-story-in-one-sentence.

30. THE CONVERSATION PROJECT, http://theconversationproject.org (last visited Feb. 15, 2016); LET'S HAVE DINNER AND TALK ABOUT DEATH, http://deathoverdinner.org (last visited Feb. 15, 2016).

31. ATUL GAWANDE, BEING MORTAL: MEDICINE AND WHAT MATTERS IN THE END (2014); ELISABETH KÜBLER-ROSS, ON DEATH AND DYING (1969).

32. MITCH ALBOM, TUESDAYS WITH MORRIE (1997).

33. For a related analysis of the healthcare debate, see Sydney Watson, *Metaphors, Meaning, and Health Reform*, 54 ST. LOUIS U. L.J. 1313, 1325–1326 (2010): "Americans know that end-of-life care and other costly care are burdening the health care system. . . . The strict father frame has no way to conceptualize government's role except as the harsh disciplinarian and punisher—not the actor one wants making end-of-life decisions for you and your loved ones," 42 U.S.C. 1395KKK (2006, Supp. 4).

34. Medicare Program; Revisions to Payment Policies Under the Physician Fee Schedule and Other Revisions to Part B for CY 2016, 80 Fed. Reg. § 70885 (Nov. 16, 2015) (to be codified at 42 C.F.R. 405, 410–411, 414, 425, 495), https://s3.amazonaws.com/public-inspection.federalregister.gov/2015-28005.pdf

35. Philippe Aries, in *The Hour of Our Death*, traces the historical trajectory of death denying from the ancient to modern world. PHILIPPE ARIES, THE HOUR OF OUR DEATH (Helen Weaver trans.,Vintage Books, 2d ed., 2013) (1981).

36. W. BRADFORD WILCOX ET AL., STRONG FAMILIES, PROSPEROUS STATES, INST. FAM. STUD. (2015), https://www.aei.org/wp-content/uploads/2015/10/IFS-HomeEconReport-2015-FinalWeb.pdf.

37. W. BRADFORD WILCOX ET AL., STRONG FAMILIES, PROSPEROUS STATES, INST. FAM. STUD. (2015), https://www.aei.org/wp-content/uploads/2015/10/IFS-HomeEconReport-2015-FinalWeb.pdf.

38. *Louisiana Data,* NATL. CAMPAIGN TO PREVENT TEEN AND UNPLANNED PREGNANCY https://thenationalcampaign.org/data/state/louisiana (last visited Feb. 15, 2016); Steven Nelson, *Census Bureau Links Poverty With Out-of-Wedlock Births*, U.S. NEWS & WORLD REP. (May 6, 2013), http://www.usnews.com/news/newsgram/articles/2013/05/06/census-bureau-links-poverty-with-out-of-wedlock-births.

39. Judith A. Seltzer & Suzanne M. Bianchi, *Demographic Change and Parent–Child Relationships in Adulthood*, 39 ANN. REV. SOCIOLOGY 275–290 (2013).

40. National Academies of Sciences, Engineering, and Medicine, FAMILIES CARING FOR AN AGING AMERICA (2016) 2–17. "Non-traditional households and complex family structures are far more common than in the past. This change has important implications for family caregiving because adult stepchildren may have weaker feelings of obligation and provide less care to their aging stepparents than their parents (Pew Research Center, 2010; Silverstein and Giarrusso, 2010; van der Pas et al., 2013). Research also shows that divorce negatively impacts the quality of intergenerational relationships between older parents and their adult children and reduces resource transfers from parents to children (Wolf, 2001). Additional

research is needed to fully understand how these trends in family structures affect the care of aging adults (Silverstein and Giarrusso, 2010; van der Pas et al., 2013)."

41. MARILYN COLEMAN & LAWRENCE GANONG, CHANGING FAMILIES, CHANGING RELATIONSHIPS 3 (1999). Page 3 offers a good synopsis of their work:

> For more than two decades, we have worked with and studied divorced and remar-ried families. Among the many things we have noticed is that traditional notions about family roles and obligations are challenged by the complex family structures that are formed following divorce and remarriage. . . . Felt obligations are expecta-tions for appropriate behavior as perceived within the context of specific, personal relationships with kin across the lifecycle. In other words, felt obligations are per-sonal beliefs held by an individual about what he or she should do to assist a spe-cific family member. . . . Filial obligations are defined as perceived obligations and expectations of adult children and elderly parents with regard to various types of services and social support that children should provide for their elders.

42. Lawrence H. Ganong et al., *Patterns of Stepchild–Stepparent Relationship Development*, 73 J. MARR. & FAM. 396, 410 (2011).

43. PAUL TAYLOR, THE NEXT AMERICA: BOOMERS, MILLENNIALS, AND THE LOOMING GENERATIONAL SHOWDOWN (2014); *The Decline of Marriage and Rise of New Families*, PEW RES. CTR. SOC. & DEMOGRAPHIC TRENDS (Nov. 18, 2010), http://www.pewsocialtrends.org/2010/11/18/iv-family.

44. Judith A. Seltzer & Suzanne M. Bianchi, *Demographic Change and Parent–Child Relationships in Adulthood*, 39 ANN. REV. SOCIOLOGY 275 (2013).

45. COLEMAN & GANONG, *supra* note 41.

CHAPTER 2

1. *Selected Long-Term Care Statistics*, FAMILY CAREGIVER ALL. (Jan. 31, 2015), https://www.caregiver.org/selected-long-term-care-statistics.

2. NATL. ALL. FOR CAREGIVING IN COLLABORATION WITH AARP, CAREGIVING IN THE U.S. 2009 5 (2009), http://www.caregiving.org/data/Caregiving_in_the_US_2009_full_report.pdf and National Academies of Sciences, Engineering, and Medicine. FAMILIES CARING FOR AN AGING AMERICA (2016). This report, cited in Chapter 1 as well, offers the most recent recap of research related to family caregiving incidence and prevalence.

3. *Id.* at 21–29.

4. For example, Family and Medical Leave Act of 1993, 29 U.S.C. §§ 2601–54, § 2612(a) (1) (2012); Y. Tony Yang & Gilbert Gimm, *Caring for Elder Parents: A Comparative Evaluation of Family Leave Laws*, 41 J.L. MED. & ETHICS 501 (2013).

5. *See, e.g.,* NINA KOHN, ELDER LAW (2013); Alicia B. Kelly, *Sharing Inequality*, 2013 MICH. ST. L. REV 967, 980 (2013); Christina Lesher et al., *Whose Bill Is It Anyway? Adult Children's Responsibility to Care for Parents*, 6 EST. PLAN. & COMMUNITY PROP. L.J. 247, 278 (2014); Katherine C. Pearson, *Filial Support Laws in the Modern Era: Domestic and International Comparison of Enforcement Practices for Laws Requiring Adult Children to Support Indigent Parents*, 20 ELDER L.J. 269 (2013). In *Health Care & Retirement Corp. of America v. Pittas*, the court applied Pennsylvania's

filial responsibility statute to find a son liable for his mother's medical rehabilitation expenses. No. 536 EDA 2011, 2012 Pa. Super. LEXIS 537 (Pa. Super. Ct. May
7, 2012).

6. *See, e.g.*, Pearson, *supra* note 5.

7. Robert H. Mnookin & Lewis Kornhauser, *Bargaining in the Shadow of the Law: The
   Case of Divorce*, 88 YALE L.J. 950 (1979).

8. Peggie R. Smith, *Elder Care, Gender, and Work: The Work-Family Issue of the 21st
   Century*, 25 BERKELEY J. EMP. & LAB. L. 351, 358 (2004) and National Academies of
   Sciences, Engineering, and Medicine. FAMILIES CARING FOR AN AGING AMERICA
   (2016) Appendix D. "Women are estimated to spend more years caregiving than
   men—on average 6.1 years or nearly 10 percent of their adult life—whereas men are
   estimated to spend on average 4.1 years or just over 7 percent of their adult life."

9. Scholars note that males tend to assist with instrumental activities of daily life, such
   as yard care or transportation, whereas females tend to assist with activities of daily
   living such as bathing or dressing, which are more vulnerable and demand more
   time each day. James N. Laditka & Sarah B. Laditka, *Adult Children Helping Older
   Parents: Variations in Likelihood and Hours by Gender, Race and Family Role*, 23
   RES. ON AGING 429, 430 (2001).

10. Douglas R. White, *Kinship, Class, and Community*, 18 WORLD CULTURES eJOURNAL
    (2011), http://escholarship.org/uc/item/5qb5z783.

11. Anne-Marie Botek, *The State of Caregiving: 2015 Report*, AGINGCARE.COM, https://
    www.agingcare.com/Articles/state-of-caregiving-2015-report-177710.htm (last vis-
    ited Feb. 25, 2015).

12. Tierra Smith, *Planning Ahead for Death? Not Many Do, and They Should*,
    DENVER POST (Aug. 6, 2015), http://www.denverpost.com/business/ci_28592689/
    planning-ahead-death-not-many-do-and-they.

13. This may be "largely inevitable," given that our study examined the caregiving rela-
    tionship "primarily from the perspective of the caregiver." Nina A. Kohn, *The Nasty
    Business of Aging*, 40 LAW & SOC. INQUIRY 506, 507 (2015).

14. The National Center on Elder Abuse offers more information on current federal
    elder justice laws. *Federal Laws*, NATL. CTR. ON ELDER ABUSE, http://www.ncea.
    aoa.gov/Library/Policy/Law/Federal/index.aspx (last visited Feb. 25, 2016).

15. Ron Acierno et al., *Prevalence and Correlates of Emotional, Physical, Sexual, and
    Financial Abuse and Potential Neglect in the United States: The National Elder
    Mistreatment Study*, 100 AM. J. PUB. HEALTH, 292–297 (2010). More reports can be
    accessed at the National Center on Elder Abuse, http://www.ncea.aoa.gov/index.aspx.

16. NATL. CTR. ON ELDER ABUSE, 15 QUESTIONS AND ANSWERS ABOUT ELDER ABUSE
    (2005), http://www.ncea.aoa.gov/Resources/Publication/docs/FINAL%206-06-
    05%203-18-0512-10-04qa.pdf.

17. *Adult/Elderly Protective Services*, LA. DEPT. HEALTH & HOSP., http://dhh.louisiana.
    gov/index.cfm/page/120/n/126 (last visited Feb. 25, 2016).

18. As the federal Administration on Aging reports, "we simply do not know for cer-
    tain how many people are suffering from elder abuse and neglect," APA, Elder
    Abuse (2016), http://www.apa.org/pi/prevent-violence/resources/elder-abuse.aspx.

19. NCEA, Statistics/Data (n.d., last visited June 23, 2016), http://www.ncea.aoa.gov/ Library/Data/index.aspx#challenges.

20. A variety of different regulations and laws deal with different aspects of elder abuse, ranging from state adult protection statutes to domestic violence laws to legal requirements that apply to institutional facilities, such as nursing homes, that serve the elderly.

21. For example, Ariz. Rev. Stat. §§ 46-451-46-459 (2014); Fla. Stat. §§ 415.101-113 (2014). The Older Americans Act, 42 U.S.C. 3001 (2014), sets out definitions of elder abuse and authorizes federal funding for the National Center on Elder Abuse.

    Unlike filial responsibility statutes, they do not impose obligations to care; and, unlike family and medical leave acts or contracts for care, they do not provide support for care. Because they neither require nor support care and because they apply to nonfamily members, we address them only briefly.

22. *See, e.g.*, Nina Kohn, *Housing and Long-Term Care*, in Elder Law: Practice, Policy, and Problems (2013); Daniel L. Madow, Comment, *Why Many Meritorious Elder Abuse Cases Are Not Litigated in California*, 47 U. San. Fran. L. Rev. 619 (2013), http://www.usfca.edu/uploadedFiles/Destinations/School_of_ Law/Academics/Co-Curricular_Programs/(7)SAN47-3Madow.pdf.

23. Cruelty to Persons with Infirmities, La. Stat. Ann. § 14:93.3 (2016).

24. *Statistics/Data*, Natl. Ctr. on Elder Abuse, http://www.ncea.aoa.gov/Library/ Data/index.aspx#problem (last visited Feb. 25, 2016). For discussion of legal aspects of elder abuse, see Nina Kohn, Elder Law: Practice, Policy, & Problems (2013); Nina A. Kohn, *Elder (In)Justice: A Critique of the Criminalization of Elder Abuse*, 49 Am. Crim. L. Rev. 1 (2012); Haya El Nasser, *As USA Grays, Elder Abuse Risk and Need for Shelters Grow*, USA Today (Jan. 10, 2012), http://www.usatoday. com/news/nation/story/2012-01-10/elder-abuse-shelters/52488726/1.

25. Lawrence H. Ganong & Marilyn Coleman, Stepfamily Relationships: Development, Dynamics, and Interventions (2004).

CHAPTER 3

1. We did not formally survey specific demographic data points but drew general observations based on autobiographical information shared in the interview, such as education history and current vocation, and family information published in the obituary, such as date of birth, spouse, and siblings. We also used interviewer observation to draw broad generalizations about income level.

2. For example, 23 Pa. Stat. and Cons. Stat. Ann.. § 4603 (West 2014); Donna Harkness, *What Are Families for? Re-Evaluating Return to Filial Responsibility Laws*, 21 Elder L.J. 305 (2014); Katherine C. Pearson, *Family (Filial) Responsibility/ Support Statutes in the United States* (Mar. 5, 2012), http://law.psu.edu/_file/ Pearson/FilialResponsibilityStatutes.pdf; Katherine C. Pearson, *Filial Support Laws in the Modern Era: Domestic and International Comparison of Enforcement Practices for Laws Requiring Adult Children to Support Indigent Parents*, 20 Elder L.J. 269 (2013).

3. Terrance A. Kline, *A Rational Role for Filial Responsibility Laws in Modern Society*, 26 FAM. L.Q. 195, 196 (1992) (five states never enacted these statutes).

4. *See*, generally, Daniel R. Mandelker, *Family Responsibility Under the American Poor Laws: I*, 54 MICH. L. REV. 497 (1956) (survey of states' filial responsibility laws and their origins).

5. See Seymour Moskowitz, *Filial Responsibility Statutes: Legal and Policy Considerations*, 9 J.L. & POLY. 709, 711 (2001); Allison E. Ross, Note, *Taking Care of Our Caretakers: Using Filial Responsibility Laws to Support the Elderly Beyond the Government's Assistance*, 16 ELDER L.J. 167, 172 (2008).

6. *See* Ross, *supra* note 88, at 173; Moskowitz, *supra* note 88, at 715. The balance between private and public responsibility has assumed center stage in ongoing debates over the deficiencies in the US social safety net, particularly with financial depressions/recessions as a backdrop. *See*, e.g., NANCY J. ALTMAN, THE BATTLE FOR SOCIAL SECURITY: FROM FDR'S VISION TO BUSH'S GAMBLE 29 (2005); Jessica Dixon Weaver, *Grandma in the White House: Legal Support for Intergenerational Caregiving*, 43 SETON HALL L. REV. 1, 74 (2013).

7. See Pearson, *Filial Support Laws in the Modern Era, supra* note 2, at 275.

8. See Moskowitz, *supra* note 5, at 717.

9. *Id.*

10. *See* Pearson, *Filial Support Laws in the Modern Era, supra* note 2, at 275.

11. *Id.* Professor Pearson notes that, at one point, the federal government precluded states from including a child's resources in determining a parent's eligibility for Medicaid and prevented states from requiring children to reimburse the government for Medicaid costs; even though the reimbursement policy has changed; "there has been little appetite in most states' welfare agencies to tie Medicaid to filial support." *Id.* at 288.

12. Louisiana law explicitly provides, "A child regardless of age owes honor and respect to his father and mother." La. Civ. Code Ann. art. 236 (2016). Louisiana also imposes financial obligations as follows:

> Descendants are bound to provide the basic necessities of life to their ascendants who are in need, upon proof of inability to obtain these necessities by other means or from other sources, and ascendants are likewise bound to provide for their needy descendants, this obligation being reciprocal. This obligation is . . . limited to the basic necessities of food, clothing, shelter, and health care.

La. Civ. Code Ann. art. 237 (2016)("Obligation of providing the basic necessities of life; ascendants and descendants; exceptions").

13. La. Civ. Code Ann. art. 238 (2016).

14. *See*, e.g., Sharon Frank Edelstone, *Filial Responsibility: Can the Legal Duty to Support Our Parents Be Effectively Enforced*, 36 FAM. L.Q. 501, 504–507 (2002).

15. *See*, e.g., Swoap v. Super. Ct. of Sacramento Cty., 516 P.3d 840 (Cal. 1973) (upholding California's filial responsibility statute against equal protection claim that the statute unconstitutionally distinguished between individuals based on wealth and ancestry).

16. Health Care & Ret. Corp. of Am. v. Pittas, 46 A.3d 719 (Pa. Super. Ct. 2012), Harkness, *supra* note 2, at 344; Mari Park, Comment, *The Parent Trap:* Health Care & Retirement Corporation of America v. Pittas, *How it Reinforced Filial Responsibility Laws and Whether Filial Responsibility Laws Can Really Make You Pay,* 5 EST. PLAN. & CMTY. PROP. L.J. 441, 446–448 (2013). Northwestern MutualVoice, *Who Will Pay for Mom's Or Dad's Nursing Home Bill? Filial Support Laws And Long-Term Care,* FORBES (Feb. 3, 2014), http://www.forbes.com/sites/northwesternmutual/2014/02/03/who-will-pay-for-moms-or-dads-nursing-home-bill-filial-support-laws-and-long-term-care/; Liz Weston, *Will You Get Dad's Nursing-Home Bill?,* Aug. 20, 2012, http://indigest.biz/2012/07/will-you-get-dads-nursing-home-bill/.

17. 23 Pa. Cons. Stat. § 4603 (2015).

18. *Son Liable for Mom's $93,000 Nursing Home Bill Under 'Filial Responsibility' Law,* WEATHERBY & ASSOCIATES (May 30, 2015), http://www.weatherby-associates.com/blog/estate-planning/2015/05/30/son-liable-for-moms-93000-nursing-home-bill-under-filial-responsibility-law/.

19. R.I. GEN. LAWS ANN. § 15-10-4 (West 2013).

20. *But see* Savoy v. Savoy, 641 A.2d 596 (Pa. Super. 1994) (mother's suit against her son resulted in his financial obligation to pay $125 per month).

21. In re Skinner, 519 B.R 613, 615 (Bankr. E.D. Pa. 2014), *aff'd,* 532 B.R. 599 (E.D. Pa. 2015).

22. Medicaid already enforces a five-year look-back period for Medicaid eligibility. *Medicaid's Asset Transfer Rules,* ELDER LAW ANSWERS (Dec. 3, 2015), http://www.elderlawanswers.com/medicaids-asset-transfer-rules-12015.

23. Brown & Fen, quoted in Brigid Schulte, *Till Death Do Us Part? No Way: The Rise in Gray Divorce,* WASH. POST: SHE THE PEOPLE (Oct. 8, 2014), http://www.washingtonpost.com/blogs/she-the-people/wp/2014/10/08/till-death-do-us-part-no-way-gray-divorce-on-the-rise/?utm_content=buffer0da25&utm_medium=social&utm_source=twitter.com&utm_campaign=buffer. The global rise in "silver separation" will also shape the international costs of elder care. *"Divorce in Twilight" or "Silver Separation" Sees Similar Trend in S. Korea and UK,* KOREA BIZWIRE (Oct. 29, 2014), http://koreabizwire.com/divorce-in-twilight-or-silver-separation-sees-similar-trend-in-s-korea-and-uk/22822.

24. See Maryalene LaPonsie, *7 Things to Know About Divorcing During Your Senior Years,* U.S. NEWS & WORLD REP.: MONEY (Apr. 24, 2015 2:37 p.m.), http://money.usnews.com/money/retirement/articles/2015/04/24/7-things-to-know-about-divorcing-during-your-senior-years; Juliette Fairley, *Easing the Financial Impact of Divorce in Retirement,* FORBES: NEXT AVENUE (Jan. 22, 2016), http://www.forbes.com/sites/nextavenue/2016/01/22/easing-the-financial-impact-of-divorce-in-retirement/#68589a8e5eef; Ben Steverman, *Divorce is Destroying Retirement,* BLOOMBURG NEWS (Oct. 17, 2016).

25. For example, LAWRENCE H. GANONG & MARILYN COLEMAN, STEPFAMILY RELATIONSHIPS: DEVELOPMENT, DYNAMICS, AND INTERVENTIONS (2004).

26. NATL. ALL. FOR CAREGIVING IN COLLABORATION WITH AARP, CAREGIVING IN THE U.S. 2009, 5 (2009), http://www.caregiving.org/data/Caregiving_in_the_US_2009_full_report.pdf.

27. Alejandro Cancino, "Poll Shows Strong Support for Paid Family Leave," (May 20, 2016), http://www.apnorc.org/news-media/Pages/News+Media/Poll-shows-strong-support-for-paid-family-leave-programs.aspx#sthash.6MJv9U5R.dpuf. "The AP-NORC Center for Public Affairs Research survey was conducted Feb. 18 through April 9, with funding from the SCAN Foundation. The nationally representative poll involved landline and cellphone interviews with 1,698 Americans age 40 or older. It has a margin of sampling error of plus or minus 3.4 percentage points."

28. Family and Medical Leave Act 29 U.S.C. § 2611 (2012).

29. *Family and Medical Leave Act*, U.S. Dept. of Labor: Wage & Hour Division, http://www.dol.gov/whd/fmla/ (last visited Feb. 28, 2016). The Labor Department defines a parent as "a biological, adoptive, step or foster father or mother, or any other individual who stood in loco parentis to the employee when the employee was a child. This term does not include parents in law." U.S. Dept. of Labor, Fact Sheet #28F: Qualifying Reasons for Leave under the Family and Medical Leave Act (2015), http://www.dol.gov/whd/regs/compliance/whdfs28f.pdf.

30. Jacob Alex Klerman et al., Family and Medical Leave in 2012: Technical Report 64 (2012, rev. 2014) http://www.dol.gov/asp/evaluation/fmla/FMLA-2012-Technical-Report.pdf.

31. Jacob Alex Klerman et al., Family and Medical Leave in 2012: Technical Report, exh. 4.4.1 (2012, rev. 2014) http://www.dol.gov/asp/evaluation/fmla/FMLA-2012-Technical-Report.pdf; *Brown v. J.C. Penney Corp.*, 924 F. Supp. 1158, 1162 (S.D. Fl. 1996); *see* Debra H. Kroll, *To Care or Not to Care: The Ultimate Decision for Adult Caregivers in a Rapidly Aging Society*, 21 Temp. Pol. & Civ. Rts. L. Rev. 403, 429–432 (2012); John A. Pearce II & Dennis R. Kuhn, *Managers' Obligations to Employees with Eldercare Responsibilities*, 43 U. Rich. L. Rev. 1319, 1334–1335 (2009); Y. Tony Yang & Gilbert Gimm, *Caring for Elderly Parents: A Comparative Evaluation of Family Leave Laws*, 41 J.L. Med. & Ethics 501 (2013).

32. S. Rep. No. 103–3, at 6–7 (1993).

33. *Supra* note 112.

34. 29 U.S.C. § 2611(11) (2012).

35. General information concerning taking FMLA with *in loco parentis* relationships can be found at https://www.dol.gov/whd/regs/compliance/whdfs28b.htm.

36. Jennifer L. Morris, Note, *Explaining the Elderly Feminization of Poverty: An Analysis of Retirement Benefits, Health Care Benefits, and Elder Care-Giving*, 21 Notre Dame J.L. Ethics & Pub. Policy 571, 595 (2007); Katie Wise, Note, *Caring for Our Parents in an Aging World: Sharing Public and Private Responsibility for the Elderly*, 5 N.Y.U. J. Legis. & Pub. Policy 563 (2002).

37. *Supra* note 112 at 104 and 106.

38. There is also the problem of elder abuse of one spouse by another in intact couples. Adult children may have to deal with this issue, too, possibly by arranging for their parents to live apart. See Betsy J. Abramson, *Wisconsin's Individual-at-Risk Restraining Order: An Analysis of the First Two Years*, 18 Elder L.J. 247, 250 (2011).

We did not ask explicitly about abuse. We analyzed the narratives for descriptions of abuse that they may not have labeled as such, and did not find any. These interviews were also voluntary. We can imagine that there were occurrences of abuse in the 1500 invited to be interviewed, but, of the 63 who came and talked for two hours, there were no reports of abuse. This was a qualitative study and not a quantitative one, so a lack of some data is a downside.

39. Parents legally remain parents until their rights are terminated. Thus, for example, regardless of their behavior, parents are legally entitled to inherit from their children. Nonetheless, in partial recognition that the quality of parenting should impact parents' expectations from their children, some states, and the UNIFORM PROBATE CODE, provide that parents whose rights could have been terminated will not be able to inherit. Unif. Probate Code § 2-114 (amended 2010); Carla Spivack, *Let's Get Serious: Spousal Abuse Should Bar Inheritance*, 90 OR. L. REV. 247, 302 (2011).

40. For a further discussion of caregiver coping mechanisms, *see* Mona DeKoven Fishbane, *"Honor Your Father and Your Mother": Intergenerational Values and Jewish Tradition*, in SPIRITUAL RESOURCES IN FAMILY THERAPY 136, 152 (Froma Walsh ed., 1999).

41. Gilbert Meilaender reflects on the ordering of loves from the universal to the particular and from the particular to the universal as implied in the Honor Commandment in *Love, Particular and Universal*, MOSAIC (Jun. 17, 2013) [response to Leon R. Kass, *The Ten Commandments: Why the Decalogue Matters*, MOSAIC (Jun. 1, 2013)], http://mosaicmagazine.com/essay/2013/06/the-ten-commandments/.

CHAPTER 4

1. For example, Cruzan v. Dir., Mo. Dept. of Health, 497 U.S. 261, 269 (1990).

2. LAWRENCE A. FROLIK & RICHARD L. KAPLAN, ELDER LAW IN A NUTSHELL 18 (6th ed., 2014).

3. See Jennifer W. Mack et al., *End-of-Life Discussions, Goal Attainment, and Distress at the End of Life: Predictors and Outcomes of Receipt of Care Consistent with Preferences*, 28 J. CLIN. ONCOLOGY 1203 (2010).

4. See Anthony L. Back et al., *When Praise Is Worth Considering in a Difficult Conversation*, 376 LANCET 866–867 (2010); Karen E. Steinhauser et al., *Factors Considered Important at the EOL by Patients, Family, Physicians, and Other Care Providers*, 284 J. AM. MED. ASSN. 2476, 2476–2482 (2000); Karen E. Steinhauser et al., *In Search of a Good Death: Observations of Patients, Families, and Providers*, 132 ANNALS INTERNAL MED. 825 (2000).

5. *See* J. Andrew Billings, *The Need for Safeguards in Advance Care Planning*, 27 J. GEN. INTERNAL MED. 595 (2012); Karen M. Detering et al., *The Impact of Advance Care Planning on End of Life Care in Elderly Patients: Randomised Controlled Trial*, 340 BRIT. MED. J. 1345 (2010).

6. *Advance Care Planning: Knowing Your Wishes Are Known and Honored if You Are Unable to Speak for Yourself*, CENTERS FOR DISEASE CONTROL AND PREVENTION, http://www.cdc.gov/aging/pdf/advanced-care-planning-critical-issue-brief.pdf (2012).

7. See Maria J. Silveira, Wyndy Wlitala, & John Piette, *Advance Medical Directive Completion by Elderly Americans: A Decade of Change*, 62 J. AM. GERIATRIC SOC. 706 (2014).

8. Cruzan v. Dir., Mo. Dept. of Health, 497 U.S. 261 (1990); Judith D. Moran, *Families, Courts, and the End of Life:* Schiavo *and Its Implications for the Family Justice System*, 46 FAM. CT. REV. 297, 301 (2008).

9. Bush v. Schiavo, 885 So. 2d 321 (Fla. 2004); Schiavo ex rel. Schindler v. Schiavo, 357 F. Supp. 2d 1378, 1382–84 (M.D. Fla. 2005); Lois Shepherd, *The End of End-of-Life Law*, 92 N.C. L. REV. 1693, 1710 (2014).

10. *See* 42 U.S.C.A. §§ 1395cc(a)(1)(q),-mm(c)(8),-(f) (2012); 42 U.S.C.A. §§ 1396a(a) (57)-(58),-(w)(2012). All hospitals that participate in Medicare or Medicaid must document information about patients' advance directives. *See* 42 U.S.C.A. § 1396a (2016).

11. LA. REV. STAT. ANN. § 40:1299.58.3 (2015).

12. LAWRENCE A. FROLIK & MELISSA C. BROWN, ADVISING THE ELDERLY OR DISABLED CLIENT, ¶ 23.07 (2d ed. 2012).

13. *See* 45 C.F.R. § 164.510 (2013). For more information and a sample HIPAA release form, *see How Can I Get a Free* HIPAA *Release Form?*, CARING.COM, http://www. caring.com/questions/hipaa-release-form (last updated May 12, 2015).

14. *See For Patients and Families,* PHYSICIAN ORDERS FOR LIFE-SUSTAINING TREATMENT PARADIGM (2012–2015), http://www.polst.org/advance-care-planning/.

15. *See History,* PHYSICIAN ORDERS FOR LIFE-SUSTAINING TREATMENT PARADIGM (2012–2015), http://www.polst.org/about-the-national-polst-paradigm/history/.

16. *See* Susan E. Hickman et al., *A Comparison of Methods to Communicate Treatment Preferences in Nursing Facilities: Traditional Practices Versus the Physician Orders for Life-Sustaining Treatment Program*, 58 J. AM. GERIATRICS SOC. 1241 (2010); Paula Span, *The Trouble with Advance Directives*, N.Y. TIMES (Mar. 13, 2015), http://www.nytimes.com/2015/03/17/health/the-trouble-with-advance-directives.html?_r=0. *See also* Jessica Nutik Zitter, *The Right Paperwork for Your End-of-Life Wishes*, N.Y. TIMES: OPINIONATOR (Apr. 29, 2015, 9:30 a.m.), http://opinionator.blogs.nytimes.com/2015/04/29/the-right-paperwork-for-your-end-of-life-wishes/?emc=edit_tnt_20150430&nlid=6440 0928&tntemail0=y&_r=0 (explaining how an advance directive is a conversation starter for laypeople whereas a POLST form becomes an enforceable physician's order).

17. H. R. 1485, Reg. Sess. (La. 2010); LA. STAT. ANN. § 40:1155.1 (2016); *see* Jenica Cassidy, *A Brief Survey of State POLST Form Distribution Practices*, 34 BIFOCAL 132, 133 (2013).

18. Catherine Seal, *Power of Attorney: Convenient Contract or Dangerous Document?*, 11 MARQ. ELDER'S ADVISOR 307 (2010).

CHAPTER 5

1. Of 306 participants, 77 (25%) had a durable power of attorney, and 45 (14%) had a living will. Of these, 226 (75%) responded that it was important to make healthcare decisions known to their doctor. Only 36 (15%) had done so. See John M. Clements, *Patient Perceptions on the Use of Advance Directives and Life Prolonging Technology*, 26 AM. J. HOSPICE & PALLIATIVE CARE 270 (2009).

2. *See* Alexia M. Torke et al., *Scope and Outcomes of Surrogate Decision Making Among Hospitalized Older Adults*, 174 J. Am. Med. Assn. Internal Med. 370, 375 (2014), http://archinte.jamanetwork.com/article.aspx?articleid=1813222.

3. L.A. Rev. Stat. Ann. § 40:1299.53 (2015).

4. L.A. Rev. Stat. Ann. § 40:1299.53(C) (2015).

5. *See* Shana Wynn, *Decisions by Surrogates: An Overview of Surrogate Consent Laws in the United States*, 36 Bifocal 10, 13 (2014). For a guide, *see Making Medical Decision for Someone Else: A How-To Guide*, The American Bar Association on Law and Aging (2009), http://www.americanbar.org/content/dam/aba/administrative/law_aging/2011/2011_aging_bk_proxy_guide_gen.authcheckdam.pdf.

6. Louisiana offers two end-of- life registries for wills and living wills. *See End of Life Registries*, Louisiana Secretary of State (2016), http://www.sos.la.gov/OurOffice/EndOfLifeRegistries/Pages/default.aspx. The Louisiana Declaration can be completed and comes into effect once an irreversible condition has been diagnosed as terminal, unless the individual has explicitly written his or her wishes should the irreversible condition not be terminal. *See Louisiana Advance Directive Planning for Important Healthcare Decisions*, CaringInfo (2015), http://www.caringinfo.org/files/public/ad/Louisiana.pdf.

7. *See* Wynn, *supra* note 11.

8. Lawrence A. Frolik & Linda S. Whitton, *The UPC Substituted Judgment/Best Interest Standard for Guardian Decisions: A Proposal for Reform*, 45 U. Mich. J.L. Reform 739 (2012); Nina A. Kohn & Jeremy A. Blumenthal, *Designating Health Care Decision-Makers for Patients Without Advance Directives: A Psychological Critique*, 42 Ga. L. Rev. 979, 986–987 (2008).

9. For example, N.Y. Pub. Health § 2982(2) (2015). ["After consultation with a licensed physician, the agent shall make health care decisions: (a) in accordance with the principal's wishes, including the principal's religious and moral beliefs."] The Uniform-Health Care Decisions Act requires that the surrogate consider the principal's "personal values." *See* Unif. Health Care Decisions Act § 5(f). Guardianship law may require similar considerations. *See, e.g.,* Minn. Stat. Ann. § 524.5–313 (2015). ("The guardian shall not consent to any medical care for the ward which violates the known conscientious, religious, or moral belief of the ward.")

10. Vanessa Raymont et al., *Prevalence of Mental Incapacity in Medical Inpatients and Associated Risk Factors: Cross-Sectional Study*, 364 Lancet 1421 (2004).

11. Sendal Mulainathan & Eldar Shafir, Scarcity: The New Science of Having Less and How It Defines Our Lives (2014).

12. Nina A. Kohn, The Nasty Business of Aging, 40 Law & Soc. Inquiry 506, 507 (2015). Kohn notes concerning Henrik Hartog's work (see Chapter 2, note 13) on inheritance that "One limitation of the study's ability to describe the bargains struck between older adults and caregivers, however, is that it examines the bargains primarily from the perspective of the caregiver. This is largely inevitable as most of the cases analyzed involve court disputes that arose after the death of the older adult ... The narrative's sympathetic attitude toward caregivers colors the

interpretation of the cases." Our study also does not include the perspectives of the deceased and those interviewed may have false confidence in their ability to interpret the wishes of their loved one and our attitude toward those interviewed may be sympathetic.

CHAPTER 6

1. Sidney Zisook & Katherine Shear, *Grief and Bereavement: What Psychiatrists Need to Know*, 8 WORLD PSYCH. 67 (2009), http://www.ncbi.nlm.nih.gov/pmc/articles/PMC2691160/.
2. *Id.* at 17.
3. *Id.; see also* M. Katherine Shear, *Complicated Grief Treatment: The Theory, Practice and Outcomes*, 29 BEREAVEMENT CARE 10 (2010), http://www.ncbi.nlm.nih.gov/pmc/articles/PMC3156458/; Julie Loebach Wetherell, *Complicated Grief Therapy as a New Treatment Approach*, 14 DIALOGUES CLIN. NEUROSCI. 159 (2012). http://www.ncbi.nlm.nih.gov/pmc/articles/PMC3384444/.
4. The Hospice Medicare Benefit provides support to the majority of mourners who experience normal grief by requiring hospice organizations to provide a minimum of twelve months of bereavement support to families of deceased patients. Hospice professionals typically aim to support mourners in a threefold approach: one, providing education about the grief process; two, offering access to support groups where stories about the deceased loved one as well as the experience of grief can be shared; and, three, offering access to mental health experts who can provide one-on-one counseling to triage any crises. "Bereavement counseling consists of counseling services provided to the individual's family before and after the individual's death. Bereavement counseling is a required hospice service, provided for a period up to 1 year following the patients' death. It is not separately reimbursable." Pub. 100–07, State Operations Manual, Appendix M, 42 CFR 418.64(d)(1), L596.
5. *See also* Mayo Clinic, *Complicated Grief*, http://www.mayoclinic.org/diseases-conditions/complicated-grief/basics/definition/con-20032765. In the years leading up to the publishing of the Major Depression entry in the *Diagnostic and Statistical Manual of Mental Disorders*, 5th ed. (DSM-5) in 2013, much controversy ensued in the bereavement community when it was announced that the "bereavement exclusion" would be removed from the diagnosis of depression with many in the hospice and social work world worried that this decision would treat grief as an illness. *Extending the Bereavement Exclusion for Major Depression to Other Losses Evidence From the National Comorbidity Survey*, 64 ARCH. GEN. PSYCHIATRY, 433–440 (2007). Clinicians stressed that trained therapists could best discern the differences between grief and depression.
6. Linda Reynolds & Derek Botha, *Anticipatory Grief: Its Nature, Impact, and Reasons for Contradictory Findings*, 2 COUNSELING, PSYCHOTHERAPY, AND HEALTH 15 (2006).
7. *Bereavement*, PSYCH. TODAY (2015), https://www.psychologytoday.com/conditions/bereavement; Zisook & Shear, *supra* note 1, (bereavement "refer[s] to the fact of the loss"). For a history of bereavement studies *see* Margaret S. Stroebe, Wolfgang

Stroebe & Robert O. Hansson, *Bereavement Research: An Historical Introduction,* 44 J. Soc. Issues 1 (1988).

8. George A. Bonanno, The Other Side of Sadness: What the New Science of Bereavement Tells Us About Life After Loss (2009); George Bonanno, *Loss, Trauma, and Human Resilience,* 59 Am. Psych. 20 (2004). Bonanno is a pioneer in bereavement research and resilience studies.

9. James William Worden, Grief Counseling and Grief Therapy, A Handbook for the Mental Health Practitioner 39 (4th ed., 2009).

10. The descriptions of these four tasks are drawn from *id.* at 37–56. He calls these tasks "grief work." *Id.* at 39.

11. Elisabeth Kübler-Ross, On Death and Dying (1969).

12. Elisabeth Kübler-Ross & David Kessler, On Grief and Grieving: Finding the Meaning of Grief Through the Five Stages of Loss (2005).

13. Paul K. Maciejewski, Baohui Zhang, Susan D. Block & Holly G. Prigerson, *An Empirical Examination of the Stage Theory of Grief,* 297 J. Am. Med. Assn. 716 (2007).

14. John Bowlby, Attachment and Loss: Vol. 3: Loss, Sadness and Depression (2001); Colin Parkes, Bereavement: Studies in Grief in Adults Life (3rd ed. 2001); Catherine M. Sanders Grief: The Mourning After: Dealing with Adult Bereavement (1989).

15. Worden cites the grief work of Sigmund Freud, Mourning and Melancholia: The Standard Edition of the Complete Works of Sigmund Freud 237–260 (Vol. 14., J. Stachey ed. and trans. 1917).

16. *Id.* at 38–39.

17. *See, e.g.,* Derek Thompson, *The Secret Life of Grief,* The Atlantic (Dec. 3, 2013), http://www.theatlantic.com/health/archive/2013/12/the-secret-life-of-grief/ 281992/.

18. Worden, *supra* note 157 at 91.

19. MercyMe, *I Can Only Imagine* (2001),https://en.wikipedia.org/wiki/I_Can_Only_ Imagine_(MercyMe_song).

20. Jette Marcussen, Frode Thuen, Poul Bruun & Lise Hounsgaard, *Parental Divorce and Parental Death—An Integrative Systematic Review of Children's Double Bereavement,* 3 Clin. Nursing Stud. (2015) (reviewing literature related to "double bereavement" of children and adolescents who experience the divorce and death of a parent and concluding that additional professional support is critical for these young people); *see* Elizabeth Marquardt, Between Two Worlds (2005)(Chapter 5, "Early Moral Forgers" and Chapter 7, "Child Size Souls," describe the coping skills of children of divorce). Marquardt does not address parent loss to death, but was involved in developing the *Homeward Bound* study as a follow-up on these previous insights. For further information on coping after divorce, see Elizabeth Krumrei, Annette Mahoney & Kenneth Pargament, *Spiritual Stress and Coping Model of Divorce: A Longitudinal Study.* 25 J. Fam. Psych. 973 (2011).

21. Joan Didion, The Year of Magical Thinking 198 (2005).

22. This quote was recited by the interviewee during the interview and taken from the transcript. The quote can be found in *The Complete Works of Ralph Waldo Emerson: Essays*, 1st series [Vol. 2] (2006).

23. Allison Kirkman, *Cemeteries and Age, in* Routledge Handbook of Cultural Gerontology 463, 465–466 (Julia Twigg & Wendy Martin eds. 2015).

24. Carole Brody Fleet, *A "Grave" Situation,* Huffington Post (Nov. 10, 2012), http://www.huffingtonpost.com/carole-brody-fleet/grief_b_1860284.html

CHAPTER 7

1. La. Rev. Stat. Ann. §§ 37:876–877 (2015).

2. We purposely choose the word "mourning" instead of "grief" to privilege the ways that family structure intersects with the public nature of acknowledging a death over the internalized and personal nature of grief.

3. Thomas G. Long & Thomas Lynch, The Good Funeral: Death, Grief, and the Community of Care 237 (2013).

4. *Death Certificates,* Louisiana State Board of Medical Examiners, http://www.lsbme.la.gov/licensure/physicians/death-certificates (last updated 2014).

5. See La. Rev. Stat. Ann. § 13:5713 (2016); *Death Investigation,* East Baton Rouge Parish Coroner's Office, http://ebrcoroner.com/death-investigation (last updated 2013).

6. See LA. Rev. Stat. § 40:41 (2016); *State Registrar & Vital Records: How to Order Death Records,* State of Louisiana Department of Health & Hospitals, http://www.dhh.state.la.us/index.cfm/page/640 (last visited Feb. 15, 2016). ["You may obtain a certified copy of a death certificate if you are the surviving spouse of the person named on the document, parent of the person named on the document, adult child of the person named on the document, sibling of the person named on the document, grandparent of the person named on the document, or an adult grandchild of the person named on the document, or the beneficiary of an insurance policy of the person named on the document (unless otherwise authorized by LA R.S. 40:41)."]

7. *U.S. Standard Certificate of Death,* Centers for Disease Control and Prevention, http://www.cdc.gov/nchs/data/dvs/death11-03final-acc.pdf (last modified Nov. 2003).

8. Marilyn Johnson, The Dead Beat: Lost Souls, Lucky Stiffs, and the Perverse Pleasures of Obituaries 29–41 (2007). (Chapter 3 chronicles the evolution of the standard obituary form from the opening phrase that begins the obituary to the date and location of death and list of survivors.)

9. Janice Hume, Obituaries in Modern Culture 152 (2006).

10. *Id.* at 16.

11. *Id.* at 12.

12. *See* James W. Green, Beyond the Good Death: The Anthropology of Modern Dying 161 (2008).

13. For example, in the Baton Rouge *Advocate,* where all obituaries or death notices appeared for our study, death notices at ten lines or fewer are free whereas obituaries costs $2.40 per line with additional costs for photos. *See Obituaries and Death*

Notice Pricing, The Advocate: Place an Obituary, http://placeads.theadvocate. com/advocate-adportal/obits/static/pricing.html (last updated 2014).

14. *See* Johnson, *supra* note 8, at 16–29. (In modern times, obituary templates are available online for laypeople as well as funeral directors at sites such as http:// www.funeralhomedirectory.com/article/obituary-examples or EverPlans, https:// www.everplans.com/articles/death-notice-templates-and-obituary-templates.).

15. Long & Lynch, *supra* note 3, at 119.

16. *See id.* at 194.

17. *Id.* at 156. (Drawing on their long experience of conducting funerals to echo this observation that "presence—the showing up, the being there—is very often all we can do. Often as not, it is enough.")

18. Macrina Cooper-White, *Cremation Is More Popular Than Ever, and Here's Why*, Huffington Post (Aug. 13, 2014, 8:47 a.m.), http://www.huffingtonpost.com/ 2014/08/13/cremation-on-the-rise-infographic_n_5669195.html.

19. *See Statistics*, Natl. Funeral Directors Assn., http://mediad.publicbroadcast-ing.net/p/healthnewsfl/files/201507/03-a_2014_cremation_and_burial_report__ 2_.pdf (last visited July 27, 2015). The Methodology on page four of the report reports that the 6% not accounted for in these statistics reflect other methods of disposition, such as donation, entombment, or removal from the state.

20. *Id.* at 2.

21. David Foos, *State Ready-to-Embalm Laws and the Modern Funeral Market: The Need for Change and Suggested Alternatives*, Mich. St. L. Rev. 1375, 1387 (2012); Tanya D. Marsh, *Rethinking the Law of the Dead*, 48 Wake Forest L. Rev. 1327, 1343 (2013).

22. *See* L.A. Rev. Stat. § 37:876 (2011).

23. *See* Cooper-White, *supra* note 18.

24. Of the fourteen cremations detailed in our study, four were buried, two were scattered, five were kept, one was unknown, and two families split the parent's ashes, keeping some and scattering some.

25. Long & Lynch, *supra* note 3 at 224.

CHAPTER 8

1. *See*, generally, Hendrik Hartog, Someday All This Will Be Yours: A History of Inheritance and Old Age (2012) (exploring nineteenth-century American inheritance disputes).

2. The law has comparatively little impact unless anyone actually goes to court. Consider what happened to Don McNay, a sophistical financial planner when his mother died. He arranged the disposition of his mother's house with his sister without formal agreement; it was only when his sister died and the husband whom she'd never divorced entered the picture that the law became directly involved. See Don McNay, *My Story*, Huffington Post: Blog (Aug. 17, 2011, 10:54 a.m.), http://www.huffingtonpost.com/don-mcnay/why-people-need-wills_ b_928921.html; David Horton, *Wills Law on the Ground*, 62 UCLA L. Rev. 1094, 1126 (2015). Studies of probate court have found relatively little litigation. Horton writes, "Previous studies of probate court found lawsuits in about 1 to 3 percent

of all estate administrations. That statistic may not seem alarming, but because 'there are millions of probates per year, one-in-a-hundred litigation patterns are very serious.' Gauged by that yardstick, my results were extraordinary: I discovered lawsuits in seventy estates (12 percent). One reason for this apparent sharp increase has nothing to do with legal or societal trends. Instead, it is that prior researchers defined "litigation" as a single cause of action: disputes over the validity of a testamentary instrument. I unearthed sixteen such will contests (5 percent). Yet as Table 3 elucidates, these cases were just a corner of the larger canvass. There were also twenty-two objections to the appointment or service of the personal representative, eighteen breach of fiduciary duty claims, nine contested heirship petitions, six efforts to recover property held by a third party, and three interpretation issues. Thus, conflict in probate appears to be far more frequent than we think." *See also* Heather K. Way, *Informal Homeownership in the United States and the Law*, 29 St. Louis U. Pub. L. Rev. 113 (2009).

3. Seven respondents explicitly mentioned the existence of a will. Eleven respondents explicitly mention that their parent or stepparent died intestate. The remaining forty-four respondents did not mention the presence or absence of a will, but settled the estate without the guidance or conflict that the presence or absence of a formal will might provide.

4. For listings of various reasons, *see, e.g.*, Heleigh Bostwick, *Don't Have a Will? 10 Common But Misguided Excuses*, LegalZoom (May 2011), http://www.legal-zoom.com/planning-your-estate/estate-planning-basics/dont-have-will-10; Richard Eienberg, *Americans' Ostrich Approach to Estate Planning*, Forbes (Apr. 9, 2014), http://www.forbes.com/sites/nextavenue/2014/04/09/americans-ostrich-approach-to-estate-planning/#7e48e7c1f07b; Reid Kress Weisbord, *Wills for Everyone: Helping Individuals Opt Out of Intestacy*, 53 B.C. L. Rev. 877 (2012).

5. In the analogous context of end-of-life planning, patients who indicated a preference for the type of life-sustaining treatment they preferred appear likely to have their wishes carried out. *See* Erik K. Frommer et al., *Association Between Physician Orders for Life-Sustaining Treatment for Scope of Treatment and In-Hospital Death in Oregon*, 62 J. Am. Geriatrics Soc. 1246 (2014).

6. This portrait, based on the *Homeward Bound* study, mirrors national statistics on the most valuable nonfinancial assets held by American households. Although the most common nonfinancial asset is a car, the most valuable such asset is a house. *See Changes in U.S. Family Finances from 2007 to 2010: Evidence from the Survey of Consumer Finances*, Fed. Res., http://www.federalreserve.gov/pubs/bulletin/2012/articles/scf/scf.htm (last updated June 22, 2012). *See*, generally, *A Quick Look at U.S. Households and Their Assets*, Urban Inst. (Dec. 9 2008), http://www.urban.org/UploadedPDF/901202_household_assets.pdf.

Among *Homeward Bound* study participants, 20% of widowed parents inherited and lived in the house a year after the death, 14% of widowed stepparents lived in the house at that point, although ongoing conflict surrounded use and ownership of those homes, and none of the widowed significant others inherited or continued to live the house, even though all were cohabiting prior to the death. Collection of

Interviews conducted by Elizabeth Marquardt & Amy Ziettlow, in Baton Rouge, LA (Oct. 12, 2011–Mar. 12, 2012) (on file with authors).

7. *Id.* Several of the deceased family members used the life insurance policy as a quick loan system or savings account. *Id.* Somewhat ironically, one respondent's family borrowed against the policy only to pay for other family burials.

8. See Susan Gary, Jerome Borison, Naomi Cahn & Paula Monopoli, Contemporary Approaches to Trusts and Estates 1–20 (2nd ed. 2014).

9. La. Civ. Code Ann. art. 1493 (2015).

10. *Id.*

11. Reliable estimates on the number of Americans who die intestate are virtually impossible to develop and would require interviews with family members of each decedent. Even probate records would distort the rate by overstating the number of people who died testate; a probate record is not opened for everyone who dies and, logically, is more likely when there is a will to administer. *See, generally*, Reid Kress Weisbord, *The Connection Between Unintentional Intestacy and Urban Poverty*, Rutgers L. Rev. Comments 1 (2012), http://www.rutgerslawreview.com/wp-content/uploads/archive/commentaries/2012/Weisbord_TheConnectionBetweenUnintentionalIntestacyAndUrbanPoverty.pdf (analyzing some of the problems in measuring rates of intestacy).

12. A.L. Kennedy, *Statistics on Last Wills and Testaments*, LegalZoom, http://info.legalzoom.com/statistics-last-wills-testaments-3947.html (last visited Feb. 15, 2016).

13. See La. Civ. Code Ann. art. 1499 (2015).

14. See La. Civ. Code Ann. art. 890 (2015).

15. *See, e.g.*, David Horton, *In Partial Defense of Probate: Evidence from Alameda County, California*, 103 Geo. L.J. 605 (2015).

16. La. Civ. Code Ann. art. 1575 (2015) ("Olographic testament. A. An olographic testament is one entirely written, dated, and signed in the handwriting of the testator. Although the date may appear anywhere in the testament, the testator must sign the testament at the end of the testament. If anything is written by the testator after his signature, the testament shall not be invalid and such writing may be considered by the court, in its discretion, as part of the testament. The olographic testament is subject to no other requirement as to form. The date is sufficiently indicated if the day, month, and year are reasonably ascertainable from information in the testament, as clarified by extrinsic evidence, if necessary. B. Additions and deletions on the testament may be given effect only if made by the hand of the testator.")

17. *See* Deborah S. Gordon, *Reflecting on the Language of Death*, 34 Seattle U. L. Rev. 379, 410–411 (2011); Ashbel G. Gulliver & Catherine J. Tilson, *Classification of Gratuitous Transfer*, 51 Yale L.J. 1, 5 (1941); John H. Langbein, *Substantial Compliance With the Wills Act*, 88 Harv. L. Rev. 489, 492 (1975).

18. *See* Alyssa DiRusso, *He Says, She Asks: Gender, Language, and the Law of Precatory Words in Wills*, Wis. Women's L.J. 22, 8–20 (2007); Daphna Hacker, *Soulless Wills*, 35 Law & Socy. Inquiry 957, 980–981 (2010) (suggesting the need to include more personal emotions in wills).

19. *See* DiRusso, *He Says, She Asks, supra* note 18; Dawn Watkins, *The (Literal) Death of the Author and the Silencing of the Testator's Voice*, 24 LAW & LITERATURE 59, 65–66 (2012).

20. *See* Courtney G. Joslin, *Marriage, Biology, and Federal Benefits*, 98 IOWA L. REV. 1467, 1495–1496 (2013) (discussing legal aspects of the stepparent–stepchild relationship); *see also* Terin Barbas Cremer, *Reforming Intestate Inheritance for Stepchildren and Stepparents*, 18 CARD. 020 J.L. & GENDER 89, 89–108 (2011) (discussing inheritance rights in stepfamilies).

21. *See* Claire M. Noël-Miller, *Former Stepparents' Contact with Their Stepchildren After Midlife*, 68 J. GERONTOLOGY 409, 410 (2013).

22. For example, R. B. Samuels, *Should I Forgive Him for the Outside Child?*, JAMAICA OBSERVER (Apr. 28, 2008), http://www.jamaicaobserver.com/magazines/all-woman/135012_Should--I-forgive-him-for-the-outside-child-. Kingston's newspaper, the *Jamaica Observer*, frequently includes questions about "outside children" in advice columns. *See id.*; Donna Hussey-Whyte, *Should the Man Tell His Wife About the Outside Children?*, Oct. 24, 2011, http://www.jamaicaobserver.com/magazines/allwoman/Should-the-man-tell-his-wife-about-the-outside-children-_9962185; *see also* Kathryn Edin et al., *A Peek Inside the Black Box: What Marriage Means for Poor Unmarried Parents*, 66 J. MARRIAGE & FAM. 1007, 1012 (2004) (referencing the use of "outside child" in non-Caribbean culture); *Outside Child*, URB. DICTIONARY (May 21, 2013), http://www.urbandictionary.com/define.php?term=outside%20 child.

23. For example, Robert B. Mincy & Hillard Pouncy, *Baby Fathers and American Family Formation: Low-Income, Never Married Parents in Louisiana Before Katrina*, CTR. FOR MARRIAGE & FAM., https://docs.google.com/viewer?url=http://americanvalues.org/catalog/pdfs/babyfathers.pdf (last visited Nov. 10, 2014).

24. *See* Lalli v. Lalli, 439 U.S. 259 (1978); Trimble v. Gordon, 430 U.S. 762 (1977); Levy v. Louisiana, 391 U.S. 68 (1968) (recognizing that Louisiana was one of the last states to recognize the equal rights of nonmarital children); Succession of Brown, 388 So. 2d 1151 (La 1980) (finding unconstitutional a Louisiana statute that distinguished between the inheritance rights of marital and nonmarital children). See also Paula Monopoli, *Toward Equality: Nonmarital Children and the Uniform Code*, 45 U. MICH. J.L. REFORM 995, 998 (2012).

25. *See* Edin et al., *supra* note 22, at 1013. The existence of a term for an "outside" child implies that an "inside" child also exists. *Id.*

26. For her to be legally entitled to inherit, she needed formal legal recognition as his child, a step he had never taken. See LA. CIV. CODE ANN. art 196 (2013).

27. *See, e.g., Life Insurance Change of Beneficiary*, METLIFE, http://eforms.metlife.com/wcm8/PDFFiles/31163.pdf (last visited Nov. 10, 2014).

CHAPTER 9

1. Rocket Lawyer, which encourages legal planning, found that most people simply "hadn't gotten around" to making a will, although it did not ask why. See *Rocket Lawyer Delivers No Excuses Estate Planning for April "Make-a-Will" Month*,

Rocket Law. (Apr. 8, 2014), https://www.rocketlawyer.com/news/article-Make-a-Will-Month-2014.aspx.

2. *See, e.g.,* Maria J. Silveira et al., *Advance Directive Completion by Elderly Americans: A Decade of Change,* 62 J. Am. Geriatrics Soc. 706 (2014); Rebecca L. Sudore & Terri Fried, *Redefining the "Planning" in Advance Care Planning: Preparing for End-of-Life Decision Making,* 153 Annals Internal Med. 256 (2010); Alexia M Torque et al., *Scope and Outcomes of Surrogate Decision Making Among Hospitalized Older Adults,* 174 J. Am. Med. Assn. 370 (2014).

3. For example, Dan K. Morhaim & Keshia M. Pollack, *End-of-Life Care Issues: A Personal, Economic, Public Policy, and Public Health Crisis,* 103 Am. J. Pub. Health e8 (2013); Paula Span, *Why Do We Avoid Advance Directives?,* N.Y. Times (Apr. 20, 2009, 9:00 a.m.), http://newoldage.blogs.nytimes.com/2009/04/20/why-do-we-avoid-advance-directives/?_php=true&_type=blogs&_r=1.

4. Inst. of Med., Dying in America: Improving Quality and Honoring Individual Preferences Near the End of Life 3–52 (2014) (you will find Chapter 3 especially helpful in analyzing the intricacies of surrogate decision-making at the end of life. Table 3-3 on p. 3–26 offers a "Summary of Patient and Family Factors in End-of-Life Decision-Making among Individuals of Different Races, Ethnicities, and Cultures," but does not include changes in family structure.)

5. Popular films can also help highlight the importance of planning ahead, especially in the light of new family structures. See, e.g., Sony Picture Classics, Amour (2014), http://www.sonyclassics.com/amour/; IMDb, Beginners, http://www.imbd.com/title/ttl1532503/ (last visited Feb. 21, 2016) (about GEN X caregiving).

6. *See* David Horton, *Testation and Speech,* 101 Geo. L.J. 161 (2012).

7. *See* Lawrence M. Friedman, A History of American Law 181 (3d ed. 2005).

8. *See* Deborah S. Gordon, *Reflecting on the Language of Death,* 34 Seattle L. Rev. 379, 384 (2011) ("Contrary to expectations, the case law supports the idea that directly infusing wills with individualized, expressive, and what some might call 'extra' language better insulates them against challenges.")

9. *See, e.g.,* Ashbel G. Gulliver & Catherine J. Tilson, *Classification of Gratuitous Transfers,* 51 Yale L.J. 1, 3 (1941); John H. Langbein, *Substantial Compliance with the Wills Act,* 88 Harv. L. Rev. 489 (1975); Karen J. Sneddon, *The Will as Personal Narrative,* 20 Elder L.J. 355, 410 (2013).

10. *See, e.g.,* Silveira et al., *supra* note 2, at 706; Sudore & Fried, *supra* note 2, at 153; Torque et al., *supra* note 2, at 174.

11. For example, Dan K. Morhaim & Keshia M. Pollack, *End-of-Life Care Issues: A Personal, Economic, Public Policy, and Public Health Crisis,* 103 Am. J. Pub. Health e8 (2013); Paula Span, *Why Do We Avoid Advance Directives?,* N.Y. Times (Apr. 20, 2009, 9:00 a.m.), http://newoldage.blogs.nytimes.com/2009/04/20/why-do-we-avoid-advance-directives/?_php=true&_type=blogs&_r=1.

12. *See* Inst. of Med., *supra* note 5.

13. *See* Reid K. Weisbord, *Wills for Everyone: Helping Individuals Opt Out of Intestacy,* 53 B.C. L. Rev. 877, 920 (2012).

14. One critical element of the advance care-planning process is naming who will make medical decisions in the event of an individual's incapacity—adding the

name of that person, the next of kin, to the drivers' license might be an interest-
ing requirement for the next twenty years as our population grays. It would make
life easier for emergency room personnel in an emergency. This name would be
revisited every time you renew your license and thus could reflect remarriages,
etc. An entire paper could address the changing role of the next of kin as a surrogate decision-maker for an incapacitated individual. To see how this question is
addressed, see, e.g., Amy Ziettlow & Naomi Cahn, *The Honor Commandment: Law,
Religion, and the Challenge of Elder Care*, 30 J. L. & Relig. 229 (2015),

15. For example, N.Y. Veh. & Traf. Law § 504(1)(a) (2016). In Louisiana, the driver's
license can include information about whether, for example, the applicant has
received a hunting license; moreover, the applicant must be asked whether he or
she would like to be an organ donor, and the state must provide information at the
motor vehicle office about organ donation. See La. Rev. Stat. Ann. § 32:410 (2016).

16. Common law marriages are an exception to this general rule; no state sanc-
tion is required at the time of the marriage. See Douglas E. Abrams et al.,
Contemporary Family Law 146–147 (4th ed. 2015).

17. Divorce itself causes numerous consequences in existing inheritance plans.
Even if the testator fails to change his or her will after a divorce, most states
have nonetheless enacted statutes that either automatically revoke or declare pre-
sumptively invalid testamentary provisions in favor of the ex-spouse. In some
states, the automatic revocation applies to designations as well. *See, e.g.*, Unif.
Probate Code § 2–804(b)(2010); Stewart Sterk & Melanie Leslie, *Accidental
Inheritance: Retirement Accounts and the Hidden Law of Succession*, 89 N.Y.U.
L. Rev. 165, 180 (2014).

18. *See* Weisbord, *supra* note 15, at 922 (listing advantages of appending the standard
form will to the state income tax form).

19. For example, Unif. Parentage Act. § 201 (2002).

20. Under the Uniform Probate Code, stepchildren will inherit in the absence of other
heirs. See Unif. Probate Code § 2–104(b) (2016) (stepchildren inherit only if
there is no surviving spouse, children, parents, siblings, children of siblings, first
cousins, or children of first cousins).

21. *See, e.g.,* Paula A. Monopoli, *Nonmarital Children and Post-Death Parentage: A Different
Path for Inheritance Law?*, 48 Santa Clara L. Rev. 857 (2008).

22. The rest of the will remains intact. At common law, marriage revoked a woman's
premarital will; in some states, marriage revoked a man's premarital will whereas
in other states, marriage and the birth of issue acted as a revocation. *See* Hulett
v. Carey, 69 N.W. 31, 34 (Minn. 1896); *Wills—Revocation by Marriage*, 34 Harv.
L. Rev. 95 (1920).

23. *See* Alicia B. Kelly, *Better Equality for Elders: Basing Economic Relations Law on
Sharing and Caring*, 21 Temple Pol. & Civ. Rts. L.J. 101 (2012); Joshua C. Tate,
Caregiving and the Case for Testamentary Freedom, 42 U.C. Davis L. Rev. 129, 177–
178 (2008) (reporting on studies showing how receipt of care influenced unequal
probate transfers to children).

24. For example, although HIPAA provides important protections for patient privacy,
its interpretation may disadvantage family caregivers. *See supra* note 146. Caregiver

contracts constitute another source of concern. *See, e.g.*, Sheena J Knox, *Eldercare for the Baby-Boom Generation: Are Caregiver Agreements Valid?*, 45 SUFFOLK U. L. REV. 1271 (2012).

25. *See, e.g.*, Ziettlow & Cahn, *supra* note 14.

26. "The roughly 6% of Medicare patients who die each year do make up a large proportion of Medicare costs: 27% to 30%." Ezekiel J. Emanuel, *Better, if Not Cheaper, Care*, N.Y. TIMES (Jan. 3, 2013), http://opinionator.blogs.nytimes.com/2013/01/03/better-if-not-cheaper-care/; *see* Alan M. Garber, Thomas E. MaCurdy, & Mark B. McClellan, *Medical Care at the End of Life: Diseases, Treatment Patterns, and Costs, in* 2 FRONTIERS IN HEALTH POL. RES. 77, 78 (Alan Garber ed., 1999) (noting similar trends).

27. *See, e.g.*, Inst. of Med., *supra* note 5 at 2–40 [showing that there are sources of support that are limited in scope such as "The National Family Caregiver Support Program, established by the Older Americans Act, as amended in 2000, which has helped increase awareness of the importance of family caregivers by establishing the caregiver as a client and providing family counseling, support groups, training, and respite care. The Affordable Care Act includes multiple references to caregivers and may help them by promoting models of care that prevent or facilitate transitions between care settings. Medicaid's Cash and Counseling program, available in about fifteen states, permits beneficiaries to pay family members modest sums for home care services in some cases. And family members of seriously injured veterans (who served after September 11, 2001) may receive a stipend, comprehensive training, medical services, and other services under the VA Program of Comprehensive Assistance to Family Caregivers.]

28. Emily Plomgren, *You Never Call, You Never Write: China's Use of Filial Responsibility Laws to Combat Consequences of Population Aging* (2015) (unpublished manuscript on file with authors).

29. *See* The FAMILY Act of 2003 (S. 1810, H.P. 3712); Sarah Jane Glynn & Jane Farrell, *Family Matters: Caregiving in America*, CTR. FOR AM. PROGRESS (Feb. 5, 2014), http://www.americanprogress.org/issues/labor/report/2014/02/05/83427/family-matters/.

30. *See The Cost of Doing Nothing* U.S. Department of Labor 13 (2015); FAMILY Act, *supra* note 32; Glynn & Farrell, *supra* note 32.

31. Martin Kitchener et al., *Institutional and Community-Based Long-Term Care: A Comparative Estimate of Public Costs*, 22 J. HEALTH & SOC. POLICY 31 (2006).

32. *Unpaid Eldercare in the United States 2011–2012: Estimates from the American Time Use Survey*, BUREAU OF LABOR STATISTICS (2013). http://www.bls.gov/news.release/pdf/elcare.pdf.

33. *See* Joan C. Williams, Robin Devaux, Patricija Petrac & Lynn Feinberg, *Protecting Family Caregivers from Employment Discrimination: Fact Sheet*, AARP PUB. POLICY INST. 3–4 (Aug. 2012), http://www.aarp.org/content/dam/aarp/research/public_policy_institute/health/protecting-caregivers-employment-discrimination-insight-AARP-ppi-ltc.pdf.

34. *See Caregiving in the U.S.: 2015 Research Report*, AARP PUB. POLICY INST. (June 2015), http://www.caregiving.org/wp-content/uploads/2015/05/2015_CaregivingintheUS_Final-Report-June-4_WEB.pdf

35. Linda Houser & Thomas P. Vartanian, *Pay Matters: The Positive Economic Impact of Paid Family Leave for Families, Businesses, and the Public*, RUTGERS: CTR. FOR WOMEN & WORK (2012).

36. For examples of options supporting paid leave, *see* Sarah Jane Glynn, *Administering Paid Family and Medical Leave: Learning from International and Domestic Examples*, CTR. AM. PROGRESS (Nov. 19, 2015), https://www.americanprogress.org/issues/labor/report/2015/11/19/125769/administering-paid-family-and-medical-leave/.

The report looks at three possible ways to fund paid family leave, using the experiences of other countries: "Individual employer requirements, in which businesses are responsible for providing paid leave; social insurance, in which risk and resources are pooled to provide a fund for wage replacement while on leave; and publicly funded programs, such as business-government partnerships, in which government works with businesses to provide workers with paid leave without expecting employers to finance the leave on their own." *CAP Outlines National Solutions to Make Paid Leave a Reality for All Americans* (2015). https://www.americanprogress.org/press/release/2015/11/19/124392/release-cap-outlines-national-solutions-to-make-paid-leave-a-reality-for-all-americans/ (press release).

37. *Administrator's Interpretation No. 2010-3*, U.S. DEPT. LAB. (June 22, 2010), http://www.dol.gov/whd/opinion/adminIntrprtn/FMLA/2010/FMLAAI2010_3.pdf

38. *See* Peggie R. Smith, *Elder Care, Gender, and Work: The Work-Family Issue of the 21st Century*, 25 BERKELEY J. EMP. & LAB. L. 351 (2004).

39. The Social Security Caregiver Credit Act, sponsored by Rep. Nita Lowey (D-NY), would institute a credit so that caregiving hours would be included in calculating an individual's Social Security benefit. Anyone who spends at least 80 hours a month caring for family members, including children under the age of 12, a senior in need of intensive care, or a chronically disabled relative would be eligible to claim the credit for up to five years. *See* H.R. 5024, 113th Cong. (2014). *See also* Brian Faler, *Clinton Proposes $6,000 Tax Credit for Family Caregivers*, POLITICO (Nov. 22, 2015, 12:13 p.m.), http://www.politico.com/story/2015/11/clinton-proposes-6-000-tax-credit-for-elderly-care-216136.

40. John Jankowski, *Caregiver Credits in France, Germany, and Sweden: Lessons for the United States*, 71 SOC. SEC. BULL. 61 (2011).

41. Natl. Council of Women's Org. & Ctr. for Cmty. Change, *Expanding Social Security Benefits for Financially Vulnerable Populations* 12–13 (2013); Shelley I. White-Means & Rose M. Rubin, *Retirement Security for Family Elder Caregivers with Labor Force Employment*, NATL. ACAD. SOC. INS. (2009).

42. See Caregiver Corps Act of 2014, S. 2842, 113th Cong. (2014) ("The bill would give the Secretary of Health and Human Services the authority to develop a toolkit and guidance for local entities to establish and implement local Caregiver Corps programs giving local faith-based groups or volunteer programs the tools to train volunteers so that they are prepared and understand how they can best support an older adult or person with a disability"); *Casey Unveils National Caregiver Corps Plan to Aid Aging Residents in Southwestern PA and Their Families Who Provide Care*, ROBERT P. CASEY JR., UNITED STATES SENATOR FOR PENNSYLVANIA (Aug. 21, 2014), https://www.casey.senate.gov/newsroom/

releases/casey-unveils-national-caregiver-corps-plan-to-aid-aging-residents-in-southwestern-pa-and-their-families-who-provide-care.

43. Fredrick Kunkle, *Aging Doesn't Always Come Naturally. Classes Are Teaching Boomers How*, Wash. Post (May 29, 2015), http://www.washingtonpost.com/local/aging-doesnt-always-come-naturally-classes-are-teaching-boomers-how/2015/05/29/150f779a-060f-11e5-bc72-f3e16bf50bb6_story.html.

44. See Ai-jen Poo, The Age of Dignity: Preparing for the Elder Boom in a Changing America 8, 32, 141–168 (2014).

45. The financial costs of caregiving are tracked. See Donald Redfoot, Lynn Feinberg & Ari Houser, *The Aging of the Baby Boom and the Growing Care Gap: A Look at Future Declines in the Availability of Family Caregivers*, AARP Pub. Policy Inst. (2013). The emotional and physical costs are also tracked and are exacerbated by conflicted histories. See W.E. Haley, D. L. Roth, G. Howard & M.M Stafford, *Caregiving Strain Estimated Risk for Stroke and Coronary Heart Disease Among Spouse Caregivers: Differential Effects by Race and Sex*, 41 Stroke 331 (2010); M. Pinquart & S. Sörensen, *Ethnic Differences in Stressors, Resources, and Psychological Outcomes of Family Caregiving: A Meta-Analysis*, 45 Gerontologist 90 (2005); P.P. Vitaliano, Z. Scanlon & H.M. Zhang, *Is Caregiving Hazardous to One's Physical Health? A Meta-Analysis*, 6 Psychol. Bull. 946 (2003).

46. A cursory review of the scholarship on caregiver abuse shows that a gap in knowledge exists. The self-help genre, including classic texts such as Virginia Morris, How to Care for Aging Parents (3d ed. 2014), does include "care for the caregiver." Additional resources concerning support for caregivers can be found through organizations such as AARP, the National Alliance for Caregiving, and the National Family Caregivers Association.

47. Lawrence H. Ganong & Marilyn Coleman, Stepfamily Relationships: Development, Dynamics, and Interventions (2004).

48. *See, e.g.*, James L. Brooks, The Unbroken Circle: A Toolkit for Congregations Around Illness, End of Life and Grief (2009). The Duke University Center for Spirituality, Theology and Health is creating new resources for chaplains and faith communities engaged in aging and end of life care. See The Foundation for End-of-Life Care, Inc., https://www.foundationeolc.org/ (last visited Feb. 16, 2016). *See also*, Amy Ziettlow, *Three Reasons Clergy Need a Healthcare App*, Huffington Post (May 21, 2014), http://www.huffingtonpost.com/rev-amy-ziettlow/3-reasons-clergy-need-a-h_b_5360063.html.

49. *Sample HIPAA Authorization Form for Family Members/Friends*, ABA Commission on Law and Aging, http://www.americanbar.org/content/dam/aba/administrative/law_aging/SampleHIPAAAuthorizationFormforFamilyMembers.authcheckdam.pdf (last accessed May 10, 2016).

50. See *Clinicians*, VITALTalk, http://www.vitaltalk.org/clinicians (last visited Feb. 16, 2016).

51. See Aisha Bonner & Eowna Young Harrison, *2014 AARP Caregiving Survey: Louisiana Registered Voters Age 45 and Older Opinions and Experiences on Critical Caregiving Issues*, AARP (Jan. 23, 2015), http://www.aarp.org/content/dam/aarp/

research/surveys_statistics/general/2015/2014-Caregiving-Survey-Louisiana-Reg-Voters-res-care.pdf.

52. *See* R.S. Brown et al., *Six Features of Medicare Coordinated Care Demonstration Programs that Cut Hospital Admissions of High-Risk Patients*, 31 HEALTH AFFAIRS 1156–1165 (2012); Margot Sanger-Katz, *Medicare to Try a Blend of Hospice Care and Treatment*, N.Y. TIMES (July 22, 2015), http://www.nytimes.com/2015/07/22/upshot/medicare-to-try-a-blend-of-hospice-care-and-treatment.html?emc=etal.

53. Alexandra Butler, *Experts on Aging, Dying as They Lived*, N.Y. TIMES: OPINIONATOR (June 17, 2015, 6:45 a.m.), http://opinionator.blogs.nytimes.com/2015/06/17/experts-on-aging-dying-as-they-lived/?_r=0.

APPENDIX A

1. Amy Ziettlow and Elizabeth Marquardt were the primary investigators of the project in years one and two. We constructed the research methodology, conducted the interviews, and began general analysis of the transcripts. Elizabeth Marquardt left the project in year three. Naomi Cahn joined the project in year three for the in-depth analysis and dissemination phase of the project.

2. Baton Rouge Statistics: Population, 230,000; 49% Caucasian, 45% African American, 3% Hispanic. Baton Rouge is and has ranked consistently in the last five years as one of the cities with the highest rates of new cases of HIV/AIDS in the United States; http://www.cdc.gov/nchhstp/newsroom/HIVFactSheets/Epidemic/Scope.htm, 52% of the population is affiliated with a faith community. http://www.city-data.com/county/religion/East-Baton-Rouge-Parish-LA.html. Baton Rouge is the capital of Louisiana and its second largest city. It is geographically located at the distinctive eastern turn of the Mississippi River, about an hour's drive directly west of on I-10 from New Orleans. The median household income (2008–2012) was $48,274, with 18.5% of its population below the poverty line. It is slightly poorer than the larger United States, which has a median income of $53,000 and a poverty rate of 14%; www.quickfacts.census.gov/qfd/states.22.22033.html (accessed Sep. 30, 2014).

3. The *Advocate* provides writing guidelines for the form of obituary:

> The introduction should include the individual's full name, age (if desired), residency, date and location of death. Next, provide all relevant biographical information, such as date and place of birth, parents, education and employment, memberships and affiliations, as well as any further information regarding residency or relocation. Then provide the name and location (if desired) for all relevant survivors, including key relatives and friends. This section can include both the living and deceased. Provide service times and locations as well as contribution information (if desired). Remember that accuracy is of utmost importance. Please be sure that dates are accurate and names, schools, and cities are spelled correctly. One picture costs $35/per day, two pictures cost $50/per day, and an icon such as a cross, adds a $15 fee;

http://placeanad.theadvocate.com/advocate-adportal/obits/static/advertise.html (accessed Sep. 30, 2014).

4. ELIZABETH Marquardt, BETWEEN TWO WORLDS: THE INNER LIVES OF CHILDREN OF DIVORCE (2005); Robert Weiss, LEARNING FROM STRANGERS: THE ART AND METHOD OF QUALITATIVE INTERVIEW STUDIES (1994).

5. After year two, Marquardt left the project and Naomi Cahn joined, bringing expertise in public policy and law analysis with an eye trained to lived application and narrative forms used in law and everyday life, specifically as used by ROBERT C. ELLICKSON, ORDER WITHOUT LAW (1991) (using a combination of interviews and ethnography of cattle farmers in a county in California to challenge the assumptions of the Coase Theorem and to put forth a new theory of social norms and order).

6. Ziettlow followed the guidance of Loren Marks, professor in the LSU School of Social Work and Program Director, Child & Family Studies, who provides researchers with "The Marks Method of Qualitative Data Analysis."

7. Qualitative work plays a unique role in both legal and theological work. We found the work of Sarah Sternberg Greene and Robert Ellickson to be especially informative, e.g., Sara Sternberg Greene, *The Broken Safety Net: A Study of Earned Income Tax Credit Recipients and A Proposal for Repair*, 88 N.Y.U. L. REV. 515 (2013); ELLICKSON, *supra* note 5.

APPENDIX C

1. JACK CANFIELD & MARK VICTOR Hanson, CHICKEN SOUP FOR THE SOUL (2012).

2. As discussed in Chapter 1, the Hospice Medicare Benefit requires that hospice organizations offer bereavement support to families for thirteen months following the death of a patient. The bereavement coordinator, chaplains, social workers, and trained volunteers at the hospice organization work together to create a Bereavement Care Plan, which includes goals and interventions, adapted to the needs of each family. Bereavement education, support groups, and one-on-one counseling are made available to each grieving family.

3. GEORGE A. Bonanno, THE OTHER SIDE OF SADNESS: WHAT THE NEW SCIENCE OF BEREAVEMENT TELLS US (2009).

4. Exodus 17:15 and 24:4, Judges 6:24, 1 Samuel 7:17, 1 Samuel 14:35, and 2 Samuel 24:25.

5. A helpful resource on family systems, spirituality, and grief is FROMA WALSH & MONICA McGoldrick, LIVING BEYOND LOSS: DEATH IN THE FAMILY (1991). Also, J.W. Nadeau, FAMILIES MAKING SENSE OF DEATH (1998), addresses how families make meaning narratively after a loss.